THE EXECUTIVE FUNCTION

FUNCTION

GUIDEBOOK

Strategies
to Help All
Students
Achieve
Success

ROBERTA STROSNIDER • VALERIE SAXTON SHARPE

CORWIN

FOR INFORMATION:

Corwin

A SAGE Company

2455 Teller Road

Thousand Oaks, California 91320

(800) 233–9936

www.corwin.com

SAGE Publications Ltd.

1 Oliver's Yard

55 City Road

London EC1Y 1SP

United Kingdom

SAGE Publications India Pvt. Ltd.

B 1/I 1 Mohan Cooperative Industrial Area

Mathura Road, New Delhi 110 044

India

SAGE Publications Asia-Pacific Pte. Ltd.

18 Cross Street

#10-10/11/12

China Square Central

Singapore 048423

Program Director: Jessica Allan

Content Development Editor: Lucas Schleicher

Senior Editorial Assistant: Mia Rodriguez

Production Editor: Amy Schroller

Copy Editor: Diane DiMura

Typesetter: Integra

Proofreader: Dennis Webb

Indexer: Molly Hall

Cover Designer: Gail Buschman

Marketing Manager: Margaret O'Connor

Printed in the United States of America

Library of Congress Cataloging-in-Publication Data

Names: Strosnider, Roberta, author. | Sharpe, Valerie Saxton, author.

Title: The executive function guidebook : strategies to help all students achieve success / Roberta Strosnider, Valerie Sharpe.

Description: Thousand Oaks, California : Corwin, 2019. | Includes bibliographical references and index.

Identifiers: LCCN 2018045092 | ISBN 9781544379289 (paperback : acid-free paper)

Subjects: LCSH: Cognitive learning. | Executive functions (Neuropsychology) | Academic achievement—Psychological aspects.

Classification: LCC LB1062 .S835 2019 | DDC 370.15/2—dc23

LC record available at https://lccn.loc.gov/2018045092

This book is printed on acid-free paper.

21 22 23 10 9 8 7 6 5

Contents

Visit the companion website at
http://resources.corwin.com/ExecutiveFunctioning
for downloadable resources such as blank templates,
modifiable versions of materials, and strategy cards.

List of Online Appendices

Visit the companion website at
http://resources.corwin.com/ExecutiveFunctioning
for downloadable resources such as blank templates,
modifiable versions of materials, and strategy cards.

Acknowledgments

We have had a variety of experiences in our teaching careers from P–12 to college-level teaching. Most of our professional lives have been spent in school settings where students were having success; however, some students were not finding success. It was the latter for whom we first saw a need for executive function skill training.

We first had the opportunity to develop and teach executive function training skills to P–12 students through a program we developed, Project Boost. Many people were responsible for helping us make Project Boost happen. We would like to thank Jim Strosnider for his dedicated work as financial officer of Project Boost as well as teaching at the camps. We thank all of our teachers including Kim Hale, Kristy Sharpe, and Kelly Sharpe for helping prepare for and teaching at Project Boost. Kim and Kelly continued to teach at every camp and provided planning for and executive function training throughout the year to students. We would be remiss if we did not mention that Kendall Hale attended every camp offered and assisted in teaching many of the skills. We thank Sophie and Brinkley Strosnider and Kendall and Jay Hale for the helpful videos they made to demonstrate their use of strategies they learned in Project Boost.

A special thank you goes out to Hannah and the Smith family for being our "first" student and family we worked with on executive functions. Hannah's success and their ongoing support were instrumental in our search for how to effectively teach executive function skills.

We thank Friends School, Hood College, Park School, our campers, teachers, and all those associated with Project Boost for giving us an opportunity to offer this program. It would not have been possible without the generous support from friends, family, and organizations such as Green-Walled Garden Club, P. Buckley Moss Foundation, and Leah Johnson with the Frederick County Child Advocacy Center for help with raising money for scholarships.

We thank our teacher candidates and graduate students at Hood College, Towson University, and Frostburg State University who were trained in and continue to teach executive function skills in their classrooms. We are grateful for your continuing to collaborate with us and allowing us to be a part of your classroom experience. Also, a special thank you to Kim Hale for making us part of her teaching experience in an ongoing partnership.

We have many colleagues and friends who have been instrumental in our successful completion of this book. We especially want to thank Dr. Debi Gartland for her years of belief in and promotion of our work. We thank Ms. Kirsten McBride, who guided and encouraged us to see our goal of writing this book to fruition. We thank Frostburg State University and Dr. Jamey Tobery-Nystrom for the opportunity to develop and offer a course in teaching Executive Function Methods. We appreciate the collaboration and encouragement we received from Dr. Steven Feifer, Dr. Oma Gail Simmons, and Ms. Jen Weaver for their collaboration and encouragement. We also thank all of the Corwin reviewers.

We have had the opportunity to present our work to teachers throughout the country. We especially thank the Council for Exceptional Children for including us in their Pre-Convention Workshops and convention presentations, and Ms. Ravae Todd of the Hawaii State Department of Education, Hilo, Hawaii, for opportunities to work with administrators, teachers, and teacher assistants in executive function skill training.

PUBLISHER'S ACKNOWLEDGMENTS

Corwin gratefully acknowledges the contributions of the following reviewers:

Bev Alfeld
Academic Performance Specialist
Crystal Lake, IL

Tamara Daugherty
Third-Grade Teacher
Zellwood Elementary
Zellwood, FL

Sarah Foster
Teacher
Colegio Anglo Colombiano
Bogota, Colombia

Deborah E. Griswold
Assistant Professor of Practice
University of Kansas, Department of
Special Education
Lawrence, KS

Vicki McFarland
Director of Federal Programs
Learning Matters Educational Group
Glendale, AZ

Kent McIntosh
Professor
University of Oregon
Eugene, OR

Erin Schons
Assistant Education Director
Children's Home Society
Sioux Falls, SD

About the Authors

Dr. Roberta Strosnider, Professor Emerita in Special Education, Towson University, Towson, Maryland, currently works as an educational consultant in the areas of learning disabilities, executive functioning, and teacher preparation. Roberta graduated from Fairmont State University (FSU) with a major in Secondary Education and in 2017 she was a recipient of an Alumna of Achievement Award from that institution. She earned her master's degree in Special Education from West Virginia University and her doctorate in Special Education from Virginia Polytechnic Institute and State University. She taught both general and special education classes in P-12 schools. She also taught at several institutions of higher education and holds faculty emerita status from Hood College, Fredrick, Maryland, and Towson University, Towson, Maryland.

Roberta received a fellowship to study HIV Prevention Education for Students with Disabilities and served as a national trainer for the Co-Teaching HIV Prevention Program. While at Towson University, she directed an off-campus teacher preparation program and received the Nasim Dil Award for her service to Small Special Education Programs. She has further served her profession as a reviewer and auditor of special education teacher education program reports for the Council for Exceptional Children (CEC). In addition, she has made contributions to the field through publications, presentations, and grants. She also served as a consultant to the Maryland State Department of Education preparing materials and online resources to provide professional development.

During her career, Roberta has been and continues to be active in advocacy efforts for students with disabilities having served as a board member and advocate for several organizations. Her work with the Frederick County, Maryland, Arc Board was recognized with the STAR Award from the Arc. The Council for Learning Disabilities (CLD) awarded her the Floyd G. Hudson Award for her contributions to the field of learning disabilities. She serves as a representative for CLD to other public policy groups such as the National Joint Committee on Learning Disabilities.

Valerie Saxton Sharpe currently works as an educational consultant in the areas of cognitive disabilities, executive functioning, and teacher preparation. Val's career path started as a special education teacher for a large Maryland school system teaching students with learning disabilities and cognitive impairments. As an administrator, she chaired the Special Education department in a comprehensive high school setting. Lastly, as an instructional specialist, she supervised and provided teacher training.

Following her career in teaching and supervision, Val prepared teachers at both Hood College and Towson University. While at Hood College, she played an integral role in the development of an assessment system to measure teacher candidate performance used for program review, reform and for accreditation purposes. As program coordinator for Towson University Elementary Education/Special Education at the Universities at Shady Grove she was known for her innovative methodology used in the preparation of teacher candidates to teach ALL students. Val was instrumental in providing teacher candidates opportunities to gain knowledge and skills in universal design, differentiated instruction, and executive function skills. She developed new Professional Development Schools (PDS) partnerships with the local school system, secured grant funding for the design and implementation of unique teacher preparation projects, wrote manuals addressing co-teaching and mentoring, and presented at PDS conferences.

For her outstanding work at Towson University, Val was awarded the Gloria E. Neubert Excellence in Teaching Award, and the Universities at Shady Grove Campus Program Director of the Year Award. She was appointed by the governor of Maryland to serve on the Maryland Professional Standards Teacher Education Board. Val also served as an invited member of the Educational Testing Service (ETS) Elementary Education Praxis II test development team.

An advocate for students with disabilities, Val has served as a national and state officer for the Council for Exceptional Children and its Division on Autism and Developmental Disabilities (DADD). For her work with DADD, she received the Special Recognition Award. Additionally, she has served on the Board of Trustees for Service Coordination of Frederick County that assists individuals with developmental disabilities to obtain services. As a member of this Board, Val supported the implementation of transition and employment services for individuals with disabilities in Maryland.

Roberta Strosnider and Valerie Sharpe cofounded Project Boost, where they wrote and taught a curriculum that provides executive-function skill training for students K–12 by building skills through the 7-Step Model explored in this book. This curriculum has been used throughout the contiguous United States and Hawaii for the professional development of teachers and administrators. The authors currently teach online courses on executive functioning and classroom management at Frostburg State University, Frostburg, Maryland.

List of Contributors

Andi Anglin-Alonso, Special Educator
Grade: Elementary
Montgomery County Public Schools,
    Maryland

Laura Beck, LMSW
High School: Executive Function Skills
    Program Designed for Students
    At-Risk
Oxford Schools, Michigan

Nadya Chacon, General Educator
Grade: 1
Montgomery County Public Schools,
    Maryland

Jessica Gray, Special Educator
Grades: K–2
Montgomery County Public Schools,
    Maryland

Kimberly Hale, General Educator
Grade: 3
Wake County Public Schools, North
    Carolina

Elisabeth Halici, General Educator
Grades: Elementary and Middle
Montgomery County Public Schools,
    Maryland

Meredith Julius, MA
High School: Executive Function Skills
    Program Designed for Students
    At-Risk
Berkley Schools, Michigan; Formerly
    Oxford Schools, Michigan

Mychael Moe, Special Educator
Grade: Ka'u High and Pahala Elementary
    School (KHPES), Ka'u High, and
    Pahala Elementary Hilo, Hawaii

Student B.
Grade: 8

Student J.
Grade: 6

Student K.
Grade: 9

Student S.
Grade: 10

Shannon Sullivan, Special Educator
Grades: Middle School
Montgomery County Public Schools,
    Maryland

Batya Toso, Special Educator
Grades: K, 4, 5
Montgomery County Public Schools,
    Maryland

Jennifer Cossette Ventura, General
Educator
Grade: 1
Montgomery County Public Schools,
    Maryland

To my husband Jim, thank you for all your love, your belief in and work to bring executive function skill training to all students, and for being a source of strength to me as I have worked on this book.

To my children, Kent, thank you for believing in and supporting me and Kim, thank you for participating as a coach in Project Boost and contributing to this book. I would also like to thank their spouses, Laura and Jamie, for all your encouragement in the writing of this book. To my grandchildren, Sophie, Kendall, Brinkley, and Jay, thank you for your love and participation in Project Boost; you are the best grandchildren ever.

—Roberta Strosnider

To my husband Mike, thank you for your never ending love, support, encouragement, and active listening skills during the writing of this book. Your thoughtful, and sometimes humorous comments were a sure sign that you understood the importance of me seeing this project through to fruition.

To my loving children, Kristy, Kelly, Jeremy, and Alex, you are the best cheerleaders a mom could have. To Kristy and Kelly, thank you for your years of participation as coaches in Project Boost.

—Val Sharpe

To all of our P–12 and higher education students, thank you for the opportunity to have a small part in your education.

—Roberta Strosnider and Val Sharpe

Introduction

During our years of working with P–12 students as teachers ourselves and our experience as observers of teachers, we found that many students had problems in executive functioning (EF) and, therefore, did not respond to general methods of teaching. They seemed anxious at the start of a new school year, yet expressed hope that things would be different in the year to come. Unfortunately, these students continued to face the same difficulties year after year because the root of their difficulties was not identified, and they did not receive interventions that specifically targeted executive function skills. We decided to write this book based on those experiences and especially as a response to results we saw in students following Project Boost, as a week-long skills camp session for students ages five to sixteen prior to the start of school.

Project Boost was designed to build students' self-confidence as they approached the new school year, and the focus was on teaching strategies that would boost their executive control. The idea was to give students a "jump start" or "boost" by introducing them to strategies that could make a difference in how they approached learning. The strategies for improving executive function skills were taught over a short period and were the focus of the week. During this period, we used the strategies and technology described in this book. Students learned basic home keys and a system for keyboarding. They each completed a short research project to practice the strategies they learned for conducting research using technology. We found that all students learned the strategies at a faster pace than we thought possible and left Project Boost with self-confidence in their new skills as they approached the upcoming school year.

The response from parents, teachers, and students was overwhelmingly enthusiastic, and all students started the school with a "Success Plan" (see chapter 1 for more information) to be shared with their teacher(s). We followed up with students intermittently throughout the school year and found that, while many of them were continuing to use the strategies they had learned during the one-week camp, the carry-over was greatest when their parents and teachers reinforced the use of the strategies. In addition, we had the opportunity to work with some of the students weekly throughout multiple academic years. With these students, we were able not only to review the skills they had learned but also to connect the strategies to their academic program working with their parents and teachers. We quickly saw that the students who made the most progress were those who had follow-up throughout the academic year. Some students returned to the summer skills camp for multiple years and eventually became peer tutors for new students.

The takeaway from that experience and our many years as educators is that students do benefit from explicit teaching of executive function skills. In recent years, we have presented our strategies at various national and local conferences, and our feedback from teachers indicated a desire and need for more information and guidance.

We wrote this book to provide teachers and others with strategies for teaching and improving students' executive function skills. The book applies to teaching students of all ages. The primary intended audience includes elementary, middle, and high school teachers, teacher educators, teacher candidates, executive function skills coaches, school counselors, school social workers, school psychologists, teacher assistants, tutors, and other related service personnel. A secondary audience is parents, who may want to reinforce the learning of the strategies.

Recognizing the daunting workloads of most teachers, every effort has been made to make the text as accessible and easy to use as possible. Chapter 1 provides a background and overview as well as tools to assist the reader in utilizing the strategies and activities described throughout the book. Subsequent chapters start with a discussion of the specific topic followed by strategies, checklists, and templates that are easily adapted to best suit the reader's students and teaching environment. A companion website, http://resources.corwin.com/ExecutiveFunctioning, is available for downloading and reproducing strategy cards, forms, and templates (see chapter 1 for more information). The Reader Outcomes provided for each chapter will assist professionals in determining their knowledge of teaching executive function skills.

Strategies have been selected to help students find academic and behavioral success, and different types of strategies will be covered in this book. Strategies used exclusively by the teacher are referred to as teaching or instructional strategies. For example, a teacher may provide a graphic organizer as a teaching or instructional strategy, or he or she may seat a student with a short attention span in close proximity to the teacher away from distractions to help. We also provide multiple learning strategies for many executive functions that teachers can teach their students to help them learn skills like spelling new words, decoding words, or writing paragraphs. Other strategies described in this book include those for regulating behavior. Some of the strategies are designed to improve executive function skills while others are compensatory strategies as they are being used as part of the scaffolding process for instruction. We realize that not all strategies work for all students. In addition, we identify supportive technology for the student.

Throughout the book, the importance of assessment is emphasized. To that end, a sample self-assessment tool for students, teachers, and parents is included. A record-keeping component is also included to assist teachers and others in determining whether a given student's use of the strategy, and ultimately executive skill functioning, has improved. ***There is also a blank data sheet for a group or whole class included at http://resources .corwin.com/ExecutiveFunctioning.*** Case studies are used as examples in each chapter to illustrate executive function strategy instruction and steps to follow when that instruction needs revision for a student. Case studies include elementary, middle, and high school students. A seventh chapter provides information regarding EF considerations when teaching students in early childhood and students who have autism spectrum disorder (ASD).

The information and checklists presented in this book are available as presented or as adapted according to Universal Design for Learning (UDL) considerations made for individual students. We are not neuropsychologists; we are educators with advanced education in special education. Between us, we have more than eighty years in the field. We have taught students with and without disabilities; students in private schools, public schools, general education settings, self-contained settings, and resource settings; and we have co-taught within inclusive settings. We have also taught students in P–12 and teacher candidates at both the undergraduate and graduate levels (both pre- and in-service teachers). Finally, both of us have served in administration for a period of time.

Children begin developing executive functions, which we define as a group of processes that allows individuals to self-regulate the ways in which they interact with their environment, while still in the crib. These skills continue to develop into young adulthood. As situations occur that require executive function skills, parents have opportunities to reinforce appropriate responses and teach skills as needed. For instance, impulse control is necessary for the safety of a child; however, it is difficult for some children to control their impulses. As these children grow into adulthood, problems with impulse control can lead to danger physically, emotionally, and academically. As students advance from grade to grade, learning becomes more complicated, and students must make advancements in how they approach learning. It is necessary for students to use metacognition to set goals, make a plan to reach those goals, implement the plans, make necessary changes to the plans, and conclude with a successful product.

It is difficult to determine how many students have executive function deficits, as there is no formal diagnosis, only a description. However, as we have looked at executive functions and how they are developed in each student, we have found a correlation between having difficulty with executive function skills and academic and social struggles in school. For example, a student having difficulty with attention and focusing may also be unable to self-regulate and may be disruptive in class.

As knowledge of the brain continues to expand, an increased amount of information about how students learn and behave has become available. More and more cases of struggling learners describe executive function deficits, yet there are no clear guidelines for addressing those deficits in the classroom. Educators are starting to accept the fact that executive functioning does underlie behavior and learning, and it is imperative that resources be made available to meet the needs of students from early childhood through postsecondary who exhibit these deficits. Also, with an increased emphasis on Universal Design for Learning (UDL) in meeting the needs of *all* students, it is imperative that teachers merge the selection of appropriate strategies and technology when planning lessons using UDL.

ABOUT THIS BOOK

Teachers today are faced with meeting a plethora of rigorous curricular demands to prepare students for college or a career. Such demands are often impacted by time challenges and constraints to keep the instructional process moving forward. The idea of adding executive function skill instruction to this list of demands can be daunting. However, it is imperative that we provide students tools that will help them learn before we attempt to teach them content. Executive function skill training provides students with a set of tools that helps build the foundation of how to learn. The notion of addressing executive function skill training within the instructional process is not new. Both the Common Core Curriculum (IDEA Partnership, 2013) and Universal Design for Learning (UDL) (Center for Applied Special Technology [CAST], 2011) note the inclusion of executive function skills. In this book, we will address questions regarding the who, what, when, and how of our 7-Step Model. The who component represents all students. Implicit instruction of strategies to assist with self-regulation addresses the what component. When speaks to the sample schedule templates we provide. Where focuses on suggested venues where the strategies can be taught. Lastly, the how attends to the manner in which teachers, paraprofessionals, school counselors, and psychologists can integrate our 7-Step Model of executive function instruction into their teaching and counseling schedule. The 7-Step Model as described here will be presented as a fluid tool that can be used in part or as whole thus providing flexibility to address class size, student needs, and type of instructional setting.

We look forward to sharing our process with you in this book.

CHAPTER 1

What You Need to Know Before Deciding to Implement Executive Function (EF) Skills Training and the 7-Step Model

Reader Outcomes

☑ You will be able to explain what executive functioning (EF) is and how students can benefit from EF skill training.

☑ You will be able to explain how Universal Design for Learning (UDL) and metacognition complement EF skill training.

☑ You will be able to identify the role of supportive technology in EF skill training.

☑ You will be able to describe the 7-Step Model and the Modified 7-Step Model.

☑ You will be able to determine how you might offer EF training in your setting.

As educators, the demands placed upon us today extend beyond the traditional mastery of content knowledge. Held to accountability standards for continual student progress, as measured in part by high-stakes testing, it is our responsibility to deliver instruction in a manner that facilitates learning for **all** students. Current inclusive practices have resulted in heterogeneous groupings of students with a variety of learning and behavioral needs within most classrooms.

Being held to high standards regarding student achievement and success is not new. In 1983, the National Commission on Excellence in Education produced a report entitled *A Nation at Risk* that communicated the strong need for major reforms in the educational process in the United States. It emphasized the need for better educational opportunities for all students (https://www2.ed.gov/pubs/NatAtRisk/risk.html). Running parallel to this cry for reform was a movement to grant inclusion to individuals with disabilities in all facets of society. As a result, legislative mandates such as the Individuals with Disabilities Education Act (IDEA, 2004), No Child Left Behind Act (NCLB, 2001) and Every Student Succeeds Act (ESSA, 2015) continued to raise the bar for educators and students. Even with accountability mandates and a focus on evidence-based practices, too many students today still experience failure or difficulty in school. In some cases, this is a result of deficits related to executive functioning, which plays a critical role in the planning, implementation, monitoring, and evaluation of adaptive behavior (Welsh, Pennington, Ozonoff, Rouse, & McCabe, 1990). The inclusion of strategies that address executive function deficits needs to become a part of our best practices repertoire.

WHAT IS EXECUTIVE FUNCTIONING (EF)?

Executive functioning is a group of processes that allows individuals to self-regulate the ways in which they interact with their environment. Executive function skills develop and improve throughout childhood and into young adulthood.

Executive functioning involves the metacognitive processes of making decisions, planning actions, and generating responses that are adaptive to environmental demands (Reynolds, Horton, & Decker, 2008). There are a variety of models for grouping executive function skills. Brown (2005) identified six clusters of executive functions, while McCloskey, Perkins, and Van Diviner (2001) listed eleven. Still other models group executive functions differently. In this book, we categorize executive function skill areas as follows (see figure 1.1):

FIGURE 1.1 Strosnider and Sharpe Executive Function Categories

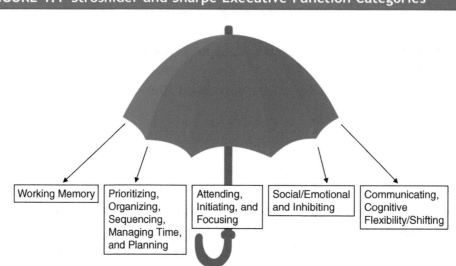

IMAGE SOURCE: www.pixabay.com/IO-images

THE EXECUTIVE FUNCTION GUIDEBOOK

- Working Memory
- Prioritizing, Organizing, Sequencing, Managing Time, and Planning
- Attending, Initiating, and Focusing
- Controlling Social/Emotional Behaviors and Impulses
- Communicating, Cognitive Flexibility/Shifting

The umbrella in figure 1.1 provides a visual of the EF categories as we organize and present them in this book. Each spoke of the umbrella includes a group of executive functions connected to chapters in the book. The EFs from left to right are covered in detail in the same sequence in chapters 2 through 6.

Executive function deficits are recognized in the DSM-5, and we know executive function (EF) deficits may lead to a plethora of inappropriate school and social behaviors. Dawson and Guare (2009) describe students with EF deficits as "smart but scattered." Researchers at the Child Mind Institute (2015) propose that executive function deficits occur two ways: externally and internally. The student has difficulty externally with behaviors and internally with thinking and learning. External behaviors associated with EF deficits may include losing assignments before turning them in, seemingly not focusing, and not getting started on tasks. Internal behaviors may include difficulty understanding what is expected, problems with taking notes, and/or problems determining what is important in a written passage. Table 1.1 outlines some signs of executive functioning deficits presented by children and adolescents.

If the student is demonstrating many of the descriptors, the next step is to provide intervention. You will find information on interventions throughout this book. As mentioned earlier, executive functions are intertwined and a student may exhibit difficulties in multiple categories. If the interventions are not effective, formal evaluation by a qualified professional may be necessary.

HOW DO ALL STUDENTS BENEFIT FROM EXECUTIVE FUNCTION SKILLS TRAINING?

Executive function skills are essential in the successful completion of life's everyday tasks. Children are not born with executive function skills, but they do have the ability to develop these skills through explicit instruction. The teaching of such skills may begin as early as preschool. As teachers and administrators, it is important to have proof that explicit training of executive function skills has proven to have positive outcomes. Sasser, Bierman, Heinrich, and Nix (2017) developed the REDI Program, which focused on teaching preschoolers the prereading skills necessary for school success in combination with the social skills needed for getting along with people. Three hundred sixty-five preschoolers from forty-four Head Start programs throughout Pennsylvania participated in this study. Participants' executive function skills were assessed prior to the skill training. The participants were classified as having either low, medium, or high executive function skills. Students were randomly selected for the control group or the REDI group. The

TABLE 1.1 Some Signs to Look for When Suspecting That Executive Function Issues Are Present

WORKING MEMORY	PRIORITIZING, ORGANIZING, SEQUENCING, MANAGING TIME, AND PLANNING	ATTENDING, INITIATING, AND FOCUSING	SOCIAL/EMOTIONAL AND INHIBITING	COMMUNICATING, COGNITIVE FLEXIBILITY/ SHIFTING
• Does not connect previous learning with current learning	• Is not goal minded and does not plan ahead	• Appears to be daydreaming in class	• Difficulty filtering inappropriate comments	• Difficulty with oral language
• Difficulty remembering sounds and words	• Time management issues such as loses track of time	• Procrastinates starting assignments	• Exhibits class clown behaviors	• May have a limited vocabulary
• Difficulty forming letters for writing	• Has difficulty determining a task sequence	• Distracted easily	• Interrupts others	• Difficulty with written language
• Forgets the sequence for spelling	• Becomes overwhelmed with long term assignments	• Fidgets	• Does not adjust emotions for different experiences	• May have an aversion to handwriting
• Forgets what has been read	• Becomes overwhelmed when there is a need to balance multiple tasks	• Has difficulty focusing on a speaker	• Recognizes behavior needs to be improved but unable to control it	• Trouble interpreting body language
• Difficulty memorizing facts	• Cannot find materials	• Asks questions or makes comments that do not match the subject at hand	• Reacts before thinking	• Difficulty understanding the intent of a verbal message
• Difficulty remembering steps of a process	• Does not record assignments	• Has to reread information multiple times	• Poor relationships with peers and adults	• Resistant to change—perseverates and is ritualistic
• Starts talking and forgets what they are saying in midsentence	• Rushes through assignments	• Insecure about how to move forward with an assignment	• May refuse to participate in class due to stress, frustration, sadness, shyness, lack of confidence, etc.	• Difficulty shifting from one activity to another
• Forgets to submit completed assignments	• Submits assignments late			• Inflexible thinking
	• Difficulty completing homework			

prereading and executive function skill training intervention was then performed. Results showed that children with low executive function skills in the REDI group had less of a decline than those in the control group. This trajectory was sustained through the third grade.

A longitudinal study, *Executive Functions Deficits in Kindergarten Predict Repeated Academic Difficulties Across Elementary School,* conducted by Morgan et al. (2018) was presented at the American Educational Research Association (AERA) 2018 annual meeting. The study tracked 11,000 kindergarten students through the third grade. A major finding of this research was that children who exhibited executive function difficulties in kindergarten, regardless of their race, socioeconomic level, or academic abilities, continued to experience academic difficulties in later years. The authors concluded that early intervention efforts are necessary before children internalize negative feelings about their academic performance and exhibit problem behaviors.

Diamond and Lee (2011) found that executive function skills training not only improved school readiness but positively impacted academic success in students ages four through twelve. As well, executive function skills continue to predict reading and math aptitude throughout a student's school and life experiences.

Currently, most students do not receive explicit instruction in executive function skills. Indeed, students struggling with these skills are often advised to try harder, pay attention, and behave. The students may try to do better, but without the right interventions, they do not know how to improve these skills. As time goes on, the difficulty they experience with executive functioning keeps dragging them into a downward spiral, and they become more and more reluctant to try.

Some students may begin a downward spiral as early as preschool. If this spiral is not stopped, it may result in retention, or worse—dropping out. While there are usually multiple reasons for poor student outcomes, there is often a similar pattern for students with executive function weaknesses. These students may

- not understand all the demands made upon them,
- find it difficult to pay attention,
- have troubling remembering what they have been taught,
- not always follow the rules,
- find it difficult to get along with others, or
- not begin work in a timely manner.

When we and parents fail to recognize these characteristics as pointing to executive function deficits, we sometimes wrongly assume that the student is simply not trying and is not well behaved. This in turn may lead to the student feeling that

- we do not care for him or her.
- the demands being made upon him or her are too hard, too easy, stupid, confusing, not meant for him/her, for example.

- he or she can do better and will try harder.

- he or she does not want to attend school any longer.

- he or she might as well not try, because success is not possible.

As time goes on, the downward spiral continues (see figures 1.2 and 1.3). While the school may implement academic interventions, these are often inadequate because the issue of executive function is not specifically addressed. Meltzer (2007) suggests you pay attention to a student's difficulties in executive function skills as early as preschool.

FIGURE 1.2 What Does the Downward Spiral Look Like?

What Does the Downward Spiral Look Like?

WHAT THE STUDENT MAY FEEL . . .		HOW THE TEACHER, PARENT OR PEER MAY INTERPRET . . .
"The demands upon me are too hard/too easy/stupid/pointless, etc."		"The student doesn't seem to care about schoolwork."
"The teacher's directions are confusing me."		"The student is not listening and following directions."
"Even when I try, I fail."		"The student needs to try harder."
"I can't sit still and pay attention in class."		"The student does not pay attention."
"I always forget what I have learned."		"The student does not remember what I have taught."
"The teacher doesn't care about me."		"The student does not respect me."
"I'll never do well in school."		"The student is not motivated."
"I don't want to go to school anymore. I might as well drop out."		"I can't get through to this student."

EXECUTIVE FUNCTION SKILLS TRAINING

Although there is evidence of a genetic predisposition to executive function deficits, timely targeted intervention can minimize the impact on students' academic and life-long success. Students cannot demonstrate skills they do not have. However, through explicit training that is targeted to a student's individual strengths and weaknesses,

FIGURE 1.3 How to Stop the Downward Spiral—Reframing One's Thinking

How to Stop the Downward Spiral

WHAT THE STUDENT NEEDS TO THINK OR UNDERSTAND . . .	POSITIVELY REFRAMING THE MINDSET	WHAT THE TEACHER, PARENT OR PEER NEEDS TO THINK OR UNDERSTAND . . .
"What are some things I like about school (i.e., getting breakfast, lunch, snacks and food for the weekend; I like this teacher; being with my friends)."		"What are this student's strengths?" (i.e., What is he or she good at academically, socially, and behaviorally?)
"I need to tell the teacher that I am having trouble with the assignment. I do want to learn."		"What is happening that is causing the student to seem to not care about schoolwork?"
"I do not mean to do some of the things that I do; I just can't seem to help it."		"Could this student have an executive functioning difficulty?"

NEXT STEPS

- Make a commitment to help the student exit the Downward Spiral.
- Reach out to professionals and other resources regarding how to proceed.

Note: Review the 7-Step Model for help in this regard.

---

executive function skills can be developed and enhanced. Our book provides a 7-Step Model for executive function skills training that incorporates Universal Design for Learning (UDL) and the use of metacognition. With this approach to explicit strategy instruction, the selected strategy is taught in a manner that is compatible with how the student learns best. As well, our book offers potentially evidenced-based strategies for students who have common executive function skill deficits. Later in this chapter we outline various approaches you might use to fit executive functioning skills training into your already full school day.

WHAT IS UNIVERSAL DESIGN FOR LEARNING (UDL)?

In the 1980s, the movement for using technology—everything from high technology, including computers, to low technology, such as highlighters—to break learning barriers and level the playing field for students with disabilities brought enlightenment to educators of all types of learners. Thus, the onset of digital texts, digital speech, and other technologies created a positive shift in instructional delivery and learning goals not only for students with disabilities, but gradually for all learners. No longer was the traditional one-size-fits-all model for instruction deemed productive in supporting learning.

The emergence of new ways to instruct students led to the development in the 1990s of Universal Design for Learning (UDL), a framework to improve and optimize teaching and learning for all people based on neuroscientific findings (Center for Applied Special Technology [CAST], 2011). UDL is founded on two premises. The first premise is that **people learn via three types of networks categorized as affective, recognition, and strategic.** Affective networks address the "why" of learning in terms of the student's feelings, values, or emotions that influence learning. Recognition networks speak to the "what" of learning and how the student identifies and processes information. Finally, strategic networks attend to the "how" of learning, including how the student plans, executes, and monitors both mental and motor tasks (Meyer, Rose & Gordon, 2014, p. 51).

The second premise consists of **three principles: Multiple Means of Representation, Multiple Means of Action and Expression, and Multiple Means of Engagement.** Multiple Means of Representation addresses "what" the student needs to learn and how this information will be presented. Multiple Means of Action and Expression refers to "how" the student will gain this knowledge and demonstrate the knowledge. Multiple Means of Engagement employs "why" the student wants to do this. Engagement is necessary for learning that is meaningful (Meyer et al., 2014, p. 59).

The onset of the UDL model focuses on designing instruction to meet the learning needs and strengths of the student. This created a paradigm shift in instructional delivery; using this model, you teach in the manner best suited to the students' diverse learning needs rather than teaching with the traditional one-size-fits-all approach. With that in mind, we have incorporated the UDL guidelines and added UDL considerations as an important component of our 7-Step Model. Figure 1.4 illustrates this incorporation.

FIGURE 1.4 UDL Guidelines Consideration

UDL Guidelines Consideration			
Executive Function Deficit:			
Multiple Means of Representation—Recognition Network WHAT is the content to be learned?	Multiple Means of Action and Expression—Strategic Networks HOW will the student demonstrate his or her knowledge and skills?	Multiple Means of Engagement—Affective Network WHY should the student want to learn this?	Based on your Considerations of the Principles, check to see that all three of these areas are considered in planning.

TABLE 1.2 Classes Without and Classes With UDL Considerations

CLASSES WITHOUT UDL CONSIDERATIONS	CLASSES WITH UDL CONSIDERATIONS
Characteristics include many of the following:	*Characteristics include many of the following:*
• Uses a *one-size-fits-all* approach to teaching	• Uses an analysis of student needs to guide instruction
• Addresses goals and objectives for the class in general	• Addresses goals and objectives based on individual needs
• May not differentiate instruction for all students	• Differentiates for all students with supportive technology available
• May require identical criterion for work completed by all students	• Groups students based on instructional and individual needs
• May group students based on one factor	• Provides opportunities for group collaboration
• May not encourage collaboration in group work	• Uses performance-based learning
• Uses grades exclusively as a measure of student achievement	• Designs classroom based on instruction and student needs
• May not consider the individual when assigning grades	• Determines grades with a variety of activities based on student needs
• Accommodates and modifies as required by legal regulations	• Accommodates and modifies for all students on an as needed basis

The implementation of UDL decreases learning barriers for all students due to the emphasis on learner variability. In providing a flexible approach to instructional design and delivery, the teacher promotes learner engagement, which is essential for learning to take place. A flexible approach to demonstrating skill fluency and mastery promotes learner participation through the following: receiving purposeful content, being motivated to learn, being resourceful and knowledgeable throughout the learning process, setting appropriate goals, and implementing strategies that support the acquisition of these goals. After over two decades of using the UDL model, there is solid evidence that this instructional delivery model is best for all students, not just those students with disabilities (Meyer et al., 2014).

Executive function training provides strategies for the teacher and student to use that help compensate for the student's areas of executive function weakness. Teaching students these strategies while incorporating UDL provides a vehicle for instructional delivery that supports the individual learning needs of each student. It is a practice that benefits all students in today's diverse classrooms. Table 1.3 illustrates how you can teach students executive function strategies while incorporating UDL.

	MULTIPLE MEANS OF REPRESENTATION—THE "WHAT" OF LEARNING: WHAT YOU CAN DO TO PRESENT THE INFORMATION	MULTIPLE MEANS OF ACTION AND EXPRESSION—THE "HOW" OF LEARNING: HOW THE STUDENT WILL ORGANIZE AND EXPRESS LEARNING	MULTIPLE MEANS OF ENGAGEMENT—THE "WHY" OF LEARNING: WHY THE STUDENT WANTS TO BE MOTIVATED TO LEARN AND REMAIN FOCUSED
Tool	• Lectures • Discussions • Books, magazines, newspapers • Guest presenters • Storytelling • Timelines • Modeling • Diagrams • Listening to music • Demonstrating • Videos • Podcasts • Role playing • Choral reading • Popcorn reading • Experiments • Games • Manipulatives • Dressing up like a character and acting a role • Pictures • Paintings • Post-it Notes	• Reports (written, oral) • Singing • Rapping • Acting • Demonstrating • Interviewing • Dancing • Diagrams • Creating videos • Creating podcasts • Dioramas • Drawing • Portfolios • Tests (written, short answer, true/false, multiple choice, dictated response) • Projects • Sequencing activities • Manipulatives • Highlighting, underlining text, bolding text • Self-assessment of learning • Post-it Note Summaries	• Background knowledge • Extending time for task completion • Color-coding • Highlighting, underlining text, bolding text • Discussions • Pro/con activities • Demonstrating • Group activities • Journaling • Summarizing information • Work centers • K-W-L-S Chart • Games • Reinforcers

TABLE 1.3 Teaching Executive Function Strategies While Incorporating UDL

	MULTIPLE MEANS OF REPRESENTATION—THE "WHAT" OF LEARNING: WHAT YOU CAN DO TO PRESENT THE INFORMATION	MULTIPLE MEANS OF ACTION AND EXPRESSION—THE "HOW" OF LEARNING: HOW THE STUDENT WILL ORGANIZE AND EXPRESS LEARNING	MULTIPLE MEANS OF ENGAGEMENT—THE "WHY" OF LEARNING: WHY THE STUDENT WANTS TO BE MOTIVATED TO LEARN AND REMAIN FOCUSED
Supportive Technology	• Videos • PowerPoints • Cameras • Computers/iPads/ APPS iPads • iPods • Microphones • Promethean boards • Prezi • Glogster • Lino • Speech to Text Software • Learning Ally (https://www. learningally.org/) • Websites • ZOOM Sessions • Facetime • Skype • Text on tape	• Videos • PowerPoints • Cameras • Microphones • Promethean boards • Prezi • Glogster • Lino • Speech to Text Software • Learning Ally (https://www. learningally.org/) • Websites • ZOOM Sessions • Facetime • Skype • Text on tape	• Videos • PowerPoints • Cameras • Microphones • Promethean boards • Prezi • Glogster • Lino • Speech to Text Software • Learning Ally (https://www. learningally.org/) • Audio text • Websites • ZOOM Sessions • Facetime • Skype • Computers/iPads/ APPS • iPods

Executive function skills training as described in this book involves your teaching students specific skill-building strategies incorporating metacognition that, in combination with UDL, help them with the following EF processes:

- Setting goals
- Self-regulating (social/emotional, inhibiting, cognitive flexibility/shifting)
- Developing a game plan for learning
- Attending to instruction
- Organizing materials and resources

- Prioritizing events and information
- Initiating work within a reasonable timeframe
- Managing time
- Communicating their learning needs
- Engaging working memory
- Self-assessing progress in the mastery and the appropriate use of strategies that support executive functioning

The practice of combining executive function skills training with Universal Design for Learning and metacognition strengthens the stage for learning because the training enables students to "tune in" to instruction in the academic, communication, and social/emotional realms. Executive function training provides strategies for you and your student to use that help compensate for the student's areas of executive function weakness.

METACOGNITION

Metacognition is defined as thinking about one's own thinking and learning (Meltzer, 2010). It provides your student with the opportunity to think about his or her

- general ability,
- competency on specific tasks,
- control over outcomes,
- causes of failure, and
- understanding the benefits of specific strategies (Reid & Leinemann, 2006).

Teaching students to use metacognition is a crucial component of the 7-Step Model of executive function skills training. The process of metacognition involves the student's understanding of his or her learning needs and applying this understanding, in combination with appropriate strategies, to successfully accomplish a task. Meltzer (2010) states, "To build their motivation, persistence, and work ethic, students need to understand their profiles of strengths and weaknesses. Doing so enables them to determine which strategies work well for them, as well as, why, where, when, and how to apply specific strategies" (p. 10). Students who use metacognition effectively plan and use techniques such as self-talk to reach their goals. The figure below represents the use of metacognition in the learning process.

CONSIDERING EXECUTIVE FUNCTIONS, METACOGNITION, UDL, AND LEARNING

Figure 1.5 outlines the considerations that both the teacher and student should address when addressing executive functions, metacognition, UDL, and learning. Both have specific elements that must be reflected upon when determining which strategy is the best choice for the student, and the role of the teacher and the student in the strategy selection process (see figure 1.5).

FIGURE 1.5 Teacher–Student Roles While Considering Executive Functions, Metacognition, UDL, and Learning

THE TEACHER	THE STUDENT
• **What are the student's needs?** • **How does the student learn best?** • **What strategies does the student know?** • **Is my lesson accessible?**	• **What am I learning?** • **What do I need to do?** • **Where do I need help?** • **Which strategy do I use?**
✓ Has a sound understanding of the student's executive function deficits.	✓ Has knowledge of the situations that create learning challenges for him or her.
✓ Presents information using a Multiple Means of Representation approach to instruction that considers the student's executive function deficits. Information is taught using a variety of modalities such as hearing, seeing (both word and graphic organizers), and touching. Alternatives for each of these modalities are offered as well.	✓ Uses metacognition to reflect on the approach to instruction that is best to facilitate his or her learning (Multiple Means of Representation) and advocates for this in an appropriate manner.
✓ Provides the student with Multiple Means of Action and Expression while considering the student's executive function deficits. A variety of response methods are provided, accompanied by the executive function strategy support and technology.	✓ Uses metacognition to think about what is being required, the possible roadblocks, and the executive function strategy and technology needed to complete any task, assignment, or assessment (Multiple Means of Action and Expression).
✓ Provides the student with Multiple Means of Engagement in terms of relevance to the student's ability and executive function deficits, optimizes the opportunity for student choice, and limits distractions. The assessment process incorporates multiple means of engagement as well.	✓ Uses metacognition to think about what he or she is learning, why this information is important to learn, and what strategies he or she must use to remain focused and participate appropriately. The student also asks questions or seeks support when needed (Multiple Means of Engagement).

This is how one teacher encourages her students to use metacognition.

Teacher Testimonial from: Batya Toso

Special Educator

Grade(s) Taught: K, 4th, and 5th

Strategy Name: Cognitive/Metacognitive Strategy Instruction

Strategy Designed for: Small group

Batya Toso

Students with disabilities were introduced to the strategy in a regularly occurring small group intervention outside the general education classroom. The two interventions were to target reading comprehension and mathematical thinking and problem solving. Initially students were taught the basic components of learning, as well as meta-cognition. Students were also taught the steps of learning or task completion using a Plan–Monitor–Evaluate frame-work. During the introduction phase, I modeled the pro-cess, had students practice the process, and identified the components as they arose.

Once students easily identified where in their learning these metacognitive components took place, I introduced them to metacognitive questions related to each compo-nent. For instance, a question relating to task knowledge could be, "What materials or resources do I need?" A possible question for strategy knowledge is, "Is the strategy I'm using working?" Students then collaboratively sorted the metacognitive questions under the headers Personal Knowledge, Task Knowledge, and Strategy Knowledge. Finally, students discussed which questions were appropriate during the Plan stage, the Monitor stage, and the Evaluate stage of learning.

IMAGE SOURCE: iStock.com/dolgachov

THE EXECUTIVE FUNCTION GUIDEBOOK

Students were then introduced to a bookmark containing a checklist encompassing each component of metacognition within the Plan–Monitor–Evaluate framework. In the beginning lessons I modeled and did Think-Alouds using the bookmark several times, together with a cloze format of guiding questions to help students come up with other questions that may be appropriate. Students then practiced use of the bookmark. The bookmark was reviewed each day and throughout the lesson as a method of ensuring we were on task; students were gradually given greater responsibility answering the questions themselves.

To help students further internalize this learning structure I made sure that any anchor charts I created followed the Plan–Monitor–Evaluate structure. For example, when focusing on the reading strategy of determining importance, I created an anchor chart listing each of the steps of the strategy under the Plan–Monitor–Evaluate headers:

Plan: What is my purpose for reading? What am I supposed to find out?

Monitor: Does what I'm reading match my purpose? Does this detail help me understand the main idea better?

Evaluate: Does the information I gathered meet my purpose? Can I summarize the most important parts of what I read?

After a six-week period, when students were more comfortable using the bookmark to guide their processes, the general education classroom teacher then began to use the bookmarks with the students during small groups.

Data

Data were collected over an eight-week period for classroom assessments in reading comprehension and math problem solving assessments with two-step word problems. Data were also collected to measure the frequency that student prompting was required to determine if improvements in student independence were made. Students using the strategy showed an improvement of 48 percent on math assessments and 42 percent on reading assessments. (Student performance in math was significantly lower at baseline than in reading.) Students showed a significantly greater decline in the frequency of prompting in a small group setting outside of the general education classroom—a 60 percent decline—than inside the general education classroom—a 34 percent decline. However, it should be noted that data measuring student independence with the checklist in the classroom were gathered for the first two weeks of generalization, whereas data for independence in the self-contained setting were gathered for six weeks.

Student Feedback

P., fifth-grade student with Other Hearing Impairment (OHI) due to ADHD:

"The bookmark helped me a lot figure out how to do what I need to do. I don't need to sit all confused anymore."

B., fourth-grade student with Specific Learning Disability (SLD):

"At first I didn't like it because it was a lot of steps to do and think, but then I started liking it because it actually made work easier. I didn't realize it made it easier until I lost my bookmark though. Stuff was harder all over again, but I asked for a new one."

L., fourth-grade student with SLD:

"It looked like a lot but then it helped me make things make sense. I knew what to do."

(Continued)

FIGURE 1.6 Cognitive/Metacognitive Strategy Instruction Poster

A version is provided in Appendix 1.6.

THINKING ABOUT
WHAT I AM DOING AND LEARNING

When working on a task I need to:

1 Plan and think about what I am doing.

+ What is the task?
+ What resources do I need?
+ What background information do I already know about this task?
+ What strategy can help me complete this task?
+ Where do I think I might have difficulty?

2 Monitor myself as I am working.

+ Am I focused and attending to the task?
+ Am I understanding what I am doing?
+ Is the strategy I selected working? If not, what other strategy might help me?

3 Evaluate my finished task.

+ Did I finish the task correctly and on-time?
+ Am I happy with my work?
+ What did I learn by doing this assignment?
+ How will I use the information that I learned?
+ What would I do differently the next time I have to complete a similar task?

SOURCE: Sharpe, Strosnider, & Toso, 2017.

FIGURE 1.7 Cognitive/Metacognitive Strategy Instruction Bookmark (Front and Back)

The bookmark front includes questions to be asked about learning. The bookmark back includes questions to be asked about self-regulation. **A version is provided in Appendix 1.7.**

METACOGNITION-KNOWLEDGE
(Toso, 2015)

Bookmark Front

BEFORE I BEGIN (PLAN)

Task Knowledge
- ☐ What is the task and expectations?
- ☐ What materials or resources do I need?

Personal Knowledge
- ☐ What do I already know about this?
- ☐ How do I learn best and what do I need?

Strategy Knowledge
- ☐ What strategy will I use to do this?

AS I WORK (MONITOR)

Task Knowledge
- ☐ Is my work matching the expectations?

Personal Knowledge
- ☐ Am I understanding?
- ☐ Is the way I'm working matching my learning needs?

Strategy Knowledge
- ☐ Is this strategy working or not working?
- ☐ What other strategy can I try?

AFTER I FINISH (EVALUATE)

Task Knowledge
- ☐ Did I complete the task appropriately?

Personal Knowledge
- ☐ What did I learn?
- ☐ How will this knowledge help me in the future?

Strategy Knowledge
- ☐ How did this strategy help me?
- ☐ What might I try next time?

METACOGNITION-REGULATION
(Toso, 2015)

Bookmark Back

BEFORE I BEGIN (PLAN)
- ☐ How am I feeling?
- ☐ What should I do to get my body and brain ready to learn?

AS I WORK (MONITOR)
- ☐ Am I focused on my task?
- ☐ How am I feeling?
- ☐ What can I do to be on task and learning?

AFTER I FINISH (EVALUATE)
- ☐ How did I do with my focus and task?
- ☐ What might I try next time?

SOURCE: Toso, 2015.

SUPPORTIVE TECHNOLOGIES

Since technology is useful in leveling the field for accessibility to learning and helps to meet the diverse learning needs of all students, each chapter of this book will address specific websites, software, and apps that support executive function skill training. We use technology as a tool to complement the strategies we teach. We choose technology tools that address multiple age groups. Please note that technology resources are developed daily. CommonsenseMedia.org is an excellent resource for teachers seeking information regarding current technology for their students. Below is an example of the supportive technology table provided in each chapter.

TABLE 1.4 Supportive Technologies Chart Example

TECHNOLOGY TOOL CATEGORY (WEBSITE, SOFTWARE, APP)	NAME OF TECHNOLOGY	EXECUTIVE FUNCTION AREA ADDRESSED	AGE GROUP
Website	Center on the Developing Child Harvard University https://developingchild.harvard.edu/	All areas	Most ages
Software	Kidspiration	Communication	K to Grade 6
iPhone App	Whiteboard	Prioritizing	All ages
iPad App	SuperNote	Organization	Grade 4 to Grade 12

THE 7-STEP MODEL FOR EXECUTIVE FUNCTION SKILLS TRAINING

Based on observations during our decades of experience, we the authors have developed a 7-Step Model for executive function skills training incorporating UDL and metacognition. This model is potentially evidenced-based, as supported by our observations, data collection and informal assessments regarding the student's ability to learn and correctly use the strategies. By addressing both learning strengths and difficulties, this approach is effective for all types of learners. The seven steps, which are explored in detail in the remainder of this chapter, are shown in figure 1.8, 7-Step Model. The completion of the steps within the model is a flexible process in that some steps may have already been accomplished when you start the process. For example, you may already know that a student has been identified with an executive function deficit in a specific area. This knowledge would eliminate step 1 of the model process. Each step of the model should be regarded as a tool to prompt your thinking in terms of how to help the student learn. This may require an open mind to different approaches to instructional planning. In addition, a Modified 7-Step Model is included later in this chapter to address the needs of teachers who wish to implement the model with an entire class.

Subsequent chapters of this book walk the reader through the 7-Step process, using examples of students of different ages who exhibit typical executive function skill deficits. The components of each step are modeled for the teacher.

FIGURE 1.8 The 7-Step Model and 7-Step Model Modified

The models presented below illustrate the basic 7-Step Model and the 7-Step Model Modified to meet the needs of teachers who want to use the model with large groups.

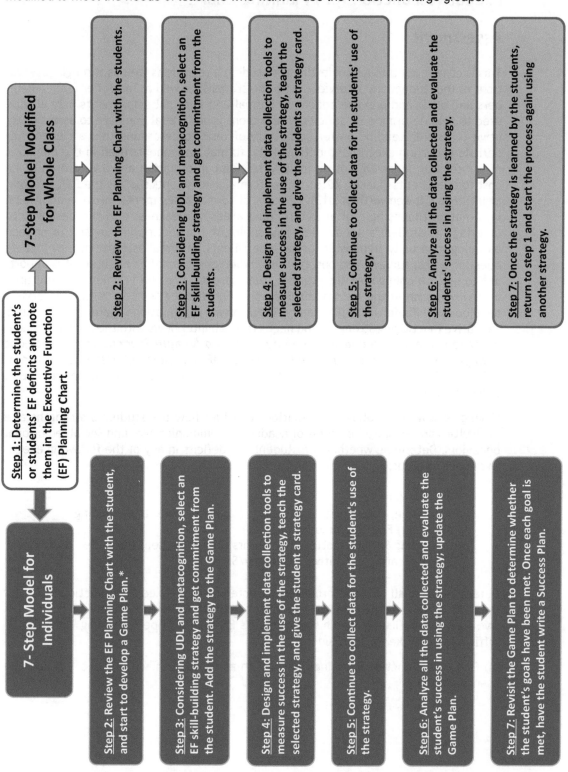

Examining Each of the 7-Steps in Detail for an Individual or Small Group

Step 1

Determine the student's EF deficits and note them in the Executive Function (EF) Planning Chart.

Assessment

This is completed through reviewing the student's records as well as through observations of the student and interviews with the student, as well as his or her family members and other and previous teachers. Formal and informal assessments may also be used to help determine EF deficits. While there is no federal mandate to assess executive functioning and no preferred battery of tests to determine that a student has deficits in certain executive function skills, formal assessments used in the diagnosis of a disability under IDEA often include relevant information and are offered at no cost to the parents (Tucker, 2015). Other formal assessments such as the *BRIEF* (Gioia, Isquith, Guy, & Kenworthy, 2013), or parts of formal assessments, provide additional information that is helpful in determining areas of weakness and the best way of meeting the student's needs. Neuropsychologists, school psychologists, or speech pathologists usually administer formal assessments. Informal assessment may include questionnaires, surveys, and observations. When questionnaires are used, it is important to get the opinions of the student, the parents, and the teacher(s). Structured interviews, such as the instrument *Executive Functioning Semi-Structured Interview* developed by Kaufman (2010), can be used to gain information regarding a student's executive functioning strengths and needs through interviews with the student, teachers, and parents. **Included in Appendix 1.15 is a Sample Student Self-Assesment Tool you can use or revise to meet the needs of your particular situation**. It provides actions for students to self-rate themselves and a column for teacher validation and comments.

Having reviewed the above information, consider how the student's strengths and difficulties are exhibited in terms of academic, communicative, and social/emotional behaviors. Determine whether the student has deficits in any of the following executive function areas:

- Working Memory
- Prioritizing, Organizing, Sequencing, Managing Time, and Planning
- Attending, Focusing, and Initiating
- Controlling Social/Emotional Behaviors, Inhibiting Behaviors
- Communicating, Cognitive Flexibility/Shifting

Determine from all of the information collected how the executive function difficulty presents. What behaviors does the learner exhibit that provide evidence of an executive function difficulty? Match the student's EF skill area personalizing what the EF difficulty looks like for the student(s).

An Executive Function Planning Chart, such as the one shown in table 1.5, may be used in this step.

Executive Function Planning

EXECUTIVE FUNCTION SKILL AREA	WHAT DOES THE DIFFICULTY LOOK LIKE FOR THIS STUDENT? (EXAMPLES)
Working Memory	Student does not remember what was read.
	Student forgets math facts and/or how to spell words known the night before.
	Student gets confused when following multistep directions.
Prioritizing, Organizing, Sequencing, Managing Time, and Planning	Student cannot find materials, glasses, and assignments.
	Student either rushes through an assignment or does not finish the task on time.
	Student's papers are sloppy and disorganized.
Attending, Initiating, and Focusing	Student needs several reminders to get started on a task or assignment.
	Student loses concentration very easily.
Controlling Social/ Emotional and Inhibiting Behaviors	Student impulsively calls out in class.
	Student makes inappropriate comments to peers and adults.
Communicating, Cognitive Flexibility/ Shifting	Student does not write coherently due to a lack of understanding language usage.
	Student's writing lacks sequencing of concepts and supporting details.
	Student may display inappropriate body language and facial expressions and/or have difficulty interpreting body language and facial expressions.
	Student is extremely slow to move from one activity on to another.
	Student finds it difficult to think about more than one thing at a time.

TABLE 1.5 Sample Executive Function (EF) Planning Chart

Step 2

Review the EF Planning Chart with the student and start to develop a Game Plan.

Reviewing the EF Planning Chart will guide the skills training for the specific executive function area. Whether you have the results of either formal or informal assessments or only informal assessments, it is important to discuss the results with the student and his or her parents. Once areas of executive functioning weakness are identified, you can begin developing the Game Plan with the student. The Game Plan starts the process of having the student "buy in" to the strategy. It enables the student to understand his or her areas of strength and difficulty. This understanding and awareness will later lead to student self-advocacy and greater independence in his or her learning process. The Game Plan includes the student's strengths, difficulties, goals for improvement, and strategies selected to enhance executive functioning through UDL and appropriate strategies.

Directions for Starting a Student Game Plan

- Base the Game Plan on the information gleaned from the records review, surveys, interviews, and the student's Executive Function Planning Chart.
- Identify the executive functions to work on based on information shared by the student and others.
- Work with the student to identify three things he or she does well and put them at the top of the Game Plan, under "What I do best." (See figures 1.9 and 1.10.)
- Work with the student to identify three goals and record them under "Things I would like to do better." ("Things I can do to help with my difficulties in school" will not be completed until the UDL planning process is finished and strategies have been selected, in step 3.)
- Consider strategies in step 3 to teach the student that will improve the executive function skill. (When selecting strategies to use for the Game Plan, consider other interventions being used in the classroom or at home to avoid duplicating efforts.)

Blank templates, modifiable versions of materials, and strategy cards can be found at http://resources.corwin.com/ExecutiveFunctioning.

FIGURE 1.9 The Student Game Plan for Elementary Students

Student Game Plan for: Kelly

What I do best: I am awesome at addition.

What I do best: My writing is very neat.

What I do best: I am a fast runner.

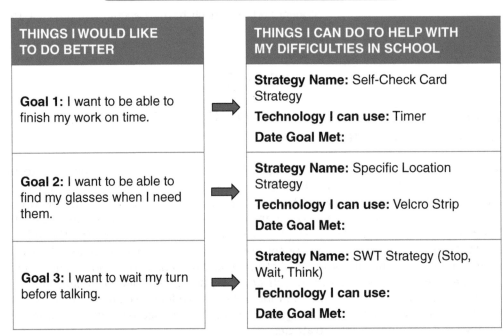

THINGS I WOULD LIKE TO DO BETTER	THINGS I CAN DO TO HELP WITH MY DIFFICULTIES IN SCHOOL
Goal 1: I want to be able to finish my work on time.	**Strategy Name:** Self-Check Card Strategy **Technology I can use:** Timer **Date Goal Met:**
Goal 2: I want to be able to find my glasses when I need them.	**Strategy Name:** Specific Location Strategy **Technology I can use:** Velcro Strip **Date Goal Met:**
Goal 3: I want to wait my turn before talking.	**Strategy Name:** SWT Strategy (Stop, Wait, Think) **Technology I can use:** **Date Goal Met:**

FIGURE 1.10 THE STUDENT GAME PLAN FOR SECONDARY STUDENTS

Student Game Plan for: <u>Matt</u>

What I like to do and feel that I do well: I am great at video games. I also like to listen to music and go to concerts. I know the words to a lot of songs. Science is my favorite subject because I like the labs.

Goals for Improvement and Corresponding Actions

GOAL 1: I would like to be able to finish my projects without waiting until the last minute.	GOAL 2: I would like to be able to find the writing mistakes before I turn in my papers.	GOAL 3: I would like to be able to get better grades on my homework.
Action 1: Backward Mapping Strategy and 9-Step Strategy	**Action 2:** COPS Strategy	**Action 3:** Home and Done Strategy
Supporting Technology: ICal	**Supporting Technology:** Spell Checker	**Supporting Technology:** Homework App
Date Goal Met:_____	**Date Goal Met:**_____	**Date Goal Met:**_____

A blank template for this chart is provided in Appendix 1.10. Blank templates, modifiable versions of materials, and strategy cards can be found at http:// resources.corwin.com/ExecutiveFunctioning.

Step 3

Considering UDL and metacognition, select an EF skill-building strategy and get commitment from the student. Add the strategy to the Game Plan.

To optimize the learning of *all* students, least of all students with executive function deficits, it is imperative to incorporate the three principles of Universal Design for Learning (UDL) into lessons: Multiple Means of Representation, Multiple Means of Action and Expression, and Multiple Means of Engagement. As a teacher, it is imperative that lessons are flexible, adaptable, and customizable, making them accessible to all learners. Following the guidelines of UDL will help ensure your lessons incorporate techniques and tools that provide options and scaffolds for executive functions.

Incorporating the metacognitive process, consider your student's learning needs, including EF deficits and strengths, to select the manner of teaching best suited to the student. Also consider the executive function and other needs of all students in the class. Decide how you will account for the student's particular executive function deficits and learning needs in the lesson, as well as in pre-, formative, and summative assessments. Select approaches, material customizations, supports, options, modifications or adaptations, and tools, including assistive technology, to include in instruction. Some supports will benefit all learners or multiple learners, while others will be applicable to only the student in question. At the same time, start thinking about EF skill-building strategies you can teach the student while modeling metacognition throughout the process.

Once you have determined the executive function skill and skills that are most important for the lesson, how the student's EF deficit will impact his or her learning, and how to design the lesson using UDL principles, consider which EF skill-building strategies to teach the student to help address the deficit. Each chapter includes several different strategies that can be used to address the EF function area addressed in that chapter.

Table 1.6 provides a structure for planning, integrating UDL and metacognition, and choosing an appropriate strategy for use with the student. The components in this table should be thought about prior to teaching the student the strategy. Table 1.6 is to be used to guide your thinking about the components involved when selecting a strategy for the student. *A blank template for this chart is provided in the Appendix 1.10, and blank templates, modifiable versions of materials, and strategy cards can be found at http://resources.corwin.com/ExecutiveFunctioning*. This process is flexible as to both your needs and the needs of your student. After a strategy is selected, add it to the student's game plan.

Questions for the student to answer are listed on table 1.7. Using these tables will lead you through a process that results in appropriate strategy selection.

TABLE 1.6 Sample Selecting a Strategy for the Student While Integrating UDL for Kelly, an Elementary Student

Student: Kelly

Executive Function Deficit: Prioritizing, Organizing, Sequencing, Managing Time, and Planning

Game Plan Goal: Goal 1: I would like to be able to finish my work on time.

MULTIPLE MEANS OF REPRESENTATION

Things for you to consider:

1. What information does the student already know?	2. What are the instructional goals for the student in relation to the executive function addressed?	3. What extended activities will be needed?	4. What enrichment activities can be implemented?	5. What will you need to incorporate when teaching the strategy?

MULTIPLE MEANS OF ACTION AND EXPRESSION

Things for you to consider:

1. How will you conduct preassessment, formative, and summative assessments for the student's learning?	2. What platforms will be permitted for the student to demonstrate mastery?

MULTIPLE MEANS OF ENGAGEMENT

Things for you to consider:

1. How will you teach the student in a manner that actively engages him or her?

TABLE 1.6 (Continued)

Based on your Considerations of the Principles for this goal, what strategy would you select that aligns with the three Principles and aligns with UDL and the Strategy Selected?

> **Name of Strategy:**
>
> **This strategy is selected because**
>
> 1. in terms of **Multiple Means of Representation, it . . .**
>
> 2. in terms of **Multiple Means of Action and Expression, it . . .**
>
> 3. in terms of **Multiple Means of Engagement, it . . .**

Once you and the student have selected a strategy, add the strategy name to the "Things I can do to help with my difficulties in school" column of the Game Plan for an elementary student (figure 1.9) or the "Action" column of the Game Plan for a secondary student (figure 1.10). Technology that supports the strategy such as websites, software, and apps should be added to these columns of the Game Plan as well.

The final phase of step 3 addresses the student's responsibility. It is important that the student take an active role in the strategy learning process. Once the strategy is selected, the student completes **table 1.7 Student Implementation of Strategy With a Focus on Metacognition and UDL Principles.** This helps the student to use the metacognitive process when responding to the questions posed, as well as taking ownership of his or her role in learning the strategy. *A blank template for this chart is available in Appendix 1.11, and blank templates, modifiable versions of materials, and strategy cards can be found at http://resources.corwin.com/ExecutiveFunctioning.*

TABLE 1.7 Student Implementation of Strategy With a Focus on Metacognition and UDL Principles

Student:

Executive Function Deficit:

Game Plan Goal:

Strategy Selected:

METACOGNITION—QUESTIONS THE STUDENT THINKS ABOUT AND RESPONDS TO

Things for you to consider:

1. What am I supposed to do?	2. Why is this strategy important for me to use and how will it help me?	3. What are the steps of the strategy?
4. Is there technology I can use?	5. What should I think about when using this strategy?	

Step 4

Design and implement data collection tools to measure success in the use of the strategy, teach the selected strategy, and give the student a strategy card.

Use the data from step 1 to show the goals the student agreed to from step 2, and design data tools to measure the use of the strategies you and the student selected in step 3 to guide the strategy instruction.

Explain the strategy to the student and model it.

Provide motivation for the strategy such as use of a reinforcement and gain a continued commitment by the student. Games such as Jeopardy, Bingo, matching, and charades can be used to reinforce recall of how to use the strategy. Each game should require the student to explain the strategy and how it helps them.

Give the student the strategy card. Have the student practice the strategy using metacognition and referring to the strategy card as needed until he or she can use the strategy with automaticity. Collect data and revise as necessary.

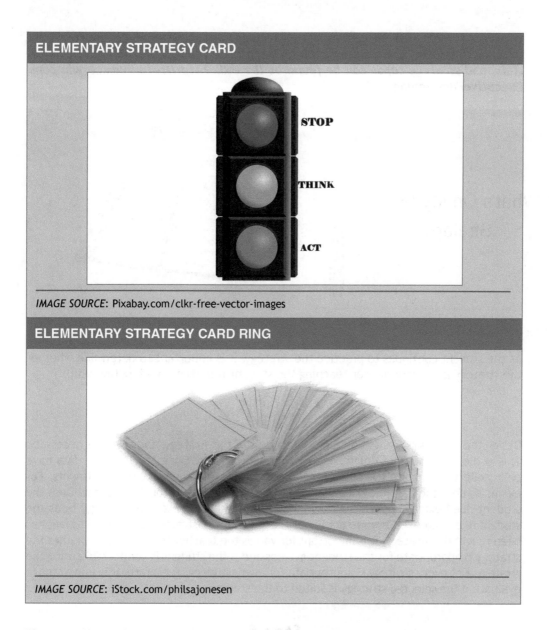

ELEMENTARY STRATEGY CARD

STOP

THINK

ACT

IMAGE SOURCE: Pixabay.com/clkr-free-vector-images

ELEMENTARY STRATEGY CARD RING

IMAGE SOURCE: iStock.com/philsajonesen

The strategy card summarizes the strategy and serves as a reminder of how to use it. It outlines the process and steps that need to be followed to successfully implement the strategy.

Directions for Making Strategy Cards

To make the card, create or purchase a 3" × 5" or business-size card. Place the name of the strategy on the front of the card, along with visuals if that is helpful for the student.

Place a description of how to use the strategy on the back of the card. It is helpful if this description is stated in the student's own words. Check the description for accuracy.

Most students with executive functioning deficits will need multiple strategies to help them with several EF skills, with separate cards for each strategy. Clip the various strategy cards together using a notebook binder ring to create a strategy ring. To do this, punch a hole in the top left of the card if you are placing the card on a strategy ring. The ring provides students with an individualized portable reference system of strategies they have learned that support their areas of executive function weakness. Older students may prefer placing their cards in a clear vinyl card sleeve in their binder.

When the student finds success using the strategy in the classroom, generalize its use to other classrooms and situations. *Blank templates, modifiable versions of materials, and strategy cards can be found at the URL: http://resources.corwin.com/ExecutiveFunctioning.*

SECONDARY STRATEGY CARD	SECONDARY STRATEGY CARD HOLDER
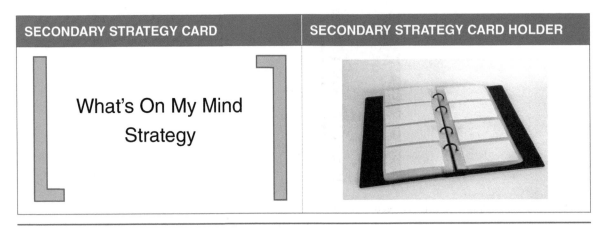 What's On My Mind Strategy	

IMAGE SOURCE: Pixabay.com/adnovak

As the student continues to practice the strategy, it is important to determine whether the strategy is appropriate for teaching the student the executive function skill.

Design the data tools, collect data on the success of the strategy, and revise as necessary. This is the baseline phase of the data collection process. Once the baseline data have been collected, analyze the data and go back and make any necessary adjustments. For example, does the baseline data show that this strategy works for the student? Does the student need extra supports such as cues to remember to use the strategy? Does the student need extended time to complete the steps of the strategy? After the student has been taught the strategy, it is important for you as the teacher to determine whether the strategy is appropriate for the student's needs and if the student is comfortable using the strategy. Not every strategy is appropriate for every student; therefore, it is important to evaluate if the selected strategy is suited to the student.

Step 5

Continue to collect data for the student's use of the strategy.

As the student is taught a new executive function skill-building strategy, you will need to determine whether the student has mastered the strategy, which includes both using the strategy correctly and generalizing it to a variety of settings. Additional assessments will be based on the progress the student makes in demonstrating the executive function skill. Over time, the student will likely be using many strategies, some of which will apply to several executive function areas, and the data being kept will be vital in determining the continued effectiveness of the strategies being used. Data collection and record keeping will be addressed in detail throughout the book. A sample data recording template such as Sample Considerations for Ongoing Data Analysis Chart (see table 1.8) assists in the strategy data collection process. *A blank template for this chart is provided in Appendix 1.12, and blank templates, modifiable versions of materials, and strategy cards can be found at http://resources .corwin.com/ExecutiveFunctioning.*

TABLE 1.8 Sample Considerations for Ongoing Data Analysis Chart

Student Name: *Kelly*
Strategy Used: *Self-Check Card Strategy*
Please write yes, no, or N/A for Not Applicable.
_____*Yes*_____ 1. The strategy is cited in the student's Ongoing Data Analysis.
_____*Yes*_____ 2. The student understands the goal of using the strategy.
_____*Yes*_____ 3. The student can explain what the strategy is and why he or she is using it.
_____*Yes*_____ 4. There is a means of collecting data to measure the student's progress.
_____*Yes*_____ 5. The tools to measure the academic or social/emotional area that the executive function deficit is impacting are appropriate.
_____*Yes*_____ 6. Daily feedback is provided for at least one week when the strategy began.
_____*Yes*_____ 7. The student is provided with reinforcement and knows his or her standing.
_____*Yes*_____ 8. Data are analyzed with the student and the revisions are made as needed.
_____*Yes*_____ 9. The selected strategy is appropriate for the student's needs.
Comments:
Number 9. Kelly is starting to generalize this strategy to other settings.

Provide time and multiple opportunities for the student to practice the strategy until he or she has memorized it. According to Center on the Developing Child at Harvard University: https://developingchild.harvard.edu/science/key-concepts/executive-function/ (2017) scaffolding helps a child to practice and learn executive function skills. This is an integral process for the child to learn to independently perform the desired executive function skill. Diamond and Lee (2011) found that only practiced executive function skills generalize across environments. It is best if these skills can be practiced daily. Once the strategy is learned, you may then add more strategies to the student's repertoire. Students should periodically review the strategies on the ring to maintain familiarity.

Step 6

Analyze all the data collected and evaluate the student's success in using the strategy; update the Game Plan.

Step 6 focuses on the assessment of the student's utilization of the strategy and its effectiveness. As the teacher, you need to determine the student's success in learning and generalizing the strategy, and whether the strategy is helping the student. Ongoing assessment should address the following questions:

- Does the student use the strategy in the noted area of executive function difficulty?
- Does the student generalize, that is, use the strategy in different scenarios?
- Has the target executive function deficit improved since the student started using the strategy?

Analysis of Data and Evaluation of Student Success Using the Strategy

Design and implement a data analysis plan to determine the strategy's effectiveness. A final assessment of the strategy needs to be completed before deciding the student has mastered the strategy. *A blank template for this chart is provided in Appendix 1.12, and blank templates, modifiable versions of materials, and strategy cards can be found at http://resources.corwin.com/ExecutiveFunctioning.*

Sample Template for Final Assessment of the Strategy

<u>Date:</u> 4/12/18

<u>Name of Student:</u> Kelly

<u>Executive Function(s) Being Addressed:</u> Initiating, Time Management, Attending

<u>Intervention Implemented? (Describe the Strategy and How It Is Being Used).</u>

The Self-Check Card was used by Kelly initially after an intermittent verbal prompt by the teacher. Kelly later checked her progress based on the use of a timer. At the end of the strategy instruction period, Kelly used the Self-Check Card independently to monitor her progress.

- ☐ **Strategy Used From:** 3/20/18   **To:** 4/10/18
- ☑ **UDL-EF Process Used**
  - Completed Executive Function Planning Chart
  - Thought through Selecting a Strategy for the Student While Integrating UDL Chart
  - Created with student a Strategy Implementation With a Focus on UDL and Metacognition Chart
  - Field-tested the strategy
  - Created strategy card for the strategy and placed on the student's Strategy Ring
  - Finalized the strategy and selected this strategy for the student
  - Taught the Strategy and kept data of usage
  - Made revisions as necessary

- ☑ **Data for Measured Results**

  Data were analyzed and showed that the strategy helped Kelly complete her work on time 12 out of 15 days.

- ☑ **Anecdotal Report of Results**

  Kelly reported that she liked using the Self-Check Card. She was happy to finish her work on time.

- ☑ **Review of Results:**

  Kelly began generalizing the use of the Self-Check Card at times when it was not required.

- ☑ **Summary Report on Game Plan Progress:**

  Although Kelly has experienced success with this strategy, she will need additional reinforcement in other situations.

Summary Report on Implications of Strategy Use on Academic Skills and Social Interactions (continue on reverse side):

Step 7

Revisit the Game Plan to determine whether the student's goals have been met. Once each goal is met, have the student write a Success Plan.

Once a goal is met, have the student write a Success Plan (figure 1.8 or appendix 1.14) outlining the steps he or she will follow as he or she transitions to using the strategy independently. Reviewing the EF Planning Chart (table 1.5) will provide information that will help in the determination of whether the student's goals have been met.

To determine whether a goal has been met, look at the data for the entire period the student has been using the strategy. Review the data with the student and discuss the following key questions:

- Does he or she feel the strategy is helping? Do the data support this perception?
- Does he or she feel it would be beneficial to continue to use this strategy?
- Does he or she feel ready to move on to another goal for this executive function?

The plan becomes a self-advocating tool the student can use for seeking the assistance he or she needs to achieve ongoing success. In this document, the student should identify the following:

- What I want to do next
- Difficulties that I may have
- Strategies I can use to help myself
- What the teacher can do to help me succeed

Note: Having met the Game Plan goals does not mean the student will no longer need UDL considerations for lessons, but it does mean the student is improving in that executive function skill.

A blank template for the Sample Student Success Plan *for both* Elementary and Secondary Students *is available in Appendix 1.14, and blank templates, modifiable versions of materials, and strategy cards can be found at http://resources .corwin.com/ExecutiveFunctioning.*

The completion of the Game Plan provides the opportunity to identify new EF deficit challenges for the student to work on. Most students experience difficulty in several areas of executive function. The next step would be to return to the executive function planning chart to determine other EF deficits to address while the student continues to maintain and generalize previously learned strategies.

Examples of how to apply the 7-Step Model for Executive Function Skills Training will be provided for each of the EFs throughout the book, as will strategies to use with different executive function skills. Case studies are used to demonstrate the entire seven-step process of executive function skills training for students with different EF skill deficits. Readers will have the opportunity to self-assess their learning with sample case studies. Templates and downloadables are provided for all strategy cards and forms so that readers can implement the 7-Step Model in their classrooms. **If you are asking yourself whether this model, as developed originally or modified, will work for you, the section below will provide information for your consideration.**

FIGURE 1.11 Sample Student Success Plan for Kelly, an Elementary Student

What I Want to Do Next

- *Goal 2: I want to be able to find my glasses when I need them.*

- *I would like to keep using my Self-Check Card when I need it.*

Difficulties I May Have

- *I still may need the teacher to remind me to stay with my work until it is finished.*

- *I lose my glasses a lot, and I need them to see.*

Strategies I Can Use to Help Myself

- *I will use the Self-Check Card for doing my work.*

- *I will be learning a new strategy to help me find my glasses.*

What the Teacher Can Do to Help

- *The teacher can check on me to see if I am using my Self-Check Card.*

- *The teacher can help me learn a new strategy for finding my glasses.*

HOW MIGHT YOU OFFER EXECUTIVE FUNCTION TRAINING IN YOUR SETTING?

Every minute of our teaching day seems filled with curricular demands and timelines, assessments of student skill mastery, and various activities that fall within our job description. Finding time to address deficits in executive function skills can be a challenge. There are several ways to integrate executive function skill training into your teaching schedule. Some overarching ideas are listed below. More detailed ideas are found throughout the book.

- **Front-load executive function skill instruction.**

  Just as you teach rules and procedures the first day or days of school, teaching students how to learn content is worthy of time before you move on to your daily instruction schedule. You will find that one to five days of skill instruction will pay off in terms of student success. If you teach in middle or high school, you will find that some students who have not demonstrated difficulty with skills such as working memory, organization, and planning in elementary school find the demands of stand-alone subjects, research projects, and the retention and retrieval of more information seems too much to handle. Indeed, some students do not hit the wall of overload until college and find that they need some help in metacognition and self-regulation to meet all the learning demands placed on them. That is why some colleges provide tips for studying in orientation and study skill classes. You will find the Modified 7-Step Model described in this book helpful for teaching executive function skills to groups. Follow the instructions in this book for teaching strategies using the Modified 7-Step Model.

SAMPLE SCHEDULE FOR FRONT LOADING EXECUTIVE FUNCTION SKILL INSTRUCTION ELEMENTARY—3RD GRADE

Monday	Explain the concept of "Learning How to Learn." Survey all students to determine how they see themselves in terms of focusing during instructional time, remembering the content delivered, being organized, planning before they act, etc.
	Tell students that one area everyone can improve upon is focusing during instructional time. Discuss with your students that there are strategies to help them improve their attention and focus during instructional time.
Tuesday	Start the first goal, focusing during instructional time. Tell the students that you will teach them a strategy that will help them focus during instructional time. Teach SLANT (Ellis, 1991) to everyone as you will be using it with the class throughout the year. SLANT (see chapter 4 for more information about the SLANT Strategy) is an attention strategy designed to physically prepare students for learning.
	Continue to use the SLANT Strategy throughout the day.

- **Integrate executive function skill instruction into "morning meeting, class meeting, or homeroom time."**

  In elementary school classes, the morning meeting is a time you may use to teach a "strategy of the week." You might follow this routine if using morning meeting time for executive function training using the strategy SLANT.

Monday	Discuss that you have observed that some students (do not single out individuals) are having difficulty following the recognized speaker in class. The recognized speaker might be the teacher or another classmate. Explain that when students are not listening to the speaker, they may miss important information like what to do next. Tell your students there is a strategy that will help them. Tell them you will teach it to them today, and they can start using it today. Teach SLANT by going over the letters in the acronym and model SLANT. Then have students practice SLANT. Tell them you will use a cue today to help them remember.
Tuesday	Review SLANT. Ask students to role play with a shoulder buddy how it looks when someone does not use SLANT. Then have them role play with their shoulder buddy how SLANT should look. Remind them to use SLANT today.
Wednesday	Compliment the students on their use of SLANT. Encourage them to keep trying to remember to do it on their own without a cue.
Thursday	Remind the students to use SLANT today. Tell them you have seen an improvement in their attention to the speaker since learning SLANT.
Friday	Compliment the students on their use of SLANT and tell them you will be adding another learning strategy on Monday.

- **Integrate executive function skill training in various academic areas.**

  Some of the strategies we describe in the book focus on reading comprehension and writing which can prove helpful in all academic areas. These strategies can be taught in your language arts classes. We also share strategies to support learning mathematics facts. Some of your students may have difficulty remembering their mathematics facts. If they have a 504 Plan or Individualized Education Program (IEP), they may have the accommodation of using a calculator when completing mathematics problems. It is helpful, however, for all students to have problem-solving skills that include finding the correct answer to problems requiring math facts without using the calculator. One of the approaches we describe in the book is skip counting to give the student an opportunity to find the answer without the calculator. In this case, we used it as a compensatory strategy.

  Academic areas requiring students to complete a long-term project or paper can be challenging in terms of executive function skills involving planning for project completion, considering content selection, organizing selected content, developing a method for reporting selected content, and time management. Strategies for supporting these executive function skills are included in this book. Although we have found high-achieving students who are interested in improving their executive function skills, it should be noted that strategies **should not be forced** on students who are already proficient in their executive function skills.

- **Integrate executive function skill instruction as needed.**

  For instance, some of your students may stand out as in need of help self-regulating their behavior, organization, and planning. This help can be provided in terms of looking at priorities in terms of behaviors endangering their path to academic success. When using this approach, you and the student will identify the executive function areas in which the student is demonstrating the most difficulty and teach strategies to the student based on his or her individual needs. Our 7-Step Model or the modified version provides a process for that instruction.

- **Offer enrichment and/or credit classes in executive function skills.**

  You may not have a time in your schedule to teach enrichment classes; however, a promising practice in some schools allows social workers, psychologists, or guidance counselors in your school to offer classes teaming with teachers, focused on executive functions. It is important to refer students demonstrating difficulty in any of the executive function areas for opportunities that address the difficulties they are experiencing.

- **Work with families to help them understand that their son or daughter needs to ultimately learn to self-regulate their academic, behavioral, and social/emotional activities to be successful.**

  Telling a student to just try harder may invalidate the fact that the student has a deficit in an executive function area. Early intervention is vital to the student's understanding that there are strategies they can use to improve opportunities for academic, behavioral, and social success. When efforts to involve family members or guardians fail, continue to correspond with them providing examples of progress their child has made academically, behaviorally, and socially. Although this practice might not result in guardians' or family members' participation, it maintains an open line of communication.

Conversation with: Meredith Julius, MA and Laura Beck, LMSW

Grade: High School Front-Loading Program

Executive Function Addressed: All Categories

Executive Function Skills Program Designed for: At-Risk Students

Laura Beck

A promising approach to teaching students-at-risk study skills with an emphasis on executive functioning is in its third year in Oxford, Michigan. School administrators requested that Meredith Julius, a licensed school psychologist, and Laura Beck, a licensed school social worker, design a general education initiative for at-risk ninth and tenth graders to reduce the disproportionality in special education referrals. Students at risk of being referred were identified and selected based on the need for intervention. This was a general education initiative to address disproportionality; therefore, no students receiving education services were included but some students with 504 Plans were enrolled. An elective course for ½ credit per semester was established so that students would receive grades and credit for the course. Julius and Beck teamed in the classroom with teachers to offer this class consisting of study skills including executive function skill instruction and assistance with current academic subjects. They created weekly lessons that were interactive using videos, modeling, and re-teaching that empowered students to self-advocate and take responsibility for their own success. Pre- and posttesting instruments were used to monitor student progress. For example, progress was monitored in terms of students handing in completed assignments. Pre- and posttest data point to promising results. Anecdotal data from teachers revealed that students have made progress in the executive function skill areas such as working memory and organization. In addition, teachers stated that students show more self-confidence since entering this program. Julius and Beck report that the extra time spent front-loading planning and instruction have resulted in a decrease in the number of referrals and subsequent evaluations for special education. The response has been well received by teachers and administrators.

FIGURE 1.12 Ideas for Implementing EF Training for Different Types of Classrooms

The chart below is provided to prompt your thinking as to how you might implement EF training for your students. The authors recognize you possess the knowledge of your students, and we value and encourage your creativity and skill in planning for them. We have taken the liberty of listing some examples.

CLASS TYPE	DELIVERY MODEL For Integration of EF Skill Training	SAMPLE STRATEGIES
PRESCHOOL–KINDERGARTEN		
General Education (Average Size Class)	Circle Time	Example using Full Class Circle Time PAW Strategy—see chapter 5
	Skill taught within curricular content or as small group	Example using Full Class Circle Time Dragon Quilt Strategy—see chapter 5
	Skill taught during first week of school while establishing rules and expectations	Example using Full Class Circle Time GOP Strategy—see chapter 2
Co-taught and/or Special Education Plug-In (Average Size Class)	Skill taught within curricular content or as small group	Example using Full Class Circle Time Dreamweaver Strategy—see chapter 6
Special Education—Self-Contained	Skill taught within curricular content, small group, or individual	Example using Full Class Circle Time PAW Strategy—see chapter 5 Example using Full Class Circle Time Dragon Quilt Strategy—see chapter 5 Example using Full Class Circle Time GOP Strategy—see chapter 2
Special Education—Resource Room	Skill taught within support group setting, small group, or individual	Example using Specific Location Strategy—see chapter 2
ELEMENTARY GRADES		
General Education (Average Size Class)	Circle Time	Example using Full Class PAW Strategy—see chapter 5
	Skill taught within curricular content or as small group	Example using Full Class Self-Check Card Strategy—see chapter 4
	Skill taught during first week of school while establishing rules and expectations	Example using Full Class GOP Strategy—see chapter 2

CLASS TYPE	DELIVERY MODEL For Integration of EF Skill Training	SAMPLE STRATEGIES
Co-taught and/or Special Education Plug-In (Average Size Class)	Morning Meeting	Example using Full Class PAW Strategy—see chapter 5
	Skill taught within curricular content or as small group	Example using Full Class Self-Check Card Strategy—see chapter 4
	Skill taught during first week of school while establishing rules and expectations	Example using Full Class GOP Strategy—see chapter 2
Special Education— Self-Contained	Review of Daily Schedule or Morning Routine	Example using Modified SLANT Strategy—see chapter 4
	Skill taught to assist with curricular content or behavior, small group, or individual	Example using Full Class Dragon Quilt Strategy—see chapter 5
	Group Practice and Review	Example using Full Class GOP Strategy—see chapter 2
Special Education— Resource Room	Review of objectives for session	Example using Visual Schedule Strategy—see chapters 2, 3
	Skill taught within curricular content, small group, or individual	Example using ABC Memory Strategy—see chapter 2
	Group practice and review	Example using Dreamweaver Strategy—see chapter 6
MIDDLE SCHOOL		
General Education (Average Size Class)	Homeroom, Activities Period, etc. Skill taught within curricular content whole group	Example using SLANT Strategy— see chapter 4
Co-taught and/or Special Education Plug-In (Average Size Class)	Homeroom Skill taught within curricular content or as small group Skill taught during first week of school while establishing rules and expectations	Example using Prewriting Strategy— see chapter 6

(Continued)

FIGURE 1.12 (Continued)

CLASS TYPE	DELIVERY MODEL For Integration of EF Skill Training	SAMPLE STRATEGIES
Special Education— Self-Contained	Homeroom Skill taught within curricular content or as small group Skill taught during first week of school while establishing rules and expectations	Example using Home Keys Keyboarding Strategy—see chapter 2
Special Education— Resource Room	Homeroom Skill taught within curricular content or as small group Skill taught during first week of school while establishing rules and expectations Support Group	Example using Home and Done Strategy—see chapter 7
HIGH SCHOOL		
General Education (Average Size Class)	Homeroom Skill taught within curricular content or as small group Skill taught during first week of school while establishing rules and expectations Support Group	Example using Backward Mapping Strategy—see chapter 3 Example using Simply Note It Strategy—see chapter 6 Example using Steps for Completing Long-Term Project Strategy—see chapter 3 Example using Big and Little Rocks Strategy—see chapter 3
Co-taught and/or Special Education Plug In (Average Size Class)	Homeroom Skill taught within curricular content or as small group Skill taught during first week of school while establishing rules and expectations Support Group	Example using Backward Mapping Strategy—see chapter 3 Example using Simply Note It Strategy—see chapter 6 Example using Steps for Completing Long-Term Project Strategy—see chapter 3 Example using Big and Little Rocks Strategy—see chapter 3

CLASS TYPE	DELIVERY MODEL For Integration of EF Skill Training	SAMPLE STRATEGIES
Special Education—Self-Contained	Homeroom	Example using Checklist Strategy—see chapters 2, 3, 4, 5, 6, 7
	Skill taught within curricular content or as small group	Example using Self-Check Card Strategy—see chapter 4
	Skill taught during first week of school while establishing rules and expectations	Example using LLUMP Strategy—see chapter 6
Special Education—Resource Room	Homeroom	Example using Self-Advocacy Strategy—see chapter 6
	Skill taught within curricular content or as small group	Example using Self-Check Card Strategy—see chapter 4
	Skill taught during first week of school while establishing rules and expectations	Example using LLUMP Strategy—see chapter 6

In the next six chapters, we will describe strategies and activities that can be used to improve or compensate for executive function skill difficulties.

Think About

- Why should you offer your students executive function skills training?

- What executive function difficulties have you observed your students experiencing?

- Think of a student or students you feel would benefit from executive function skill training.

- How would the strategy instruction be staffed?

- Where you would hold the training (i.e., classroom, library, counselor's office)?

- When would you offer the training (i.e., Morning Meeting, Class Meeting, Daily Schedule Review)?

CHAPTER 2

Working Memory and Supportive Strategies

> **Reader Outcomes**
>
> ☑ You will be able to identify factors that suggest problems in the executive function skill area of working memory.
>
> ☑ You will be able to identify how difficulties in working memory impact a student's behavior, social/emotional well-being, and academic success.
>
> ☑ You will be able to identify strategies to use to address difficulty in working memory.
>
> ☑ You will be able to record student progress and make instructional changes based on the data.

WHAT IS WORKING MEMORY?

Working memory is at the foundation for learning. According to Cooper-Kahn and Foster (2013) working memory is "the ability to temporarily hold information in one's head to use it to complete a task" (p. 10). Working memory is sometimes referred to as short-term memory, but the problem is that short-term memory is linked more closely to long-term memory than what we previously thought. Kaufman (2010) defined working memory as "the cognitive mixing bowl in which new information is combined with background knowledge to allow for comprehension of spoken and written language" (p. 7). It is comprised of auditory memory (remembering what you hear) and visual-spatial memory (remembering what you see), but it is the efficient use of working memory that allows students to solve multistep mathematics problems and synthesize pertinent information into a research paper.

Working memory is a critical factor in school success. It helps students with things such as

- retrieving information from long-term memory and holding on to it long enough to use it (short-term memory);
- hindsight (learning from the past), forethought (being able to plan by remembering the information), anticipatory set (to predict based on memory), sense of time (to remember events and activities), and awareness of self-storing and remembering appropriate behaviors (Tam, 2014, pp. 351–353);
- remembering instructions, especially with complex tasks; and
- paying attention and staying on task.

Students who have problems with working memory may experience the following:

- Have difficulty remembering sounds and words and forget what they have read
- Have difficulty memorizing facts
- Have difficulty remembering the steps of a process and stop in the middle if they start the process at all
- Start talking and forget what they are saying in midsentence
- Have difficulty forming letters for writing and remembering the sequence for spelling
- Have difficulty remembering directions for completing assignments especially as directions become more complex
- Initiate a task, then stop before completing it
- Have a blank stare on their face
- Check the work of others to see what they are doing
- Consistently make the same errors in spelling and math
- Demonstrate poor self-checking skills
- Complete assignments but forget to submit them
- Have difficulty remembering rules and procedures
- May not profit by what they have previously learned
- May not be able to predict what is going to happen based on previous experience

FIGURE 2.1 How Working Memory Builds on Long-Term Memory in the Learning Process

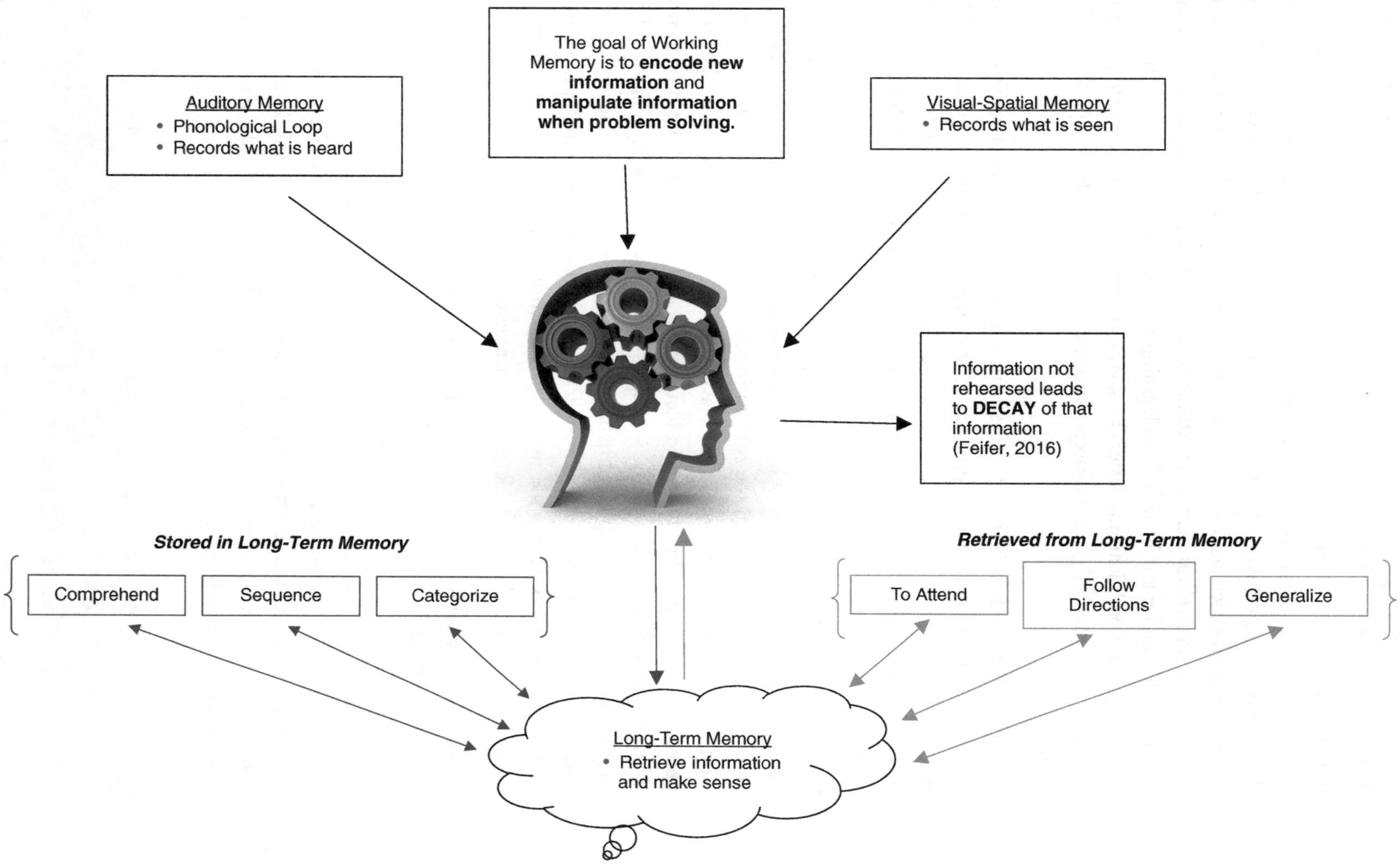

Auditory Memory
- Phonological Loop
- Records what is heard

The goal of Working Memory is to **encode new information** and **manipulate information when problem solving.**

Visual-Spatial Memory
- Records what is seen

Information not rehearsed leads to **DECAY** of that information (Feifer, 2016)

Retrieved from Long-Term Memory

To Attend

Follow Directions

Generalize

Long-Term Memory
- Retrieve information and make sense

Stored in Long-Term Memory

Comprehend

Sequence

Categorize

SOURCES: iStock.com/pavlen

HOW DOES A DIFFICULTY IN WORKING MEMORY IMPACT STUDENT ACHIEVEMENT?

Students who have difficulty in working memory face numerous challenges in the classroom. Moyes (2014) reminds us that our students in general forget 90 percent of what they learned within the first thirty days and much of it soon after class ends. If we want them to remember, we need to repeat information often (p. 66). It is helpful if that information is repeated in different ways. Students with working memory problems face even larger hurdles, and many benefit from learning that involves sensory activities. This can be accomplished with learning letters by saying the letter, tracing the letter, and making the letters in sand. This is a multisensory approach that can have a positive influence on memory.

Kaufman (2010) states, "Given the dramatic impact that comparatively weak working memory can have on academic functioning, it is important that instruction be delivered in ways that minimize amount of information (e.g., directions, content) students with working memory problems must hold at any one time on their smallish 'cognitive desktops'" (p. 84).

The behavior and social/emotional well-being of a student may also be impacted by a deficit in working memory. In school, when a student has difficulty remembering rules and procedures, it may appear the student is not trying or is purposefully not complying with the rules and procedures of the classroom. This inability to remember rules and procedures may cause the student to feel anxious and confused about how to respond. Without intervention and specific strategies to help with working memory, the child may fall into a downward spiral of behavioral and social/emotional issues. According to Moyes (2014), it is important to consider the student's struggle with working memory and reward remembering while not punishing forgetting. We go a step further and advocate rewarding the appropriate use of strategies also.

In addition, a working memory deficit has social/emotional implications beyond the academic setting. If not sufficiently addressed in school, a working memory deficit may impact a person throughout his or her lifetime. Each day, a person with a working memory deficit struggles to remember tasks that need to be completed in the home and work settings, as well as important events and meetings, dates and times for medical appointments, social gatherings, and the like. The inability to remember this kind of important information can result in the loss of jobs and friendships, leaving the person with feelings of failure, low self-esteem, loneliness, and frustration.

SUPPORTIVE STRATEGIES WITH CARDS FOR WORKING MEMORY

The following are examples of supportive strategies to teach students that can help them with goals related to the EF area of working memory. It is important to note that all strategies will not work for all students. Step 3 in the 7-Step Model provides help in choosing appropriate strategies for students while considering UDL and metacognition, and step 4 will guide you through the teaching process. Steps 5, 6, and 7 address data tools for the assessment of strategy effectiveness, revision if needed, and the celebration of success with the strategy or strategies before moving on. **Blank templates, modifiable versions of materials, and strategy cards can be found at http://resources.corwin .com/ExecutiveFunctioning**.

MNEMONICS

Scruggs and Mastropieri (2000) report student success with the use of mnemonics. A popular mnemonic, **E**very **G**ood **B**oy **D**oes **F**ine, is used to learn and remember the notes on the treble clef. The possibilities are endless for constructing mnemonics specific to learning tasks. Scruggs and Mastropieri (2000) also advocate using the alphabet to aid memory. The ABC Memory Strategy does just that. This strategy is designed to support the ability to use working memory.

ABC MEMORY STRATEGY (FOR A LIST OR A PROCESS)

To use the ABC Memory Strategy, start by choosing a theme. Next, think of words related to that theme beginning with letters of the alphabet, in order (A–Z). For example, if the theme is the seven continents and the task is to recall them the ABC Memory Strategy would prove helpful. The letter A would be paired with four continents and when put in alphabetical order they would be Africa, Antarctica, Asia, Australia in that order. The student would find no continents starting with the letters, B, C, or D so these letters are skipped. There is a continent starting with the letter E and that is Europe. The student would find no continents starting with the letters, F, G, H, I, J, K L or M so these letters are skipped. There is a continent starting with the letter N and that is North America. The student would find no continents starting with the letters, O, P, Q, or R so these letters are skipped. There is a continent starting with the letter S and that is South America. This makes the seventh continent, so once these are learned in order, the task of recalling and naming the seven continents in ABC order is complete.

Flashcards are used to help the student remember the information. To create the flashcards, print the letter of the alphabet on the front of the card and the word that begins with that letter on the back of the card. A graphic representation of the word may also be used for unfamiliar words. Apps like StudyBlue can also be used to create flashcards for the ABC Memory strategy. When there are multiple items for a particular letter, such as A for the continents, the four A cards in alphabetical order could be numbered 1, 2, 3, and 4.

Start by having the student learn the word on the back of the card that corresponds to the letter on the front for the seven cards, in alphabetical order (i.e., letters A–Z). Have the student follow the steps below to commit the words to memory:

- **Read** the letter (A) on the front of the card and the word (e.g., *Africa*) on the back of the card.

- **Say** the letter (A) on the front of the card and the word (e.g., *Africa*) on the back of the card.

- **Look** at the letter on the front of the card (A), and without turning the card over, state the word (continent) associated with that letter (e.g., *A—Africa*).

- **Put the card out of sight** and think about the letter on the front of the card (A). Without looking at the card, **say the continent associated with that letter** (e.g., *A—Africa*). If successful, proceed to the next letter. If unsuccessful, go back to the first step and follow the steps until successful.

- **After successfully learning the first card**, proceed to the second card and follow the same steps to learn it. Once learned, include the previous cards for review.

- **Continue** until the words on all seven cards have been memorized. Going forward, always include the previous cards for review while the student is learning the new cards. This builds success for the student.

- **Commit to memory** by saying the name of the continents faster and faster. This step also improves processing speed.

The student will find this process motivating when he or she sees how much easier it is to learn and remember information. Our data from 2008 through 2012 showed students remembering up to twenty items in a week's time using this strategy. Often, no more than seven letters as in the seven continents will be used, but for other lists additional letters can be added following the same process. It is important to continuously review the cards already learned as the student continues to add more cards and words to his or her memory bank.

FIGURE 2.2 ABC Memory Strategy for a List

Continent A-1 **A**	Picture of Africa on the back
Continent A-2 **A**	Picture of Antarctica on the back
Continent A-3 **A**	Picture of Asia on the back

FIGURE 2.3 ABC Memory Strategy Process

The strategy card for ABC Memory Strategy summarizes the steps of the process.

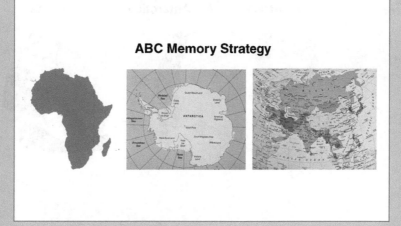

ABC Memory Strategy

- **Read** the letter (A) and the continents.
- **Say** the letter (A) and the continents.
- **Look** at the letter and from memory, state the continent.
- **Put the card out of sight** and think about the letter and the continents associated with the letter.
- **After successfully learning the first card**, proceed to the second card.
- **Continue** until you have learned the information on all seven cards.
- **Commit** to memory the new cards, reviewing all cards learned each day.

SOURCES: Pixabay.com/openclipart-vectors; iStock.com/meshaphoto; and iStock.com/pawel_gaul

CAN YOU SEE IT IN YOUR MIND ASSOCIATION STRATEGY?

You have some terms you need to remember. Using the same cards, let's pair them with something you know well. Think of a place you can visualize such as your bedroom. Associate the first term with something or someplace in your room. Imagine the spear for Africa on the dresser, the stuffed penguin for Antarctica by the lamp, and a stuffed panda bear for Asia in the corner. Then when it is time to remember the names of the continents, in your mind, look around your room for the items. This will help you recall the names (Strosnider, Sharpe, & Weaver, 2017).

GOP STRATEGY FOR ELEMENTARY STUDENTS

GOP is a mnemonic strategy for remembering the steps of the process of unpacking materials for class. It is also helpful to use with students who have difficulty transitioning from one subject to another or one classroom to another.

FIGURE 2.4 Can You See It in Your Mind Association Strategy

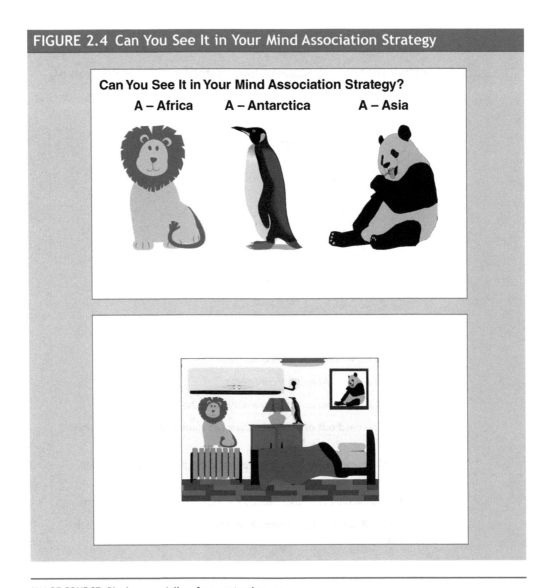

IMAGE SOURCE: Pixabay.com/clker-free-vector-images

There are three steps of GOP for the beginning of class:

1. **G**et your backpack and take out your notebook.

2. **O**pen your notebook to the pocket inside the front cover.

3. **P**lace your Strategy Ring or Strategy Cards on your desk.

GOP STRATEGY FOR SECONDARY STUDENTS

GOP is a mnemonic strategy for remembering the steps of the process of recording homework assignments.

FIGURE 2.5 GOP Strategy Card for Elementary Students

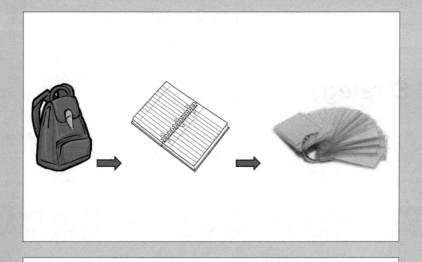

1. **G**et your backpack and take out your notebook.
2. **O**pen your notebook to the pocket inside the front cover.
3. **P**lace your Strategy Ring or Strategy Cards on your desk.

SOURCES: Pixabay.com/artsybee; Pixabay.com/openclipart-vectors; and istock.com/philsajonesen

There are three steps of GOP for the beginning of class:

1. **G**et your notebook.

2. **O**pen your notebook to the homework page.

3. **P**ut the assignment in the homework column.

OR

1. **G**et your device.

2. **O**pen your phone to the homework app or to the camera.

3. **P**ut your homework assignment in the app **or** take a photo of the assignment.

FIGURE 2.6 GOP Strategy Card for Secondary Students

GOP Strategy	*This is what I need to do at the end of every class:* **G**et your notebook. **O**pen the notebook to the homework page. **P**ut the assignment in the homework column. Or **G**et your device. **O**pen your phone to the homework app or to the camera. **P**ut your homework in the app or take a photo.

CONCRETE EXTERNAL STORAGE SYSTEMS

Cooper-Kahn and Dietzel (2008) suggest using concrete storage systems to help students remember information. A concrete external storage system differs from the normal visuals provided in the classroom for all students in that it can be personalized, and the student does not have to differentiate it from all the posted classroom visuals. The idea behind this strategy is to have students store their thoughts in a physical place from which they can be easily retrieved. Examples of concrete external storage systems include to-do lists, oral information put into notes, cues for listening, technology such as *Mindjet Manager*, templates for different types of assignments, photos (see clean desk photo—Image 2.2 below), and dictated responses. In terms of photos, we have found students respond well to personalized photos as short-term memory prompts. An example is provided below. Students, using devices, can take photos and store the pictures. Instant cameras can be used in the classroom to document papers and materials.

PREWRITING GRAPHIC ORGANIZERS

Writing can be laborious for students with working memory executive function skill deficits. Given the task of writing (an essay, paper, long response, etc.), some students find it difficult to remember the points they would like to make first, second, or third, for example. Prewriting activities produce a concrete written plan for writing a paper (Harris & Graham, 1996).

Teachers may design graphic organizers to help students remember what they want to write and the order in which it should be written. The student completes the organizer before beginning to write. The process helps the student to retrieve and list points to be included in order before starting to write. The teacher can provide chapter and page numbers to help with the sequencing. The next step is to check to make certain that the evidence points are in the correct order. Some students with EF issues also benefit from an organizer that includes important vocabulary words. The student then uses the graphic organizer to guide his or her writing. Story maps, graphic organizers, concept maps, sequence templates, and the like are typically used with students at the elementary level. However, they can be useful for all students. Figure 2.9 is an example of a prewriting graphic organizer for an individual student at the secondary level.

The student can keep a photo of his or her completed graphic organizer to refer to as needed.

FIGURE 2.7 Prewriting Graphic Organizer

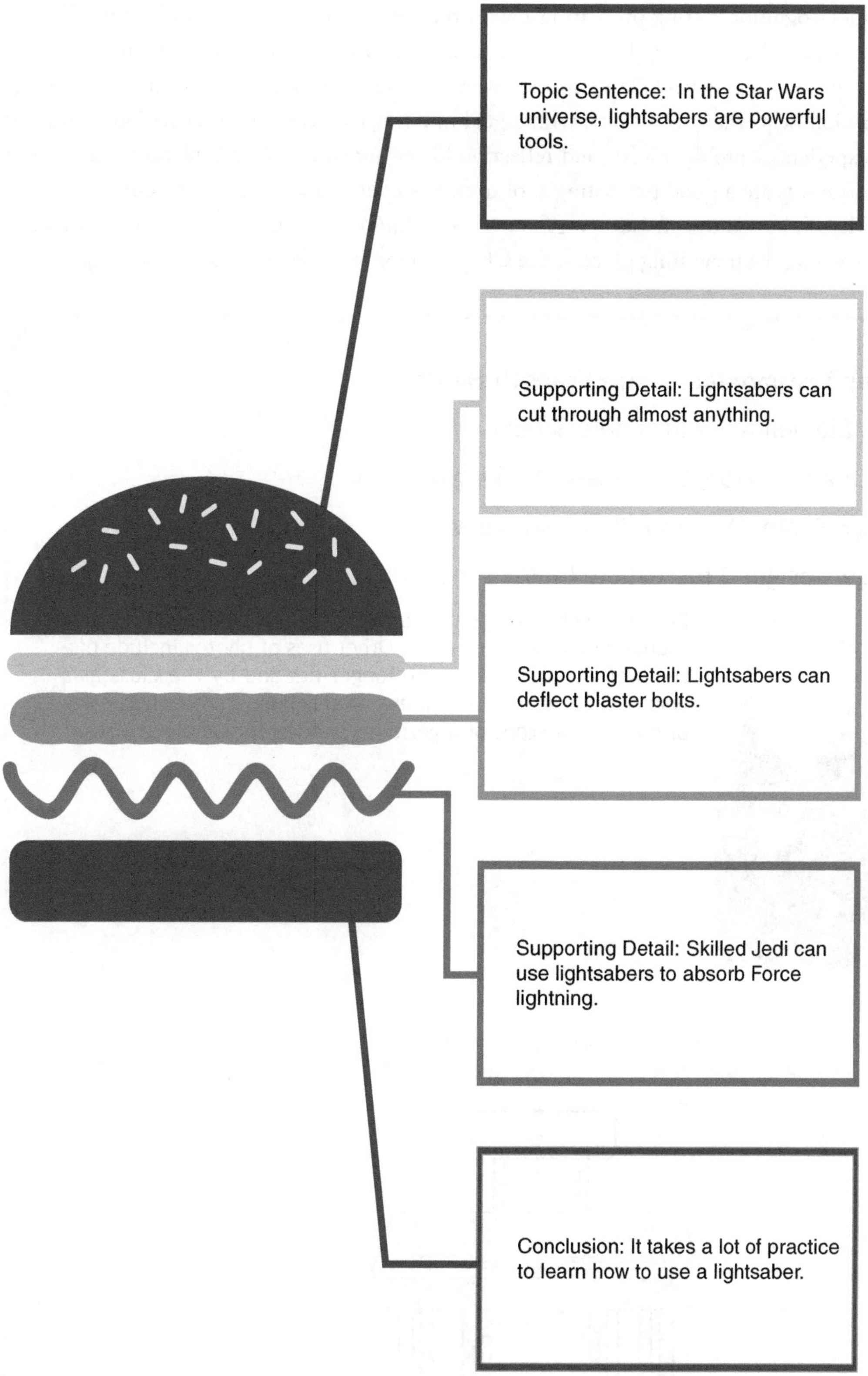

Topic Sentence: In the Star Wars universe, lightsabers are powerful tools.

Supporting Detail: Lightsabers can cut through almost anything.

Supporting Detail: Lightsabers can deflect blaster bolts.

Supporting Detail: Skilled Jedi can use lightsabers to absorb Force lightning.

Conclusion: It takes a lot of practice to learn how to use a lightsaber.

Adapted from Understood.org,https://www.understood.org/~/media/
f27fa769f3c74e3298981008d4f771c2.pdf

It is helpful to model prewriting and allow the student to practice it until it becomes part of his or her regular writing process. While modeling the process, point out that using metacognition during prewriting makes the writing process faster and more efficient. Not only does this step help the student **remember** the purpose and content of what to write, it also involves talking through what the student is thinking. This use of metacognition helps the student plan with a goal in mind, connect new information with prior experiences, problem solve, and reflect on his or her success in completing a task. Venn diagrams are a good prewriting tool to help students brainstorm and **remember** their ideas. The use of software programs such as *Kidspiration* and *Inspiration* are useful in teaching the prewriting process. See Chapter 6 for more details about prewriting.

Teacher Testimonial from: Elisabeth Halici

Grade: Elementary and Middle School

Executive Function Addressed: Working Memory

Strategy Name: Desktop Photo Strategy

Strategy Designed for: Whole Class or Individual

Each student has a picture on his or her desk of how the desk should look when class ends. Other uses of photos include pictures of visuals that are no longer needed by the class as a whole, pictures of the homework assignment from the board, or pictures of steps or algorithms needed to complete tasks.

Elisabeth Halici

IMAGE 2.2 Sample Concrete External Storage System

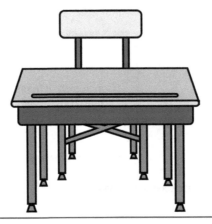

IMAGE SOURCE: Pixabay.com/openclipart-vectors

TASK ANALYSIS

Task Analysis, in this situation, is the process of analyzing and implementing the steps needed to successfully complete a goal. When analyzing a task, it is important to consider the student's developmental and working memory levels.

For example, your students may find a task analysis for completing the morning routine helpful. A classroom routine for a middle schooler broken into individual tasks may include

- entering the classroom and taking your assigned seat;

- taking your class notebook or folder, pencil or pen, and text out of your backpack;

- placing your backpack on the back of your chair;

- reading the objectives for the class;

- completing the class warm-up or drill in your notebook; and

- sitting quietly and waiting for further instructions from your teacher.

VISUAL SCHEDULES

Visual Schedules with reminders are another simple and effective visual aid.

FIGURE 2.8 Visual Schedule Example

DAY	TIME	ACTIVITY	REMINDERS
Monday	9:00am–10:00am	Language Arts	Bring your book.
	10:00am–10:05am	Get ready for Mathematics	
Tuesday	10:05am–11:00am	Mathematics	Be sure to hand in your completed work.
	11:05am–12:00am	Physical Education	Change shoes.

SOURCES: Book: Pixabay.com/janjf93, Paper and Pencil: Pixabay.com/clker-free-vector-images, Shoes: Pixabay.com/openclipart-vectors

VISUAL-KINESTHETIC STRATEGIES—WHAT I SEE AND DO

For students who learn best by seeing and doing, Meltzer (2010) includes the Human Number Line Strategy. In this strategy, students walk forward for addition and backward for subtraction. It can be as simple as 2 + 2 or as complex as reversing because of parentheses in a problem such as 2 + (-2).

VISUAL AND AUDITORY MEMORY STRATEGY

CONCENTRATION GAMES

The use of concentration games gives students an opportunity to strengthen their working memory. Games can be constructed around any information students need to remember. In addition to traditional memory match card games, many concentration games are available as apps, including **Memory Matches** and **Find the Pair Memory Matching Cards**.

VISUAL SEQUENTIAL MEMORY STRATEGY

CHUNKING

The process of chunking information during instructional delivery helps the student to connect to the material. When learning a long list of sequential pictured items, it is helpful to chunk the list into sections appropriate for the student. For example, you may want to start with three pictures at a time and progress to as many as seven at a time. The **iMimic App** is a good source of technology to reinforce visual sequential memory.

AUDITORY SEQUENTIAL MEMORY STRATEGY

Like in visual sequential chunking the process of chunking information during instructional delivery helps the student to connect to the material. When learning a long list of spoken items, it is best to initially state three items to the student, gradually increasing the amount of stated items to seven. The **Simon App** is a good source of technology to reinforce auditory sequential memory.

STRATEGIES TO AID STUDY

Students need to know the status of the results of their study. Do they know it now, or do they need more study before moving on? One means of determining whether more study is needed is for the student to attempt to teach the information to someone else. The Teach-It Strategy provides an opportunity for students to self-check their own understanding of the information. This strategy is described below.

TEACH-IT STRATEGY

Using your notes, teach the material to someone else.

As you taught it, did you feel that you knew and understood it?

Did the person you taught understand and learn the material you were teaching?

If you answered no to any of these questions, you need to study the material in a different way and try again.

FIGURE 2.9 Teach-It Strategy Card for Elementary Students

Teach-It Strategy

When using the Teach-It Strategy

- Using your notes, teach the material to someone else.

- As I taught it, did I feel that I knew and understood it?

- Did the person I taught understand and learn the material I was teaching?

- If I answered no to any of these questions, I need to study the material in a different way and try again.

IMAGE SOURCE: iStock.com/lisegagne

FIGURE 2.10 Teach-It Strategy Card for Secondary Students

Teach-It Strategy

When using the Teach-It Strategy

- Using your notes, teach the material to someone else.
- As I taught it, did I feel that I knew and understood it?
- Did the person I taught understand and learn the material I was teaching?
- If I answered no to any of these questions, I need to study the material in a different way and try again.

STUDY CUBE RECALL STRATEGY

This strategy can be used as a short-term memory activity for elementary, middle, and high school students to recall, reinforce, or study information that has been taught. It can be used in different ways: to define vocabulary; respond to specific questions; role play appropriate social interactions; and recall the chemical elements of the Periodic Table, historic timelines, and mathematic algorithms and theorems. To implement this activity, take a cube and label each side of the cube with the word or symbol you wish to have the student recall or study. For example, if you are reviewing vocabulary words, you could place one word on each side of the cube. Then have the student toss the cube and read and define the word on the top side of the cube. If a student has difficulty responding to the information posted, he or she should place a Post-it arrow marking that side of the cube. The arrow will serve as a reminder of the information that still needs to be learned.

FIGURE 2.11 Sample Cube for the Study Cube Recall Strategy

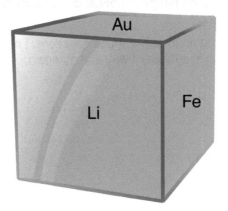

IMAGE SOURCE: Pixabay.com/openclipart-vectors

FIGURE 2.12 Study Cube Recall Strategy Card for Elementary Students

Study Cube Recall Strategy

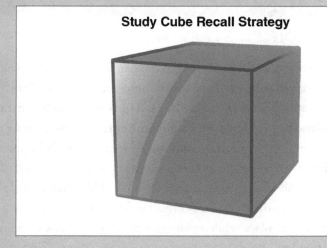

1. Place one word or symbol on each side of the cube.

2. Toss the cube and answer the question, define the word, or name the symbol located on the top of the cube. Continue tossing the cube until you have answered all of the items on the cube.

3. Place a Post-it arrow on any item you have trouble with. The arrow will serve as a reminder of the information that you need to study more.

IMAGE SOURCE: Pixabay.com/openclipart-vectors

FIGURE 2.13 Study Cube Recall Strategy Card for Secondary Students

Study Cube Recall Strategy

1. Place one word or symbol on each side of the cube.

2. Toss the cube and answer the question, define the word, or name the symbol located on the top of the cube. Continue tossing the cube until you have answered all of the items on the cube.

3. Place a Post-it arrow on any item you have trouble with. The arrow will serve as a reminder of the information that you need to study more.

Quizlet is an example of an app that can be used for ongoing study or for making mock tests.

Kahoot is a game that teachers and students can use in review of material and practicing the retrieval of facts.

POST-IT NOTE MODIFIED STRATEGY

The Post-it Notes, also known as Sticky Notes, have been found useful to students for many years as reminders of various tasks. One use of these notes has been for students to record the main idea about information read. **The Post-it Note Modified Strategy is a modification that addresses problems we found students demonstrating with the original strategy.** It is useful for improving working memory through improved focus, attention, and processing speed. It can be used in a variety of ways but is most often used when a student is doing a self-read in a multichapter book. This strategy helps when a student who is reading independently reads slowly, has difficulty remembering what he or she has read, loses his or her place while reading, or needs to go back to reread before conferencing with the teacher. The strategy involves two components. First, the student uses a timer to time how long it takes him or her to read each page. Second, the student jots down brief notes summarizing the main ideas of the page on a Post-it Note after each page is read.

Teach the Post-it Note Modified Strategy to the student by modeling it. Also, model metacognition by stating aloud the thought process. For example, you might say,

- "I am going to use the Post-it Note Modified Strategy to help me read more quickly and remember what I have read."

- "To use this strategy, I need the book or paper I am reading, a pencil, a timer, and Post-it notes."

- "I need to follow these steps to complete the Post-it Note Modified Strategy:
  - First, I am going to write my name and today's date on the Post-it Note.
  - Next, I will start the timer and start reading. When I finish reading each page, I will stop the timer and write down how much time it took me to read the page, as well as the page number.
  - Then, I will write the main idea on the Post-it Note and stick it on the page. I will do this for all the pages in the assignment.
  - Finally, I will take my book and notes to conference with my teacher and refer to the notes to help me remember what I read. I will ask myself if I was able to remember most of the details from what I read. If not, I will ask the teacher what I need to do to remember more of the details. For example, should I read slower, or read fewer pages at a time?
  - This strategy helps me, so I need to practice it until using it becomes easy for me."

You may wish to start by having the student complete one page and one Post-it Note, then checking the note for accuracy. Once the student demonstrates success, you may increase the number of pages you assign.

As students reach high school, the reading requirements are too complex for this strategy. E-books and programs such as **Voice Dream** and **Learning Ally** are helpful. In addition to hearing the book read, students can read along, highlight, and take notes right in the book with these programs.

A sample completed Post-it Note Modified Strategy would look like this:

Post-it Note Modified Strategy Example

Amanda (Mummies in the Morning)

Date: 2/1

Pages: 3

Times: 2 minutes

Idea:
Jack and Ann found a tree in the woods and Jack heard a noise.

IMAGE SOURCE: Pixabay.com/openclipart-vectors

Student Testimonial from: S.

Grade: Middle School

Executive Function Addressed: Communication-Written

Strategy Name: Post-it Note Modified

Strategy Designed for: Individual

I used this strategy in middle school to read books that were at my independent reading level. It really helped me. Before I used this strategy, I read the pages and looked at the words, but I could not remember the main idea. I had to go back and reread the pages several times. When I started timing myself, I realized I was reading slowly because I was not reading with the purpose of finding the main idea. With the timer, I was actually reading the words and writing the main idea without going back over the pages again and again. Now that I am in high school, my reading is more difficult, and I use *Learning Ally*, an online e-reader, which is one of my accommodations.

(Continued)

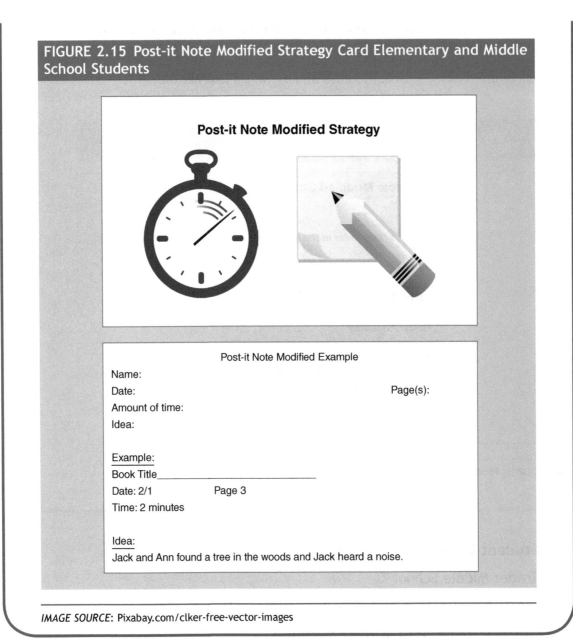

Post-it Note Modified Strategy

Post-it Note Modified Example

Name:

Date: Page(s):

Amount of time:

Idea:

Example:

Book Title_____

Date: 2/1   Page 3

Time: 2 minutes

Idea:

Jack and Ann found a tree in the woods and Jack heard a noise.

IMAGE SOURCE: Pixabay.com/clker-free-vector-images

VISUAL AIDS

Research shows that tapping into visual learning can be an effective way of supporting and improving both the remembering and retrieval aspects of working memory (Kouyoumdjian, 2002; https://www.psychologytoday.com/us/blog/get-psyched/201207/learning-through-visuals). Visual aids include word walls, bulletin boards built around useful information, charts listing rules, checklists, and sequential graphic organizers. These aids can be useful for representing algorithms, rules, steps of a process, and so on.

The Use of Teacher Visuals discussed by: Kimberly Hale, Elementary School Teacher

Grade: 3rd

Visuals Designed for: Whole Class

Number Lines and Skip Counting Charts

Number lines and skip counting charts can be used as compensatory visual supports that can help students with working memory deficits solve math problems. They help demonstrate concepts while also reinforcing memory of the facts. While the goal is for students to ultimately demonstrate automaticity, use of a number line chart, as shown below, provides support for the student who is struggling to keep up. Some students understand a concept but forget the math facts; they can use number lines to move ahead in conceptual instruction while still working on automaticity of facts. Use of the number line chart shown below can simplify the practice of math facts with the reinforcement of solving problems correctly.

Elisabeth Halici demonstrating the use of visuals

Students can use premade number lines or make their own. Several number lines can be represented in a number line chart, such as the one shown below:

FIGURE 2.16 Addition and Subtraction Number Line Chart*

1	2	3	4	5	6	7	8	9	10	11	12	13	14	15	16	17	18	19	20
21	22	23	24	25	26	27	28	29	30	31	32	33	34	35	36	37	38	39	40
41	42	43	44	45	46	47	48	49	50	51	52	53	54	55	56	57	58	59	60
61	62	63	64	65	66	67	68	69	70	71	72	73	74	75	76	77	78	79	80
81	82	83	84	85	86	87	88	89	90	91	92	93	94	95	96	97	98	99	100

*Print this chart on a full sheet of 8 ½" x 11" paper or poster board. Laminate for students so they can use an erasable marker if desired. *Reproducible Addition and Subtraction Number Line and Skip Counting Charts may be found and downloaded from http://resources.corwin .com/ExecutiveFunctioning.*

Teach the student how to use the number line. For example, to find the answer to the problem, "What is the sum of 13 + 2," show the student how to solve by placing a marker (or finger) on the number 13 and moving it forward 2 numbers. This lands on number 15. Therefore, 13 + 2 = 15.

For the problem, "What is the difference in the equation 20 − 8?" the student would place a marker (or finger) on the number 20 and move it back 8 numbers, landing on the number 12. Therefore, 20 − 8 = 12.

SKIP COUNTING STRATEGY

Forward and backward skip counting (also known as counting-by-numbers) is a memory strategy for helping students learn mathematics facts (e.g., number tables) and solve problems. It can also be used as a compensatory strategy for students who have been unsuccessful in learning their facts after receiving appropriate instruction and interventions. Students in a five-day EF Summer Camp experience mastered skip counting forward and backward by 2s, 3s, 4s, 5s, and 10s. Some were also able to master 6s, 7s, 8s, and 9s. The strategy involves memorizing number tables with the assistance of a visual aid known as a skip counting chart, shown below.

FIGURE 2.17 Skip Counting Chart

X	1	2	3	4	5	6	7	8	9	10
1	1	2	3	4	5	6	7	8	9	10
2	2	4	6	8	10	12	14	16	18	20
3	3	6	9	12	15	18	21	24	27	30
4	4	8	12	16	20	24	28	32	36	40
5	5	10	15	20	25	30	35	40	45	50
6	6	12	18	24	30	36	42	48	54	60
7	7	14	21	28	35	42	49	56	63	70
8	8	16	24	32	40	48	56	64	72	80
9	9	18	27	36	45	54	63	72	81	90
10	10	20	30	40	50	60	70	80	90	100

Starting with 10s, 5s, and 2s, have students recite number tables (for all numbers between 1 and 10) in a choral fashion orally or silently, both forward and backward (e.g., "10, 20, 30, 40, 50 … 100, 90, 80, 70 …"), consulting with the skip counting chart as necessary. Determine how high to go based on the level of the student. Since the 10s table is most familiar, start by having the student count by 10s, followed by 5s, and then 2s. When those numbers are learned, proceed to 3s, 4s, 6s, 7s, 8s, and finally 9s. Have the student practice each number table until it is mastered, then move on to the next one. By increasing the speed of recitation, the student will approach automaticity (processing speed).

While use of the skip counting chart is helpful for students when they are first learning the strategy, automaticity is the goal. Some students will require the visual support of the charts longer than others to master the facts. Phase out the charts as a student reaches fluency. As new types of problems are first being learned, once again allow the student to use the charts.

Being able to skip count helps with solving mathematics equations, such as finding the product in multiplication, the quotient in division, lowest common denominators, and factors. For example, a student multiplying 3×4 would skip count multiples of 3 four times, saying "3, 6, 9, 12, so the answer is 12!" For division problems, a student dividing $21 - 7$ would skip count backward by seven, saying "21, 14, 7. That is three skips, so the answer is 3!"

The Skip Counting Chart can provide support to students who have difficulty remembering number tables. Using the chart pictured above, the student would count across from the number being multiplied the number of spaces for the multiplier. For instance, to solve, "What is 10×2?" the student would place a finger on the number 10 in the first column, and go to the X column and down to 2 (to the column with the header 2). The answer is the number in the cell where row 10 intersects column 2, or 20. Once students can solve problems in one direction, demonstrate how reversing the numbers in a multiplication equation arrives at the same answer (i.e., 2×10 also intersects at 20).

Keep in mind that the goal is for the student to memorize the number tables so they can skip count the numerals without looking at the chart. A student who has memorized the number tables would skip count the answer to 10×2 by saying, "10, 20; $10 \times 2 = 20$." Another example, for the problem 8×7, the student would say "8, 16, 24, 32, 40, 48, 56; $8 \times 7 = 56$."

The chart can also be used for factoring and division.

FIGURE 2.18 Skip Counting Strategy Card for Elementary Students

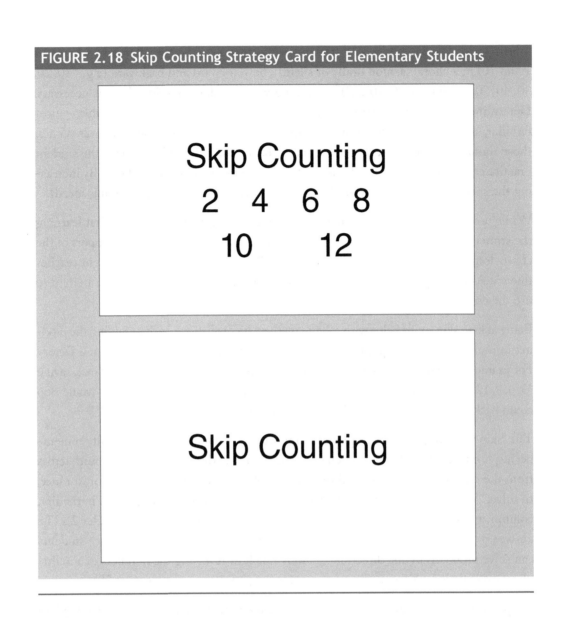

Skip Counting

2   4   6   8

10   12

Skip Counting

FIGURE 2.19 Skip Counting Strategy Card for Secondary Students

Skip Counting | Skip Counting

MULTISENSORY INPUT

A multisensory approach incorporates multiple senses such as hearing, smelling, seeing, tasting, and touching, which promotes activation of several parts of the brain and provides multiple pathways for input of the content to be learned. While it is important not to overstimulate students, it is well known that students remember better when more than one sense is used in the learning process. Programs designed for students with disabilities often employ a multisensory approach; however, such an approach—which is aligned with the principles of UDL—can be helpful to many students. Examples of multisensory input include

- allowing students to walk, stand, skip, for example, while a lesson is being delivered,
- providing students with a visual cue,
- having students listen to themselves recite a mnemonic,
- pairing a smell with a word or name, and
- having students trace sandpaper letters of a word as they spell the word.

HOME KEYS KEYBOARDING STRATEGY

The Home Keys Keyboarding Strategy, based on the memory sequence of the alphabet, is used to teach keyboarding skills to children as young as age six. It is developmentally designed to teach finger placement in the order of the alphabet familiar to most students. Corresponding dots of different colors are placed on students' fingers and letters on the keyboard. Students match the color of the dot on their finger to the dots on the keyboard. Once the fingering for each letter is mastered, the same process using color coding matching dots on the corresponding fingers and matching numbers and symbols on the keyboard is used. Letters already in short-term memory are continually practiced for automaticity. Once automaticity is achieved, the student retrieves that information from long-term memory to generalize his or her typing skills in various situations.

For younger students who cannot manipulate the correct fingering, start by having them use their pointer fingers only. Use a string of yarn to divide the keyboard so the students know which pointer finger to use for which letters. Anything to the left of the yarn means the student uses the left pointer finger and anything to the right of the yarn means the student uses the right pointer finger. Students in an EF Summer Camp, with no knowledge of Home Keys, were able to learn the Home Keys and correct fingering of the rest of the alphabet in a five-day experience.

KEYBOARDING RAP

Students find it helpful to sing or rap about the location of the letters. Students ten years of age and older enjoy making a rap or song to help them remember the finger placements. Younger students enjoy a poem included in the Diana King Keyboarding Program (King, 1986).

FIGURE 2.20 Home Keys Keyboard

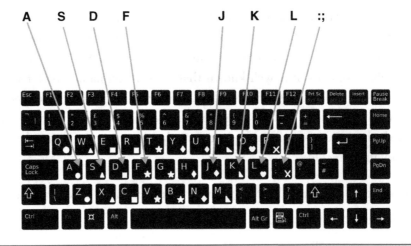

IMAGE SOURCE: Pixabay.com/clker-free-vector-images

FIGURE 2.21 Home Keys Keyboarding Strategy Card for Elementary Students

Home Keys Keyboarding Strategy

- Put your fingers on the home keys, matching the color of the sticker on your finger to the color of the sticker on the home key letter.

- Practice moving from the home keys to all the letters of the alphabet in ABC order.

- Say or sing the rap.

- Practice, practice, practice to increase your typing speed.

IMAGE SOURCES: iStock.com/s-cphoto and Pixabay.com/clker-free-vector-images

THE EXECUTIVE FUNCTION GUIDEBOOK

FIGURE 2.22 Home Keys Keyboarding Strategy Card for Secondary Students

Home Keys Keyboarding Strategy	• Put your fingers on the home keys.
	• Practice moving from the home keys to all the letters of the alphabet in ABC order.
	• Say the letters in a rap.
	• Practice, practice, practice to increase your typing speed.

STRATEGIES FOR SYNTHESIZING RESEARCH INTO A REPORT

The use of technology can help students access their outline, rough draft, notes from resources, and citations quickly and easily. Most allow the teacher and student to share documents so the teacher can quickly assess the student's progress. Google is one example.

Student Testimonial from: B.

Grade: 5th

Executive Function Addressed: Working Memory, Organization, Planning, Sequencing

Strategy Name: Online Research Strategy

Strategy Designed for: Individual

My assignment was to complete research on a person I admire. I used Google Tools to complete my research on Audrey Hepburn. My teacher gave us an online organizer to fill in an outline of what I need to know about my person. I followed the outline and filled it in as I found the information about her. My teacher could go in and check how I was doing and make suggestions. I can store my notes and sources online. When I started writing my rough draft, I followed the outline. I worked on it at school and at home. I liked using Google Tools, because I did not forget where I was in writing my paper. Everything I wrote was there for me and my teacher.

SUPPORTIVE TECHNOLOGIES

With the onset of technology, new instructional tools and supports are now available to meet the diverse learning needs of all students. Many of these tools integrate a UDL platform, are highly engaging and interactive, and may be used to reinforce instructional content or executive function skills. We use technology to compliment and support executive function skill training. Below are some of the technology tools we have found to be beneficial when teaching executive function skills and strategies.

TABLE 2.1 Sample Supportive Technologies

TECHNOLOGY TOOL CATEGORY (WEBSITE, SOFTWARE, APP)	NAME OF TECHNOLOGY	EXECUTIVE FUNCTION AREA ADDRESSED	AGE GROUP
Website	Center on the Developing Child Harvard University https://developingchild.harvard.edu/	All areas	Most ages
Website	Child Mind Institute https://childmind.org/	All areas	Most ages
Website	Common Sense Educationhttps://www.commonsense.org/	All areas	
Website	Intervention Central Response to Intervention — RTI Resources http://www.interventioncentral.org/	All areas	Most ages
Website	https:/www.Kahoot.com	All areas	Most ages
Website	https://www.Khan Academy.com and Khan Academy App LD Online www.ldonline.org/	All areas	Most ages
Website	Understood.org https://www.understood.org	Working memory	All ages
Website	Brain Pop	Working memory	All ages
iPhone App	Chegg Flash Cards	Working memory	All ages
iPhone App	Google Classroom	Working memory	Grades 3 to 12
iPhone App	Explain Everything	Working memory	Grades 3 to adult
iPhone App	Homework	Working memory	All grades

TECHNOLOGY TOOL CATEGORY (WEBSITE, SOFTWARE, APP)	NAME OF TECHNOLOGY	EXECUTIVE FUNCTION AREA ADDRESSED	AGE GROUP
iPhone App	Kahoot App	Working memory	Grades 3 to 12
iPhone App	Lino	Working memory	All ages
iPhone App	Memory Matches	Working memory	PreK to Grade 3
iPhone App	Mindjet Manager	Working memory	Grades 1 to 12
iPad App	Mindmeister	Working memory	All ages
iPad App	Number Blast	Working memory	K to Grade 12
iPad App	Number Recall	Working memory	PreK to Grade 2
iPad App	Number Track	Working memory	PreK up
iPad App	One Note	Working memory	Grades 4 to 12
iPhone App	Quizlet	Working memory	Grades 2 to 12
iPhone App	Read to Kids	Working memory	PreK to Grade 2
iPhone App	Remember the Milk	Working memory	All grades
iPhone App	Sono Flex	Working memory	PreK up
iPad App	Starfall	Working memory	PreK to Grade 3
iPad App	Study Blue	Working memory	Grades 4 to 12
iPad App	Super Note	Working memory	Grades 4 to 12
iPad App	Timer	Working memory	PreK to 12
iPad App	What is the Next Integer?	Working memory	PreK to Grade 12

CASE STUDY: AMANDA

We will now look at the case study of Amanda (*see Appendix 1.1 for her full case study*), an eight-year old student in the third grade with executive function deficits in several skill areas. In this chapter, the 7-Step Model for Executive Function Skills Training explained in chapter 1 will be applied to the area of working memory.

The questions that need to be considered to determine the appropriate executive function interventions that will support Amanda's learning needs are these:

1. What are Amanda's executive function needs? (The step 1 process will answer this question.)

2. What are the strategies that can be used to support Amanda's executive function needs? (The step 3 process will answer this question.)

3. How should the effectiveness of the selected strategies in supporting Amanda's executive function needs be measured? (The step 4 and step 5 processes will answer this question.)

4. Do the selected strategies work? (The step 6 process will answer this question.)

The following example shows how to address one of Amanda's goals for working memory difficulties using the 7-Step Model. *The model is not a lock-step procedure but merely a template to guide your thinking. Your flexibility and creativity in using this model to meet your needs and the needs of your student are encouraged.*

The 7-Step Model

Step 1

Determine the student's EF deficits and note them in the Executive Function Planning Chart (table 2.2).

Assessment

As described in chapter 1, the assessment process is completed through reviewing the student's records as well as through observations of the student and interviews with the student, as well as his or her family members and other and previous teachers. Formal and informal assessments may also be used to help determine EF deficits. *(See Sample Student Self-Assessment Tool in Appendix 1.15.)*

Key Questions

1. How are the student's strengths and difficulties exhibited in terms of executive functions?

After a thorough review of Amanda's records, including current test scores on standardized tests, report card grades, work samples, observations of Amanda in academic and social settings, and interviews with her, Amanda's previous teachers, and her parents, the following strengths and needs in working memory are identified:

Amanda's Strengths
- She is very pleased with herself on the occasions when she has remembered her materials and glasses.
- She likes helping the teacher with tasks.

- She remembers dances and enjoys teaching them to others.
- She knows the sounds of most of the single consonants and all the long vowels.
- She remembers letter formation for all manuscript letters.
- She remembers names of parts of the body and bones. She also remembers to follow the rules in science lab exercises.

Amanda's Difficulties

- She has difficulty remembering the sounds of the short vowels and is inconsistent in all the consonant combinations. It is a lengthy process for her to sound out a multisyllabic word. When she encounters a word she does not know, she spends so much time and energy sounding it out that she forgets what she read before and after.
- She has difficulty remembering what she reads. As stated above, decoding sometimes causes her to lose track of what she is reading. When she knows the words, however, there is still a problem remembering what she has read. When silently reading, she often needs to reread a page because she does not remember what she reads. This makes answering comprehension questions or stating the main idea very difficult for her. Interventions in reading have helped her; however, Amanda is still behind her peers.
- She has difficulty remembering math facts—skip counting. She likes to write numbers but does not like to practice math facts. She has pretty much given up on learning them and tries to make marks on her papers and count those. As math problems become increasingly complex for her, it becomes more likely "the making marks practice" will result in a calculation error.
- When she is required to solve multistep problems, she forgets the algorithm for doing so.
- She forgets what the various mathematics signs mean.
- She does not remember what she needs to do to be prepared at the start of each class.
- She does not follow multistep directions.
- She has difficulty remembering class routines.
- She has difficulty benefitting from hindsight or foresight.
- She has difficulty remembering where she has placed items.

Amanda also has difficulties with other Executive Function Skills as can be seen on the Executive Function Planning Chart below. *Blank templates, modifiable versions of materials, and strategy cards can be found at http://resources.corwin.com/ ExecutiveFunctioning.*

Executive Function Planning

For the purpose of this chapter, the focus will be Amanda's executive function deficit in the area of working memory.

2. Is there an executive function deficit in working memory?

Looking at the information presented in answer to question 1, it is established, in addition to other deficits, that there is an executive function deficit in working memory.

3. How does the difficulty in working memory present?

The **Executive Function Planning Chart** specifies how Amanda's working memory difficulties present. If Amanda were eligible for services, an IEP objective for this goal might read, Amanda will answer reading comprehension questions with 90 percent accuracy using her Post-it Notes she writes while reading in a timed situation.

TABLE 2.2 Executive Function (EF) Planning Chart

EXECUTIVE FUNCTION SKILL AREA	WHAT DOES THE DIFFICULTY LOOK LIKE FOR THIS STUDENT? (EXAMPLES)
Working Memory	She does not remember what she has read. She forgets math facts and/or how to spell words she knew the night before. She gets confused when following multistep directions.
Prioritizing, Organizing, Sequencing, Managing Time, and Planning	She cannot find materials, glasses, and assignments. She either rushes through an assignment or does not finish the task on time. Her papers are sloppy and disorganized.
Attending, Initiating, and Focusing	She needs several reminders to get started on a task or assignment. She loses concentration very easily.
Controlling Social/Emotional and Inhibiting Behaviors	She impulsively calls out in class. She makes inappropriate comments to peers and adults.
Communicating, Cognitive Flexibility/Shifting	She does not write coherently due to a lack of understanding language usage. Her writing lacks sequencing of concepts and supporting details. She may display inappropriate body language and facial expressions and/or have difficulty interpreting body language and facial expressions. She is extremely slow to move from one activity on to another. She finds it difficult to think about more than one thing at a time.

Step 2

Review the EF Planning Chart with the student and start to develop a Game Plan.

As described in chapter 1, this will guide the skill training for the specific executive function area of working memory. After reviewing the assessment results with Amanda and her parents, we completed the Executive Function Planning Chart in step 1. Once Amanda's areas of executive function weaknesses needing immediate attention are identified, you can begin to develop Amanda's Game Plan. This will give Amanda an opportunity to "buy in" to the process. This understanding and awareness will later lead to student self-advocacy and greater independence in Amanda's learning process. Amanda's Game Plan includes the student's strengths, difficulties, goals for improvement, and strategies selected to enhance executive functioning through UDL and appropriate strategies. See chapter 1 for directions on starting a student Game Plan. *Blank templates, modifiable versions of materials, and strategy cards can be found at http://resources.corwin.com/ExecutiveFunctioning.*

FIGURE 2.23 Amanda's Game Plan for Working Memory

Student Name: <u>Amanda</u>

> **What I do best:** I am very helpful to my teacher.

> **What I do best:** I try very hard even when I get confused.

> **What I do best:** I am really good at science and love doing science experiments.

THINGS I WOULD LIKE TO DO BETTER	THINGS I CAN DO TO HELP WITH MY DIFFICULTIES IN SCHOOL
Goal 1: I would like to read faster and remember what I have read.	**Strategy Name:** To be determined after completing step 3 **Technology I can use:** **Date Goal Met:**
Goal 2: I would like to learn and remember my math facts and how to solve problems.	**Strategy Name:** To be determined after completing step 3 **Technology I can use:** **Date Goal Met:**
Goal 3: I would like to remember what I need to do to be prepared for my classes.	**Strategy Name:** To be determined after completing step 3 **Technology I can use:** **Date Goal Met:**

Step 3

Considering UDL and metacognition, select an EF skill-building strategy and get commitment from the student. Add the strategy to the Game Plan.

What are the strategies that can be used to support Amanda's executive function needs? Think about how you would respond to the following questions:

- What are Amanda's learning needs and challenges in terms of UDL (Multiple Means of Representation, Multiple Means of Action and Expression, Multiple Means of Engagement)? See table 2.3.
- What approaches and supports will be used to help Amanda access the lesson, given her working memory deficit? Examples include the following:
  - checking for understanding
  - allowing extra processing time
  - providing her with a notepad and pencil so she can write cue words as a reminder of what she wishes to say
  - chunking the number of steps needed to complete a task and having her complete one section at a time
  - using graphic organizers
  - providing prewriting activities
  - scaffolding information taught
  - incorporating supportive technology
- What strategies will be taught to Amanda and added to her Game Plan?
  - Select from those described in the first part of the chapter, other resources, or those you have used previously.
  - Use the **Selecting a Strategy for the Student While Integrating UDL Chart**, table 2.3, as a tool to prompt your thinking in terms of selecting the appropriate strategy that matches Amanda's learning needs and challenges. Written completion of this chart is not necessary. *A blank chart can be found in Appendix 1.10, and blank templates, modifiable versions of materials, and strategy cards can be found at http://resources.corwin.com/ ExecutiveFunctioning*. A sample thought process for working memory is provided below.

TABLE 2.3 Selecting a Strategy for the Student While Integrating UDL

Student: Amanda

Executive Function Deficit: Working Memory

Game Plan Goal: Goal 1: I would like to read faster and remember what I have read.

MULTIPLE MEANS OF REPRESENTATION				
Things for you to consider:				
1. What information does the student already know? *Amanda is making strides in reading (standardized testing reading scores have improved.) She has trouble with reading comprehension.* *The demands on her working memory need to be minimized.*	**2. What are the instructional goals for the student in relation to the executive function addressed?** *She needs to read two to three pages and remember the information read so she can summarize main ideas.*	**3. What extended activities will be needed?** *Use a multisensory approach that includes reading selected pages, accurately recording details from these pages on Post-it Notes, and timing with a stopwatch app how long it takes to read each page.*	**4. What enrichment activities can be implemented?** *Have Amanda practice reading information on teacher selected websites, newspaper ads and posters, timing how long it takes to read each page and recording details on Post-it Notes.*	**5. What will you need to incorporate when teaching the strategy?** • *Connect background knowledge, preteach prerequisite information.* • *Model the expected process for using Post-it Note Modified, strategy cards, and other materials.* • *Provide simple verbal directives and visual support of the process using a checklist of steps to be completed.* • *Check for understanding and accuracy in completing Post-it Notes* • *Provide extended time for task completion.*

(Continued)

TABLE 2.3 (Continued)

MULTIPLE MEANS OF ACTION AND EXPRESSION

Things for you to consider:

1. How will you conduct preassessment, formative, and summative assessments for the student's learning?

For preassessment, Amanda will be asked to read three pages and state the main ideas of what she has read.

For the formative stage, provide Amanda with reading materials accompanied by audio text, Post-it Notes, a timer, a pencil, and extended time. Model the Post-it Note Modified Strategy process.

For the summative stage, provide Amanda with reading materials, Post-it Note Modified, a stopwatch, a pencil, and extended time. Model the Post-it Note Modified Strategy process.

The accuracy and number of main ideas Amanda provides on her Post-it Notes will be used to determine whether outcomes are met.

2. What platforms will be permitted for the student to demonstrate mastery?

Demonstrate mastery through the completion of graphic organizers, checklists, summarizing information read, sequencing details read, talking about her answer, drawing pictorial representation of the information read.

MULTIPLE MEANS OF ENGAGEMENT

Things for you to consider:

1. How will you teach the student in a manner that actively engages the student?

- *Have the student engage in creating goals that encourage success.*

- *Have the student use metacognition to self-monitor the process to be completed.*

- *Have the student collect data using a tally sheet to record the number of details the student remembered and recorded compared to the total number of details the teacher expected to be recorded. This shows the effectiveness of the strategy to help attain goals.*

- *Allow the student to share the ideas he or she has for remembering details of what he or she reads.*

TABLE 2.3 (Continued)

Based on your Considerations of the Principles for this goal, what strategy would you select that aligns with the three Principles and Align with UDL and the Strategy Selected?

Name of Strategy: *Post-it Note Modified Strategy*
This strategy is selected because it

1. *minimizes working memory demands and allows her to chunk information* (Multiple Means of Representation).

2. *helps her identify key concepts through highlighting main ideas and recording these details of what has been read and provides her the opportunity to sequence details of what is read* (Multiple Means of Action and Expression).

3. *provides her the opportunity to demonstrate mastery of lesson and the mastery and the effectiveness of the strategy using metacognition and self-monitoring* (Multiple Means of Engagement).

---

o Think about the components of the **Student Implementation of Strategy With a Focus on Metacognition and UDL Chart**, table 2.4. This chart should be completed with the student. It is a tool that helps the student to buy in to the strategy learning process. *A blank chart can be found in Appendix 1.11, and blank templates, modifiable versions of materials, and strategy cards can be found at http:// resources.corwin.com/ExecutiveFunctioning*.

o Once you and the student have selected a strategy, add the strategy name to the "Things I can do to help with my difficulties in school" column of the Game Plan for an elementary student or the "Action" column of the Game Plan for a secondary student.

Figure 2.24 shows Amanda's completed Game Plan, which lists her goals and the strategies she and her teacher have decided she will learn to strengthen her EF skills in the area of working memory. Given her issues, additional strategies such as Skip Counting, Check List, GOP, and supportive technology would be taught to Amanda to further strengthen this skill area.

TABLE 2.4 Student Implementation of Strategy With a Focus on Metacognition and UDL Principles

Student: Amanda

Executive Function Deficit: Working Memory

Game Plan Goal: Goal 1: I would like to read faster and remember what I have read.

Strategy Selected: Post-it Note Modified Strategy

METACOGNITION—QUESTIONS THE STUDENT THINKS ABOUT AND RESPONDS TO

Things for you to consider:

1. What am I supposed to do?

*Use the **Post-it Note Modified Strategy** so that I can read faster and remember what I have read.*

2. Why is this strategy important for me to use and how will it help me?

This strategy will help me read faster and remember what I have read.

3. What are the steps of the strategy?

I will follow the steps on my strategy card so that I know what I need to do to read faster and remember what I read.

- *Write name and date.*
- *Start timer; read one page.*
- *At the end of the page, stop timer, write the page number, the main idea, and the length of time it took to read the page on the Post-it Note.*
- *Stick the Post-it Note to the page.*
- *Use notes to remember what I read.*
- *Go to the next page.*

4. Is there technology I can use?

- *Colored pens and color-coded Post-it Notes to record what I have read*
- *Recording software for writing the information I have read and remember, for example, Kidspiration, Wave Pad, Voice*
- *Checklist apps that show the correct way to show the steps I need to take when using this strategy and check off each step as completed, for example, Wunderlist, Stripes, List Away*
- *Timer apps to time my reading (Multiple Means of Engagement), for example, Alarm Clock HD, Tabata Stopwatch, Interval*
- *Post-it Note apps to record what I have read (Multiple Means of Action and Expression), for example, Lino, All Notes, Sticky Note*

5. What should I think about when using this strategy?

When using this strategy, I need to think about

- *starting the timer before I start reading, and turning it off when I finish reading.*
- Going to the next page as soon as I have finished the Post-it Note for each page.

Student Name: Amanda

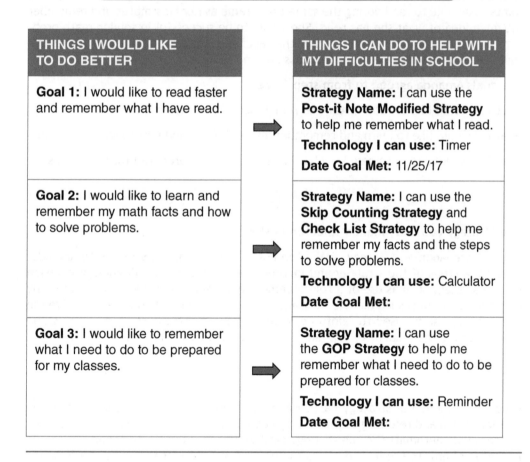

> **What I do best:** I am very helpful to my teacher.

> **What I do best:** I try very hard even when I get confused.

> **What I do best:** I am really good at science and love doing science experiments.

THINGS I WOULD LIKE TO DO BETTER	THINGS I CAN DO TO HELP WITH MY DIFFICULTIES IN SCHOOL
Goal 1: I would like to read faster and remember what I have read.	**Strategy Name:** I can use the **Post-it Note Modified Strategy** to help me remember what I read. **Technology I can use:** Timer **Date Goal Met:** 11/25/17
Goal 2: I would like to learn and remember my math facts and how to solve problems.	**Strategy Name:** I can use the **Skip Counting Strategy** and **Check List Strategy** to help me remember my facts and the steps to solve problems. **Technology I can use:** Calculator **Date Goal Met:**
Goal 3: I would like to remember what I need to do to be prepared for my classes.	**Strategy Name:** I can use the **GOP Strategy** to help me remember what I need to do to be prepared for classes. **Technology I can use:** Reminder **Date Goal Met:**

Step 4

Design and implement data collection tools to measure success in the use of the strategy, teach the selected strategy, and give the student a strategy card.

The following illustrates how step 4 would be applied to the Post-it Note Modified Strategy which addresses Goal 1.

The data from Step 1 show that

Amanda spends a lot of time rereading because she gets off task between words, sentences, paragraphs, and pages. This causes her to have to reread to find her place and to find the main idea of what she is reading. It ends up taking a long time for her to read a selection and she does not remember the main ideas. The skills Amanda needs to learn this strategy are reading in the time allotted, reading with the purpose of finding the main idea, and recording the main idea. She will need to remember, use the timer, record the time it took, as well as write the main idea on the Post-it Note. When she does not read and remember the main idea, she tends to earn a low grade on the assignment.

We talked with Amanda about her difficulties and started to develop a Game Plan.

Amanda understands that many of her difficulties relate to working memory. She wants to be able to read during the same time frame as her classmates and remember the main idea of what she has read. She wants to be successful in solving math problems but finds it difficult to remember the facts and what to do. She also wishes she could remember what she needs for class and the routine.

The goals Amanda agreed to from step 2 are

Goal 1: I would like to read faster and remember what I have read.

Goal 2: I would like to learn and remember my math facts and how to solve problems.

Goal 3: I would like to remember what I need to do to be prepared for my classes.

The Strategy you and Amanda selected in step 3 is

Post-it Note Modified Strategy. Teach the Post-it Note Modified Strategy to Amanda. **Model** the steps of the strategy and incorporate metacognition. Provide motivation for the strategy such as use of a reinforcement and gain a continued commitment by the student. Games such as Role Play and Sequencing a List of the Steps involved in the strategy can be used to reinforce recall of how to use the strategy. Each game should require the student to explain the strategy and how it helps him or her.

Give the student the strategy card. Have the student practice the strategy using metacognition and referring to the strategy card as needed until he or she can use the strategy with automaticity. The strategy card summarizes the strategy and serves as a reminder of how to use it. It outlines the process and steps that need to be followed to successfully implement the strategy. To make the card, create or purchase a 3" x 5" or business-size card. Place the name of the strategy on the front of the card, along with visuals if that is helpful for the student. Place a description of how to use the strategy on the back of the card. It is helpful if this description is stated in the student's own words. Check the description for accuracy. Punch a hole in the top left of the card if you are placing the card on a strategy ring. This strategy ring will provide Amanda with an individualized portable reference system of strategies that supports her EF skills in working memory.

FIGURE 2.25 Post-it Note Modified Strategy

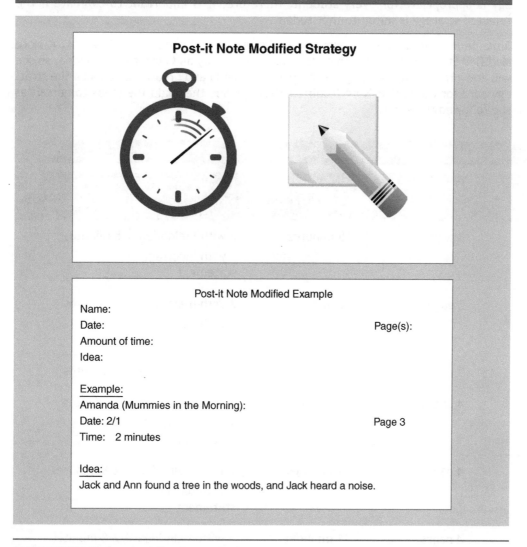

Post-it Note Modified Strategy

Post-it Note Modified Example

Name:

Date: Page(s):

Amount of time:

Idea:

Example:

Amanda (Mummies in the Morning):

Date: 2/1   Page 3

Time: 2 minutes

Idea:

Jack and Ann found a tree in the woods, and Jack heard a noise.

IMAGE SOURCE: Pixabay.com/clker-free-vector-images

As the student continues to practice the strategy, it is important to determine whether the strategy is appropriate for teaching the student the EF skill working memory.

Design and collect data and revise as necessary.

Design the data tools, collect data on the success of the strategy, and revise as necessary. *A blank reproducible baseline data chart is available at http://resources .corwin.com/ExecutiveFunctioning*. This is the baseline phase of the data collection process. Once the baseline data has been collected, analyze the data and go back and make any necessary adjustments. For example, does the baseline data show that this strategy works for the student? Does the student need extra supports such as cues to remind her to use the strategy? Does the student need extended time to complete the steps of the strategy? After the student has been taught the strategy, it is important for you as the teacher to determine whether the strategy is appropriate for the student's needs and if the student is comfortable using the strategy. Not every strategy is appropriate for every student; therefore, it is important to evaluate if the selected strategy is suited to the student.

Amanda incorporates metacognition as she uses her strategy card. The Post-it Note Modified Strategy is to help Amanda read more quickly and note the main ideas so she will know them after reading several pages. Amanda and I read the steps on the strategy card for the Post-it Note Modified Strategy. She then said the steps to herself as she followed the steps.

TABLE 2.5 Baseline Data for Amanda's Usage of the Post-it Note Modified Strategy

DATE	ASSIGNMENT	READING TIME	USE OF POST-IT NOTES	AVERAGE TIME PER PAGE
11/15	3 pages	15 minutes	2 with main idea 1 with incorrect statement	5 minutes
11/16	3 pages	12 minutes	2 with main idea 1 with partial statement	4 minutes
11/17	3 pages	12 minutes	3 with main idea	4 minutes
11/22	4 pages	12 minutes	3 with main idea 1 with incorrect statement	3 minutes
11/23	4 pages	11 minutes	3 with main idea 1 with partial statement	2.8 minutes
11/24	4 pages	11 minutes	4 with main idea	2.8 minutes

Analyze the baseline data and go back and make any necessary adjustments. For example, does the baseline data show that this strategy works for Amanda? Does Amanda need extra supports such as cues to remind her to use the strategy? Does Amanda need extended time to complete the steps of the strategy?

After Amanda has been taught the strategy, it is important for you as the teacher to determine whether the strategy is appropriate for Amanda's needs and if she is comfortable using the strategy. You may need to revise the selected strategy or choose another strategy that is more appropriate for her needs after looking at data.

Step 5

Continue to collect data for the student's use of the strategy.

Determine the student's success in learning and generalizing the strategy. Considerations for Ongoing Data Analysis Chart, table 2.6, provides points you as the teacher need to consider as you continue to analyze the data addressing the student's correct use and generalization of the selected strategy. The teacher's responses to the questions considered in table 2.6 are posted below. **Blank templates, modifiable versions of materials, and strategy cards can be found at http://resources .corwin.com/ExecutiveFunctioning.**

As explained in step 1, we need to determine whether Amanda has mastered the strategy, which includes both using the strategy correctly and generalizing it to a variety of settings. Complete table 2.6 Sample Considerations for Ongoing Data Analysis Chart for Amanda.

TABLE 2.6 Sample Considerations for Ongoing Data Analysis Chart

Student Name: *Amanda*
Strategy Used: *Post-it Note Modified Strategy*
Please write yes, no, or N/A for Not Applicable.

_____yes_____	1. The strategy is cited in the student's Ongoing Data Analysis.
_____yes_____	2. The student understands the goal of using the strategy.
_____yes_____	3. The student can explain what the strategy is and why he or she is using it.
_____yes_____	4. There is a means of collecting data to measure the student's progress.
_____yes_____	5. The tools to measure the academic or social/emotional area that the executive function deficit is impacting are appropriate.
_____yes_____	6. Daily feedback is provided for at least one week when the strategy began.
_____yes_____	7. The student is provided with reinforcement and knows his or her standing.
_____yes_____	8. Data are analyzed with the student and the revisions are made as needed.
_____yes_____	9. The selected strategy is appropriate for the student's needs.

Comments

Amanda likes using the timer and Post-it Notes. She is proud of her progress. Her main difficulty is determining and writing the main idea. One revision discussed was to make the main idea a multiple choice. She asked to continue with the strategy because she remembers it better when she writes it down.

For the Post-it Note Modified Strategy, the same data chart was used as used in baseline data collection.

TABLE 2.7 Data Chart for Post-it Note Modified Strategy Use

DATE	ASSIGNMENT	READING TIME	USE OF POST-IT NOTES TO RECORD MAIN IDEAS	AVERAGE TIME PER PAGE (COMPUTED WITH CALCULATOR)
12/1	Read 5 pages in the book, *Mummies in the Morn*.	15 minutes	Used 3 Post-it Notes with 4 main ideas	Average time per page: 3 minutes
12/2	Read 5 pages in my book.	15 minutes	Used 5 Post-it Notes with 4 main ideas 1 Post-it Note incomplete	Average time per page: 3 minutes
12/3	Read 6 pages in my book.	20 minutes	Used 6 Post-it Notes 2 Post-it Notes incomplete	Average time per page: 3.30 minutes
12/4	Read 5 pages in my book.	13 minutes	Used 4 Post-it Notes with 4 main ideas	Average time per page: 2.60 minutes
12/8	3 pages	15 minutes	Used 2 with main idea 1 with incorrect statement	Average time per page: 5 minutes
12/9	3 pages	12 minutes	Used 2 with main idea 1 with partial statement	Average time per page: 4 minutes
12/10	4 pages	12 minutes	Used 3 with main idea	Average time per page: 3 minutes
12/15	5 pages	15 minutes	Used 5 with main idea 1 with incorrect statement	Average time per page: 3 minutes
12/16	5 pages	12 minutes	Used 5 with main idea 1 with partial statement	Average time per page: 2.40 minutes
12/17	3 pages	9 minutes	Used 3 with main idea	Average time per page: 3 minutes

Amanda did not have this class every day, so she was only using it during this time. We discussed her progress, and Amanda agreed she would try the strategy next week at home. Her parents agreed this would be a way to help her read and comprehend in the evening instead of her refusing to read at home as had been the case before.

Step 6

Analyze all the data collected and evaluate the student's success in using the strategy; update the Game Plan.

In analyzing Amanda's success in learning and generalizing the Post-it Notes Modified Strategy and whether it has helped her, there are overarching questions:

- Did she use the strategy in the noted area of executive function difficulty?
- Did she generalize, that is, use the strategy in different scenarios?
- Has the target executive function deficit improved since Amanda started using the strategy?

We can answer these questions by completing the **Final Assessment of The Strategy**. A final assessment of the strategy can be used to analyze all the data collected, evaluate Amanda's success, and evaluate the effectiveness of the strategy. *A blank template for the* **Final Assessment of the Strategy** *can be found in Appendix 1.13, and blank templates, modifiable versions of materials, and strategy cards can be found at http://resources.corwin.com/ExecutiveFunctioning*.

Review the data recording tool and completed **Final Assessment Template** to determine:

- Does Amanda use the strategy in the noted area of executive function difficulty?
  - Yes, Amanda has used the Post-it Note Modified Strategy diligently; however, she tends to write very short phrases for the main idea. She likes using the timer and likes having the Post-it Notes to look back at for review of the main ideas.
- Does Amanda generalize?
  - Amanda has started to use this strategy in other classes and while completing homework when reading content.
- Has the noted executive function deficit improved since Amanda started using the strategy?
  - Yes, Amanda has performed better on items requiring her to remember what she has read, and her speed has improved as well.

Conclusion: Based on the data, Amanda is improving in the working memory area using the Post-it Note Modified Strategy. Amanda will continue to use this strategy, and she will use it independently.

Step 7

Revisit the Game Plan to determine whether the student's goals have been met. Once a goal is met, have the student write a Success Plan.

To determine whether Amanda's first goal has been met, look at the data for the entire period she has been using the strategy. Review the data with her, and discuss with her the following key questions:

- Does she feel the use of the strategy is helping? Do the data support this perception?
  The data for goal 1 show that Amanda has been successful on goal 1 using the Post-it Note Modified Strategy. (Goals 2 and 3 will be considered separately.)

Sample Template for Final Assessment of the Strategy

Date: 12/17/17

Name of Student: Amanda

Executive Function(s) Being Addressed: Working Memory

Intervention Implemented? (circle one) Y/N

Describe the Strategy and How It Is Being Used:

Post-it Note Modified Strategy

1. Start the timer.
2. Read the assigned page.
3. When finished reading, stop the timer and record the time it took to read the page on the Post-it Note.
4. Write name, date, page number, and main idea also on Post-it note.

☑ **Strategy Used From:** 11/14/17 **To:** 12/17/17

☑ **UDL-EF Process Used:**

- Completed Executive Function Planning Chart
- Thought through Selecting a Strategy for the Student While Integrating UDL Chart
- Created with student a Strategy Implementation With a Focus on UDL and Metacognition Chart
- Field-tested the Post-it Note Modified Strategy
- Created strategy card for Post-it Note Modified and placed on Amanda's Strategy Ring
- Finalized Post-it Note Modified Strategy and Selected this Strategy for Amanda
- Taught the strategy and kept data of usage
- Made revisions as necessary

☑ **Data for Measured Results:** Two weeks of data from step 5. (See completed Post-it Note Modified Strategy Chart)

☑ **Anecdotal Report of Results:**

- Liked using the timer and read more quickly because she was cognizant of the timer
- Voluntarily read sections to find the main idea

☑ **Review of Results:**

- Improved focus on what she read
- Increased amount read in a specific period
- Increased comprehension and vocabulary

☑ **Summary Report on Game Plan Progress:**

The Post-it Note Modified Strategy has helped Amanda to attain **"Goal 1:** I would like to remember what I have read and read it more quickly."

Accomplished 12/17/2017.

Summary Report on Implications of Strategy Use on Academic Skills and Social Interactions:
Amanda uses the Post-it Note Modified Strategy independently and accurately while reading. The strategy has helped to improve Amanda's silent reading rate and reading comprehension as measured on Post-it Notes.

FIGURE 2.26 SAMPLE SUCCESS PLAN FOR AMANDA (WORKING MEMORY GOAL 1)

What I Want to Do Next

I want to be successful and read faster and remember what I've read.

Difficulties I May Have

- *I have trouble remembering what I read.*
- *I reread things a lot to remember main points. This makes me unable to finish my work on time.*

Strategies I Can Use to Help Myself

To help me remember what I read I can use the Post-it Note Modified Strategy. For this strategy, I need to have Post-it Notes, a pen, what I am reading, and a timer.

What the Teacher Can Do to Help

When I use the Post-it Note Modified Strategy, the teacher will check what I have written on my Post-it Notes to make sure that I have remembered all the information that is important.

- Does she feel it would be beneficial to continue to use this strategy? Amanda feels the strategies have helped her, and the data support this.
- Does she feel she is ready to move on to another goal for this executive function? Amanda says she feels ready to move onto another goal. She will continue to implement the Post-it Note Modified Strategy.

After each goal on the student's Game Plan has been met, help her write a personal Success Plan to communicate what she plans to do to have a successful school year and self-advocate for the assistance she needs to help her on this journey towards success. This should identify the following:

- What I want to do next
- Difficulties that I may have
- Strategies I can use to help myself
- What the teacher can do to help

Figure 2.26 is the sample template for Amanda's working memory goal 1. *A blank template can be found in Appendix 1.14, and blank templates, modifiable versions of materials, and strategy cards can be found at http://resources.corwin.com/ExecutiveFunctioning.*

WHAT HAPPENS THEN?

When all three goals on the Game Plan are met, it is time to identify new challenges on which to focus. Few students experience difficulty in only one executive function. While Amanda will continue to work on strengthening her working memory, there are other executive function area deficits to be addressed. The next step would be to return to the EF Planning Chart to determine which EF deficits to address.

Summary

Working Memory is at the core of learning. Most learners find manipulating multiple pieces of memory to solve a problem challenging. For those with working memory deficits, it is extremely difficult to do so. While a deficit in working memory looks different for each student, most students with working memory deficits have difficulty remembering academic content, completing multistep projects, and remembering directions, rules, and routines. These difficulties and others have a negative impact on student achievement, behavior, and social/emotional well-being, leading some into the Downward Spiral discussed in Chapter 1. Supportive strategies both to improve working memory and to compensate for working memory deficits are available for teachers and students, who can work together toward student success. Concrete external storage systems, mnemonics, multisensory strategies, and study strategies are just a few of those described in this chapter. Supportive technologies, some of which are listed in the chapter, are available to assist in the improvement of EF skills. Finally, the 7-Step Model is presented in this chapter for an elementary student presenting difficulty in working memory among other deficits. Through this example in working memory, you can see how these steps come together working with an individual student. For those using the 7-Step Model Modified it is helpful to see and select the parts of the model that will fit your particular situation. We encourage teachers, regardless of whether they are using the 7-Step Model or 7-Step Model Modified, to use their knowledge, judgement, and creativity to determine what their program will look like, keeping in mind that on-going assessment, determination of what is needed, the consideration of UDL and metacognition in the choice of strategies, the implementation of strategies, and the commitment of the student are all vital components for a successful implementation of Working Memory Executive Function Skills Training.

Practice

- Practice the 7-Step Model for working memory using one of the case studies in the Appendix. Note that there is another case study for a middle school student, Emily. (*See Appendix 1.3.*) As well, there are two case studies for students in secondary school. Carlos is the secondary student we will focus on in chapters 4 and 5.

- Note any challenges and successes you experienced and review the content in chapter 1 for background information relating to this chapter.

- Practice the 7-Step Model for one of your students.

Prioritizing, Organizing, Sequencing, Managing Time, Planning, and Supportive Strategies

Reader Outcomes

☑ You will be able to identify factors that suggest problems in the executive function skill area that includes prioritizing, organizing, sequencing, managing time, and planning.

☑ You will be able to identify how difficulties in prioritizing, organizing, sequencing, managing time, and planning impact the student's behavior, social/emotional well-being, and academic success.

☑ You will be able to identify instructional strategies for teachers and learning strategies for students to use to address difficulty in prioritizing, organizing, sequencing, managing time, and planning.

☑ You will be able to record student progress and make instructional changes based on the data.

WHAT IS PRIORITIZING, ORGANIZING, SEQUENCING, MANAGING TIME, AND PLANNING?

Prioritizing, organizing, sequencing, managing time, and planning are five executive function skills that are closely linked. To better see this linkage, let's first look at each separately.

PRIORITIZING

Dawson and Guare (2010) define prioritization as "The ability to create a roadmap to reach a goal or to complete a task. It also involves being able to make decisions about what's important to focus on and what's not important" (p. 8). Dawson and Guare link the skill of planning to prioritizing. Kaufman (2010) notes that planning is part of strategizing and states, "It is the quality and specificity of these plans and strategies that will determine in large part whether people achieve their goals" (p. 4). As teachers and parents, it is our role to determine a young child's priorities. But, as they get older, they are tasked with making decisions regarding the importance of an activity. In order for students to prioritize in class, they need to determine what task at hand is the most important to complete and then rank subsequent tasks in order of importance.

ORGANIZING

"Planning and organization is the ability to manage current and future-oriented task demands in a systematic, efficient manner" (Cooper-Kahn and Dietzel, 2008, p. 53). Organization and planning affect many areas of our everyday functioning. Meltzer (2010) divides the executive function of organization as space and materials in one context and ideas in the other. These executive function skills include not only the organization of items and planning of events, but the organization of our thinking and what we have learned, as well as the planning of our time to complete tasks.

SEQUENCING

Kaufman (2010) states that "the quality of learning and production is the ability to properly sequence the information that enters and exists in the mind" (p. 4). Students struggle when their mind does not take in and process information in a sequential manner. It is the process of sequencing that creates an automatic link to the delivery of the instructional material and the learned connections made by the student. Such students may have difficulties with following routines, steps to solve a mathematics problem, and formulating plans.

MANAGING TIME

Managing time is "The capacity to estimate how much time one has, how to allocate it, and how to stay within time limits and deadlines. It involves a sense that time is important" (Dawson & Guare, 2009, p. 17). According to Kaufman (2010), there is a multitude of research supporting time management as multidimensional in that it is interconnected with planning, prioritizing, and organizing. Kaufman believes that time management skill difficulties "can take two forms" (p. 5). The first form involves the skills of organization and planning, while the second form evolves from the student's lack of sense of time. The first form of time management difficulty results in the student not planning for the completion of an assignment which results in the student "rushing" and producing a product of poor quality. The second form of time management difficulty is due to the student's inability to keep track of time. In such a situation, the student assumes he or she has plenty of time to complete an assignment and is frequently shocked when "suddenly" the assignment due date has arrived. Losing track of calendar dates and days of the week is another characteristic of this time management difficulty (p. 5).

PLANNING

As the student gets older, the role of planning gradually becomes more the student's responsibility than the parents. Planning is a skill that needs to be effectively modeled for the student, providing opportunities across settings for the student to practice and generalize this skill. Much like the difficulties associated with deficits in prioritizing and time management, students lacking the ability to plan and organize often do not meet assignment deadlines, become anxious and frustrated because they need to "rush" to complete a task, or make overlapping plans that cause conflicts. Cooper-Kahn and Foster (2013, pp. 46–47) link planning with time management while Dawson and Guare (2009, p. 17) link planning with prioritizing.

WHAT DOES A DIFFICULTY IN PRIORITIZING, ORGANIZING, SEQUENCING, MANAGING TIME, AND PLANNING LOOK LIKE?

Prioritizing

Students who have problems in prioritizing

- have difficulty determining goals,
- have difficulty determining which tasks must be completed first and submitting incomplete assignments or not submitting assignments at all,
- may not make time to study.

Organizing

Students who have problems in organizing

- write down assignments but forget where they recorded them,
- lack organization in terms of content flow in written work,
- are unable to find personal items,
- forget materials needed to complete class and homework assignments,
- have a messy desk,
- have a messy binder and be unable to find papers and other materials needed for class.

Sequencing

Students who have problems in sequencing

- have difficulty recollecting the order of steps to complete assignments,
- omit details or sequence them incorrectly,

- do not follow the sequence of steps of an algorithm in solving math problems,
- do not remember the sequence of details read and have difficulty completing assignments because of this.

Managing Time

Students who have problems in managing time

- do not complete homework and state that extracurricular activities consumed homework time,
- submit assignments late,
- rush through assignments and do not check their work before handing them in,
- perseverate on one task and do not complete others.

Planning

Students who have problems in planning

- do not plan for long-term assignments,
- appear to be overwhelmed and/or anxious.

HOW DOES A DIFFICULTY IN PRIORITIZING, ORGANIZING, SEQUENCING, MANAGING TIME, AND PLANNING IMPACT STUDENT ACHIEVEMENT?

While some students come to our classrooms able to plan and organize their thoughts, activities, and materials, others come to our classrooms "living by the moment" without a care for planning and organizing. Students begin formal instruction to plan and organize in preschool through activities like sorting, classification, and labeling. These skills are important prerequisites to the executive skills of planning and organizing, however, some students have difficulty making a connection between the skills and life. Some adults also have not made that connection. Some adults plan at the last minute only to be disappointed when those plans do not work out. They may also have difficulty locating personal and work-related items causing difficulty with personal and work relationships.

If a deficit in prioritizing, organizing, sequencing, managing time, and planning is not addressed in childhood, it will continue to create difficulties for the individual into adulthood. The inability to organize a personal schedule, plan, or manage time may cause the individual to miss important work and social events. The inability to prioritize tasks may interfere with multitasking and completing tasks on time and thus compromise the individual's performance in the workplace. Adults who struggle with the sequencing needed to perform ordinary tasks, such as following a recipe to cook a meal, self-care, or following a travel itinerary, may become overwhelmed and frustrated at the challenge of managing daily tasks.

We recommend involving students at a young age in planning family and class events, being taught to organize their thoughts and materials, and working with others for the greater good. Family and school events provide a structure for such instruction. Children can be involved in planning an event such as their birthday celebration and practice task analysis, prioritizing and organizing as plans are made. By involving children at an early age, adults can role model, while at the same time giving children age and developmentally appropriate tasks to complete. As these children grow, they can move into helping with more and more decisions that require them to plan and organize. In summary, we concur with Dawson and Guare (2009) who suggest teaching planning and prioritizing in the following manner:

- "Create plans for your child when young."
- "Involve your child as much as possible in the planning process."
- "Use things the child wants as a jumping-off point for teaching planning skills."
- "Prompt prioritizing by asking your child what needs to get done first." (p. 234).

Reading, writing, and mathematics achievement is also at risk when students have trouble prioritizing, organizing their thoughts, managing time, and planning. Having classes in different locations and being responsible for bringing the right materials to each class can be challenging for students with deficits in this area.

Deficits in this area may also cause students to struggle with completing their classwork and homework. Behavior and social emotional well-being are also impacted by deficits in prioritizing, organizing, sequencing, managing time, and planning. When a student has difficulty in these executive functions, it may appear the student is not trying or is purposefully not completing assignments when in reality, he or she may be overwhelmed by classwork, projects, papers, and studying for tests and does not know what to do or what questions to ask. Feelings of anxiety or behavioral outbursts may occur as a result. Without intervention and specific strategies to address a deficit in this EF skill area, the student may become anxious and confused. This situation may lead the child into the Downward Spiral of behavioral and social/emotional well-being issues described in chapter 1, figure 1.2.

While teacher-provided structure is necessary when working with students with EF weaknesses in the area of prioritizing, organizing, sequencing, managing time, and planning, teacher-provided structure alone is not sufficient. Students need to learn skills that will help them benefit from instruction. Therein lies the challenge for us as teachers and our students alike. Learning and, ultimately, achievement suffer when students do not approach learning with a goal in mind and a plan to reach that goal. Students must learn to plan by identifying the tasks to be completed, estimating the time required to complete tasks, sequencing tasks in order of priority, gathering the needed materials, and following their plan. The organization involved in setting and managing one's schedule is vital for success.

SUPPORTIVE STRATEGIES WITH CARDS FOR PRIORITIZING, ORGANIZING, SEQUENCING, MANAGING TIME, AND PLANNING

The following are examples of supportive strategies to teach students that can help them with goals related to the EF area of Prioritizing, Organizing, Sequencing, Managing Time, and Planning. It is important to note that all strategies will not work for all students. Step 3 in the 7-Step Model provides help in choosing appropriate strategies for students while considering UDL and metacognition, and step 4 will guide you through the teaching process. Steps 5, 6, and 7 address data tools for the assessment of strategy effectiveness, revision if needed, and the celebration of success with the strategy or strategies before moving on. ***Blank templates, modifiable versions of materials, and strategy cards can be found at http://resources.corwin.com/ExecutiveFunctioning.***

PRIORITIZING STRATEGIES

Big Rocks Little Rocks Strategy for Setting Priorities

This strategy is based on the Big Rocks exercise described by Covey and Harris (1999) in *The 7 Habits of Effective Teens*. It is useful for helping students understand the importance of prioritization. It involves using a vase and different size rocks (including fine sand) to demonstrate the importance of determining tasks that need completion and performing these tasks in order of priority. The sand and rocks represent tasks the student needs to do. Big rocks represent the most important tasks, with smaller rocks representing less important ones, and sand representing the least important tasks. The vase represents the capacity to get things done.

Start by demonstrating that if all the things that need to be done (represented by all the sand and rocks) are dumped into the vase without any prioritization, all the rocks and sand may not fit. Although it seems like there is not enough room in the vase to fit everything, dump out all the rocks and sand and show the student that by prioritizing and strategizing (adding big rocks before sand) it is possible to make everything fit. This illustrates how little rocks (low-priority items) can get in the way of reaching your goals and underscores the importance of prioritizing the big rocks (high priority items).

Teach the student this strategy by having the student

- make a list of all the things he or she does in a day,

- identify what tasks must take priority,

- label three of the largest rocks with the highest-priority tasks and put those into an empty vase,

- list less important tasks and use smaller rocks and sand to represent these,
- add the rest of the rocks and sand to the vase in order from largest to smallest.

Explain that, as with the rocks, a student needs to prioritize his or her assignments and tasks and tackle them from most important to least to make everything fit.

Below is a sample strategy card for Big Rocks Little Rocks Strategy.

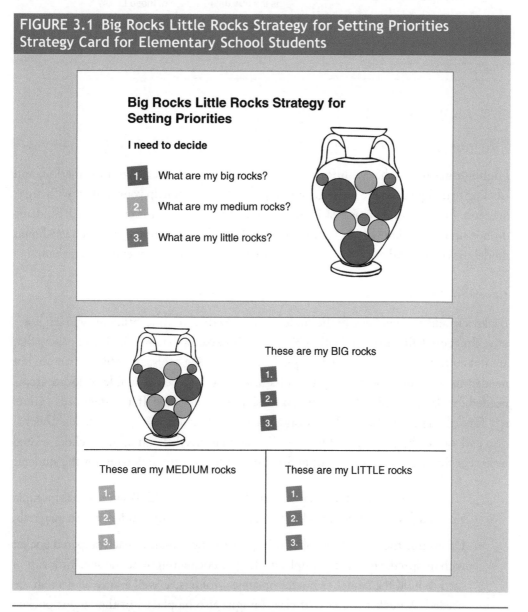

FIGURE 3.1 Big Rocks Little Rocks Strategy for Setting Priorities Strategy Card for Elementary School Students

IMAGE SOURCE: Pixabay.com/clker-free-vector-images

Since the EF skills of prioritizing and sequencing tend to overlap, please refer to Steps for Completing a Long-Term Project Checklist Strategy under **Sequencing Strategies** section of this chapter for additional considerations.

Determining Some Priorities	• What are the tasks that I need to complete first? When is the due date for each of these tasks? • What are the tasks that I need to complete second? When is the due date for each of these tasks? • What are the tasks that I need to complete last? When is the due date for each of these tasks? • Do the assignment due dates match how I have prioritized the tasks? If not, what do I need to change?

ORGANIZING STRATEGIES

The Importance of Highlighting, Color-Coding, and Labeling

Highlighting to emphasize information, color-coding to categorize information, and labeling to designate where items go are simple tools that can help your student with organization. Tasks are often made easier when something important is emphasized. Students do not necessarily know how to use these tools to their advantage, so teachers should model the correct and effective use of these tools and encourage students to use them.

Backpack Organization Strategy for Elementary Students

Backpacks add another layer to the student's organization routine. Students with an executive function deficit in organization often have backpacks that are filled with papers that are not correctly filed and often crumpled, broken writing tools, and objects that are not needed in the school setting. This results in the student being unable to locate items needed for class, as well as for working on assignments at home. If a student uses a strategy for keeping his or her backpack organized, the student may experience less frustration and assume better responsibility for the materials needed and used in school related tasks. For the Backpack Organization Strategy, we suggest the following for the student:

- Use a clear backpack that is appropriately sized for the child's age and has multiple zippered pockets. A clear backpack makes it easier for the student to see materials.

- Determine the use for and label, using a permanent marker, each zippered pocket with its specific use. For example, the largest pocket might be the specific location used to hold the student's binder or subject folders, as well as any books that are needed. A pocket folder that clasps might also be placed in the largest pocket. Papers for parents to sign, or to hold papers that do not have a designated location can be stored in the pocket folder. The middle-size pocket might be designated for portable devices. The smaller pockets can be labeled for items like writing tools and rulers. **Note:** The arrangement of materials in the backpack will vary depending on individual needs and local policies.

- Teachers and parents need to model the appropriate placement of items and provide opportunities for student practice. Initially, the teacher and parent will need to check the student's backpack to see if the items have been placed in the appropriate pocket. Once the student has learned the strategy, periodic checks should be made by the teachers and parents to make sure the student has continued to use the strategy correctly.

Note: For younger students, we suggest using small photos showing the designated content for each pocket. The photo can be glued to the inside of each pocket. As well, each pocket can be labeled.

FIGURE 3.3 Backpack Organization Strategy Card for Elementary Students

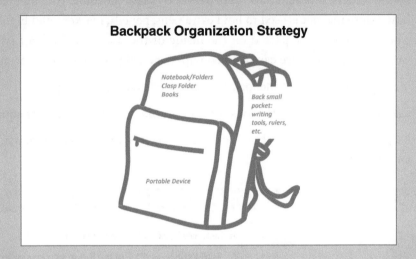

Backpack Organization Strategy

Notebook/Folders
Clasp Folder
Books

Back small pocket: writing tools, rulers, etc.

Portable Device

Where to put things in my backpack

- Largest pocket—my binder or folders, books, clasp folder
- Middle-size pocket—my portable device
- Small pocket—my writing tools, rulers

IMAGE SOURCE: Pixabay.com/clker-free-vector-images
*THIS CARD CAN BE TAILORED TO INDIVIDUAL NEEDS AND LOCAL POLICIES.

Locker Organization Strategy for Middle and High School Students

The Locker Organization Strategy is designed for middle and high school students who visit their lockers in a variety of schedules. These changes in schedule make it even more important for the locker to be organized in such a way that the student can enter and exit quickly with the right materials. That organization will be influenced by the student's personal challenges with keeping their materials in order. We recognize that some students carry all of their materials with them all day so as not to have to visit the locker at all. With the correct strategy in place, the student can make use of the locker as it was designed to be used. This Locker Organization Strategy provides students with a roadmap for finding items in their locker quickly and efficiently.

With the Locker Organization Strategy, the student is taught to

- use the top inside shelf of the locker to place folders, books, notebooks, spare notebook paper, for example. The textbook covers are color-coded to distinguish which books are used during which day and part of the day.

- use the inside part of the locker door to post the color-coded (in terms of textbooks, folders and materials needed) weekly class schedule. A container with a heavy-duty magnet is used to hold extra pens, pencils, markers, and highlighters. The last thing to be posted on the inside of the door is a To-Do List for the week. Remaining space can be filled with personal photos, pictures, or messages.

- use the hooks inside of the locker for hats and coats, for example.

- use the bottom floor of the locker for items like projects and sports equipment.

- keep a photo of the organized locker taken by the student as a visual roadmap of locker content locations.

FIGURE 3.4 Locker Organization Strategy Card for Secondary Students

Locker Organization Strategy

To Keep My Locker Organized I Need to Use the

- TOP INSIDE SHELF of the locker to place folders, books, notebooks, spare notebook paper, etc.

- INSIDE PART OF THE LOCKER DOOR to post the color-coded weekly class schedule, a container with a heavy-duty magnet, and a To-Do List for the week.

- HOOKS INSIDE OF THE LOCKER for hats, coats, etc.

- BOTTOM FLOOR OF THE LOCKER for projects, sports equipment, etc.

*THIS CARD CAN BE TAILORED TO INDIVIDUAL NEEDS AND LOCAL POLICIES.

Binder Organization Strategy for Older Elementary Students

The binders of students with executive function deficits often appear sloppy, with pages not secured in their binders, as well as missing and misfiled assignments. Teaching students a strategy for organizing all the papers and materials they need for class in their binders is a useful way to strengthen the EF skill of organization. Start by discussing with the student what he or she likes in his or her binder and incorporate those preferences. Then walk the student through the process organizing his or her binder by doing the following:

- Use a large three ring binder that zips closed as a central repository for all papers, assignments, and other materials needed for class, such as pencils and strategy cards. (Older students may need separate notebooks of folders for each class.)

THE EXECUTIVE FUNCTION GUIDEBOOK

- Clip a large, clear pocket with a zipper into the binder for storing items like pencils, erasers, and highlighters.

- Clip the strategy ring onto one of the binder rings. (If using strategy cards without the ring, store them in the front of the binder in a clear plastic business card holder that clips into the binder.)

- Use tabbed dividers to create separate sections for each subject.

- Create a homework section with three parts:

  1. Homework to be completed, materials or supplies needed, and due date

  2. Homework that is partially completed

  3. Homework that is complete and ready to be handed in

Below is a sample strategy card for Binder Organization Strategy.

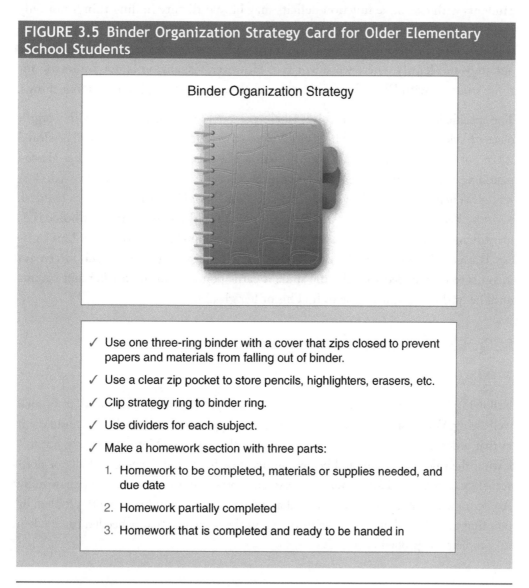

FIGURE 3.5 Binder Organization Strategy Card for Older Elementary School Students

Binder Organization Strategy

✓ Use one three-ring binder with a cover that zips closed to prevent papers and materials from falling out of binder.

✓ Use a clear zip pocket to store pencils, highlighters, erasers, etc.

✓ Clip strategy ring to binder ring.

✓ Use dividers for each subject.

✓ Make a homework section with three parts:

  1. Homework to be completed, materials or supplies needed, and due date

  2. Homework partially completed

  3. Homework that is completed and ready to be handed in

IMAGE SOURCE: Pixabay.com/openclipart-vectors

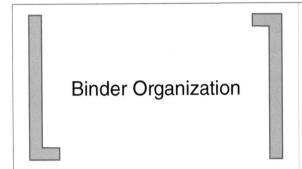

Binder Organization

- Use a divider for each subject area:
  - ○ **Record of assignments**
  - ○ **Homework partially completed**
  - ○ **Homework completed and ready to hand in**
  - ○ **On-going in class assignments**
- Insert business card sheet into binder in a place that is easily located.
- Bring pens, pencils, erasers each day.

Specific Location Strategy

Students with executive function deficits may have difficulty finding things not only due to memory issues, but also due to difficulty with sequencing events. For example, when we lose something, we often find it through a visualization process of retracing our steps to identify where we saw it last. However, visualizing is not automatic for some students with EF deficits, so they need alternative strategies for finding things.

The specific location strategy involves labeling frequently misplaced items with a bright piece of Velcro. Attach a matching color Velcro strip to the place the item will be stored when not in use. For instance, if your student repeatedly cannot find his or her glasses, matching Velcro strips can be placed on the eye glasses case and on the student's desk at school. Whenever the student is not using the case, have him or her affix it to the desk with the Velcro strip. Urge the student's parents to use the same strategy at home (i.e., identifying a place where the glasses will be kept and applying Velcro strips). This strategy is especially effective when used with a self-monitoring chart. A reinforcement menu is recommended whereby the student earns points from the teacher and parents until he or she is routinely able to find his or her glasses.

SEQUENCING STRATEGIES

The Importance of Cueing

Following steps in order is important for academic, behavioral, and social/emotional well-being. When students know what they are supposed to do but do not complete it in that order, consequences include solving a mathematics problem incorrectly, not following the rules accurately, and becoming upset or frustrated. Cueing verbally or nonverbally can guide students toward the next appropriate step academically or behaviorally. An example might involve cueing a student who is solving a multistep math problem by pointing to a chart that shows the next step in the sequence that is needed to be taken to complete the problem correctly.

Specific Location Strategy

Place a strip of Velcro on the object.

Place the matching strip in the location where the item should be stored.

Affix the object to the Velcro strip where it will be stored whenever object is not in use.

IMAGE SOURCE: iStock.com/curtoicurto

Steps for Completing a Long–Term Project Checklist Strategy

An example of a checklist that is useful for older students is Steps for Completing a Long-Term Project. The steps for this are as follows:

- Record the assignment in writing or on an app.

- Visualize how you would like the completed project to look.

- Make a list of all the tasks you need to complete it.

- Estimate how long each task will take.

- Set priorities.

- Backward Map the tasks from the due date, giving yourself some time to check over the project and revise if necessary.

- Gather the materials needed.

- Ask for clarification if needed.

- Start the project.

- Check your progress with the Backward Map to make certain you are on track to finish each part at the time you have set for yourself.

- Complete the project and check it for content and mechanics.

- Revise the project and turn it in.

Below is a sample strategy card for Steps for Completing a Long-Term Project Checklist Strategy. This strategy addresses a higher-level task completion and is appropriate for secondary students.

FIGURE 3.8 Steps for Completing a Long-Term Project Checklist Strategy Card for Secondary School Students

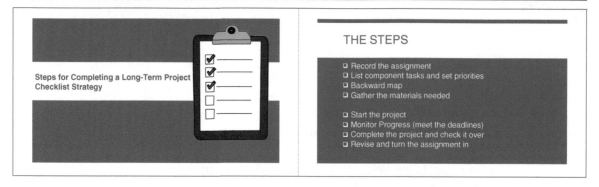

Steps for Completing a Long-Term Project Checklist Strategy

THE STEPS

- ☐ Record the assignment
- ☐ List component tasks and set priorities
- ☐ Backward map
- ☐ Gather the materials needed

- ☐ Start the project
- ☐ Monitor Progress (meet the deadlines)
- ☐ Complete the project and check it over
- ☐ Revise and turn the assignment in

MANAGING TIME

Time Needed Strategy for Time Management

For students to plan for successful, on-time completion of assignments (or of component tasks within assignments), they need to be able estimate and allot sufficient time, which requires having a sense of time and how long it takes them to complete tasks. A sense of time can be taught in several ways, including helping students understand how to estimate the time needed to complete a task. Begin with explicit instruction in the estimation of time needed to complete a task. Most students are familiar with the time needed to watch a favorite television show, so they can comprehend how long thirty minutes or one hour is.

To help a student with estimating time needed, explain to the student, for instance, that he or she has three short homework assignments and ask him or her to estimate how long it will take to complete them all. If the student seems unable to predict a length of time, suggest a frame of reference that is familiar, such as thirty minutes (e.g., "the length of one episode of *Sheldon*). Using that frame of reference, have the student estimate how much time each task will take. Add two minutes for a transition break between assignments. Then have the student time himself or herself with a stopwatch and record how long each task takes to complete. Add up the actual time it took the student to complete all three tasks plus breaks and review the results with the student. Were the student's estimates close to the actual time it took to complete the tasks? Have the student continue to estimate the time needed for assignments and periodically review the accuracy of these estimations. Being able to accurately estimate the time it takes to complete various tasks or assignments will help the student plan for completing tasks both in class and at home.

Example for a 30-minute time period

- **Assignment 1**—Read a page. Using the Post-it Note Modified Strategy, summarize the main points.
  - Estimated time: 5 minutes
  - Actual time: 6 minutes
  - Break: 2 minutes—At the end of each assignment, there is a 2-minute break that will be added to the total time of the assignment.
  - Total time: 8 minutes
  - Time remaining: 22 minutes

- **Assignment 2**—Complete a page of math problems.
  - Estimated time: 10 minutes
  - Actual time: 12 minutes
  - Break: 2 minutes—At the end of each assignment, there is a 2-minute break that will be added to the total time of the assignment.
  - Total time: 14 minutes
  - Time remaining: 22 – 14 = 8 minutes

- **Assignment 3**—Complete a one-paragraph character sketch.
  - Estimated time planning: 5 minutes
  - Estimated time writing: 5 minutes
  - Actual time planning: 5 minutes
  - Actual time writing: 6 minutes
  - Total time: 11 minutes
  - Time remaining: 8 – 11 = –3 minutes (exceeded time)

In this case, discuss with your student how consistently he or she underestimated the time it would take to answer or respond to the question by a few minutes; encourage revision of the estimates to come closer to the actual time. Explain that once your student can estimate with accuracy, he or she will be able to schedule in segments so that there will be time to complete all assignments.

Below is a sample strategy card for Time Needed for Time Management Strategy.

FIGURE 3.9 Time Needed for Time Management Strategy Card for Elementary School Students

Time Needed for Time Management Strategy

Time Needed for Time Management Strategy

10 min
5 min
25 min

Estimate the time needed for each assignment or the component tasks of an assignment

Add up estimated time needed for all assignments or tasks to determine estimated total work time needed

Periodically time how long each assignment takes to actually complete and compare to estimate to make sure estimates are on target

SOURCES: iStock.com/bsd555 and Pixabay.com/clker-free-vector-images

FIGURE 3.10 Time Needed for Time Management Strategy Card for Secondary School Students

Time Needed for Time Management Strategy

- Estimate the time needed to complete each assignment.
- Add up the estimated time for all assignments.
- Note the total time I need to complete all assignments.
- Note the actual start and completion time for each assignment and determine if my estimated time for completion of all assignments was accurate. **Readjust estimated time as needed and remember for future assignments.**

THE EXECUTIVE FUNCTION GUIDEBOOK

PLANNING STRATEGIES

Student Testimonial from: K. and J. as told by K.

Grade: K.—8th, J.—5th

Executive Function Addressed: Planning and Time Management

Strategy Name: How Do I Spend My Time?

Strategy Designed for: Individual or Whole Class

We used pennies to find how we spent our time. J. had 24 pennies for 24 hours in the day. I had 168 pennies for the number of hours in a week. My brother J. listed everything he did in one 24-hour day and the amount of time he spent doing it. I listed everything I did for a 168 hour week and the amount time I spent doing it. A penny was then taken from our piles for each hour we had spent. We were both surprised that we had pennies left over! We did not think we had any time for ourselves but it turned out we just needed to plan our time including time for having fun.

Planners

While there are planners that are designed to assist in recording multiple types of information, we encourage our students to match the planner to their individual needs. For students who receive a school planner, we encourage the removal or marking out of information that does not directly match the students' needs. For instance, we have helped students design personal planners that meet their individual needs by modifying existing planners or designing planners unique to the student. The important point is that all students need to have an online or paper planning tool to guide them in their day to day life. Online calendars are also useful as back-ups.

Backward Mapping Strategy for Planning

This is a planning strategy that can be tailored to the needs of the student. It is important to reinforce each step until your student has success with the method. First, task analyze and divide the assignment into phases with your student. Then estimate how long each phase will take. Next, have your student circle the due date of the assignment on a calendar and work backward until each phase of the project has its own due date. Be sure to schedule the phases in order (i.e., research before writing). Have your student leave time at the end for checking over his or her work and making revisions where needed. The project should be completed with corrections a few days before it is due to account for unexpected circumstances. *A reproducible calendar and blank templates, modifiable versions of materials, and strategy cards can be found at http://resources .corwin.com/ExecutiveFunctioning.*

FIGURE 3.11 Sample of a Backward Mapping Calendar

Sample of a Backward Mapping Calendar

March 2018

SUNDAY	MONDAY	TUESDAY	WEDNESDAY	THURSDAY	FRIDAY	SATURDAY
1 • Read Famous Person Project information and content required outline or graphic organizer. • Make list of questions I have about the assignment.	**2** • Ask the teacher the questions I have. • Decide who I will choose for project.	**3** • Go online to find 5 resources for project.	**4** • Read 2 of the 5 resources and make summary notes online or on 3x5 Post-its.	**5** • Read 2 of the 5 resources and make summary notes online or 3x5 Post-its.	**6** • Read 1 of the 5 resources and make summary notes online or 3x5 Post-its.	**7** • Arrange Post-it note summaries by topic about the famous person online or on a table.
8 • Decide which topics need more information and make a list of the topics online or on a 3 x 5 Post-it note.	**9** • Find needed topic information online or in the library.	**10** • Read new resources and make summary notes online or 3 x 5 Post-it notes. • Place notes under correct topic.	**11** • Arrange online notes or 3 x 5 Post-its to match the content outline or graphic organizer sequence.	**12** • Write project intro. • Write about first outline section.	**13** • Write about second and third outline section.	**14** • Write about last outline section. • Write conclusion.
15 • Proofread intro and first section. • Make corrections.	**16** • Proofread remaining sections and conclusion. • Make corrections.	**17** • Have a peer proofread your paper and give you feedback.	**18** • Make any edits. • Proofread your final product.	**19** • Pack your project to take to school	**20** **Famous Person Project due —hand in to teacher.**	

Below is a sample strategy card for Backward Mapping Strategy.

FIGURE 3.12 Backward Mapping Strategy Card for Elementary School Students

Backward Mapping Strategy

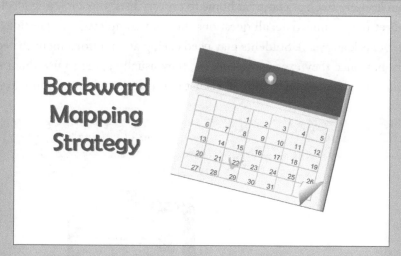

- Mark the project due date on the calendar.
- Determine the important parts of the project. Estimate the time needed to complete each part.
- Count backward from the project due date and set completion dates for each part. **Be sure to leave a few days before the due date to review and revise your project.**
- Hand in the project on or before the due date.

IMAGE SOURCE: Pixabay.com/openclipart-vectors

FIGURE 3.13 Backward Mapping Strategy Card for Secondary School Students

Backward Mapping	<ul><li>Mark the project due date on the calendar.</li><li>Determine the essential components of the project. Estimate the time needed to complete each component.</li><li>Count backwards from the project due date and set completion dates for each component. **Be sure to leave a few days before the due date to review and revise your project.**</li><li>Hand in the project on or before the due date.</li></ul>

Checklist Strategy

Checklists and to-do lists are a helpful tool in planning that students can use to keep track of what they need to do. They can be used for any number of processes and routines, from keeping track of chores at home to grocery lists to completing all elements a of worksheet (e.g., name, date, all questions on front completed, all questions on back completed, check answers). Students may need cueing and reinforcement to begin using checklists, but once they experience success, they usually agree to use them regularly. Work with your student to develop a checklist that is thorough but not too long.

FIGURE 3.14 Example Checklist Strategy Card for Elementary School Students

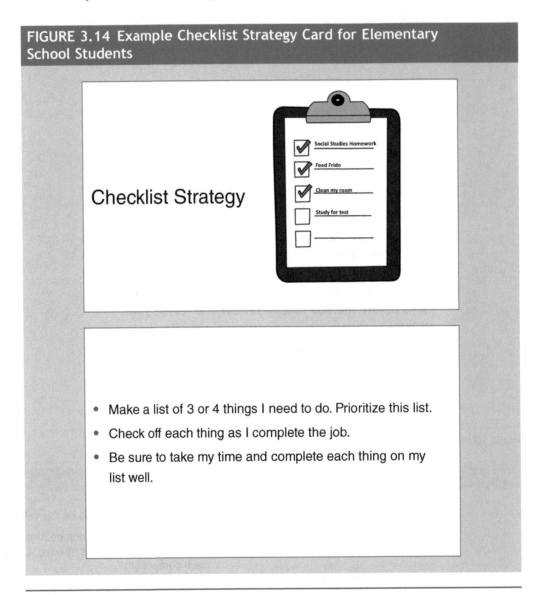

Checklist Strategy

- Social Studies Homework
- Feed Frido
- Clean my room
- Study for test

- Make a list of 3 or 4 things I need to do. Prioritize this list.
- Check off each thing as I complete the job.
- Be sure to take my time and complete each thing on my list well.

IMAGE SOURCE: Pixabay.com/clker-free-vector-images

Teacher Testimonial from: Andi Anglin-Alonso

Special Educator, Resource

Grade(s) Taught: Elementary

Executive Function Addressed: Organizing, Prioritizing, Sequencing, Managing Time, and Planning

Strategy Name: Visual Schedule for Planning

Strategy Designed for: Individual Student

ABOVE: Andi Anglin-Alonso

Students with executive function deficits often have a difficult time processing and planning throughout the day. Visual schedules are a good way for them to map out their day and week for the completion of routines.

I teach a student in a plug-in/pull-out resource setting who continually asked off-topic and non-school-related questions. In fact, this behavior consumed 56 percent of his instructional day. To remedy this situation, I developed a visual schedule for this student to plan times when he can ask off-topic and nonschool-related questions. This allowed the student to recognize and plan for appropriate times when he was permitted to ask his questions. Prior to implementing the Visual Schedule for Planning Strategy, I discussed it with the student and he agreed to try it. The student worked with me to select the pictures used in the schedule and the times when he would be permitted to ask his off topic and nonschool-related questions. The initial times for questioning were designated for the beginning of the lunch period before going to the cafeteria and at the end of his school day in the Resource Room while he packed his materials for home. Baseline data was collected on the student's use of this visual weekly schedule. An analysis of the baseline data revealed that the original times (beginning of the designated sessions) selected for off-topic and or unrelated questions was not working because the student had difficulty transitioning from asking his questions to completing his scheduled school work. This resulted in my moving the time scheduled for the student to ask off-topic and nonschool-related questions to midday during the last 5 minutes of his lunch period when he visited me in the Resource Room and at the end of the day when he returned to the Resource Room to pack his materials for home. I was consistent in implementing this visual schedule and the student adhered to it. Data after 1 week showed that the revised times for asking questions were working.

Below is an illustration of the final visual schedule I used with the student.

(Continued)

FIGURE 3.15 Visual Schedule for Planning When to Ask Off Topic and Nonschool-Related Questions

MONDAY	TUESDAY	WEDNESDAY	THURSDAY	FRIDAY
Language Arts	Language Arts	Language Arts	Language Arts	Language Arts
SS/Science	SS/Science	SS/Science	SS/Science	SS/Science
Math	Math	Math	Math	Math
LUNCH				
Afternoon Preparation—Student can ask off-topic questions the last 5 minutes.				
Language Arts	Language Arts	Language Arts	Language Arts	Language Arts
Art	PE	Singing in the Choir	Class Meeting or Media Center	Technology Lab
Resource Support Student can ask off-topic questions the last 5 minutes	Resource Support Student can ask off-topic questions the last 5 minutes	Resource Support Student can ask off-topic questions the last 5 minutes	Resource Support Student can ask off-topic questions the last 5 minutes	Resource Support Student can ask off-topic questions the last 5 minutes

SUPPORTIVE TECHNOLOGIES

Technology plays an integral role in meeting the diverse learning needs of all students, by integrating a UDL platform and reinforcing instructional content. It is engaging and interactive, making it appealing to many students. We use technology as a tool to complement and support executive function skill training. Below are some of the technology tools we have found to be beneficial when teaching executive function skills and strategies.

TABLE 3.1 Sample Supportive Technologies

TECHNOLOGY TOOL CATEGORY (WEBSITE, SOFTWARE, APP)	NAME OF TECHNOLOGY	EXECUTIVE FUNCTION AREA ADDRESSED	AGE GROUP
Website	Center on the Developing Child Harvard University https://developingchild.harvard.edu/	All areas	Most ages
Website	Child Mind Institute https://childmind.org/	All areas	Most ages
Website	Common Sense Education https://www.commonsense.org/	All areas	
Website	Intervention Central Response to Intervention – RTI Resources http://www.interventioncentral.org/	All areas	Most ages
Website	LD Online www.ldonline.org/	All areas	Most ages
Website	Understood.org https://www.understood.org/		Most ages
iPhone App	Whiteboard	Prioritizing	All ages
iPhone App	Glogster	Prioritizing	All ages
iPad App	Priority Matrix	Prioritizing	Grade 4 to adult
iPad App	One List—Prioritized To-Do List	Prioritizing	Preschool to adult
iPhone App	Activity Order	Organization	Preschool to Grade 1
iPhone App	Glogster	Organization	All ages
iPhone App	Homework	Organization	Grade 1 to Grade 12
iPhone App	Lino	Organization	All ages
iPhone App	myHomework	Organization	Grade 1 to Grade 12

(Continued)

TABLE 3.1 (Continued)

TECHNOLOGY TOOL CATEGORY (WEBSITE, SOFTWARE, APP)	NAME OF TECHNOLOGY	EXECUTIVE FUNCTION AREA ADDRESSED	AGE GROUP
iPhone App	TheHwApp	Organization	Grade 3 to adult
iPad App	Glogster	Organization	All ages
iPad App	Notebook	Organization	Grade 1 to Grade 12
iPad App	OneNote	Organization	Grade 4 to Grade 12
iPad App	SuperNote	Organization	Grade 4 to Grade 12
iPad App	Todoist: Organize your life	Organization	K to adult
iPhone App	123 Number Math Game	Sequencing	Preschool to K
iPhone App	Activity Order—Lite	Sequencing	K to adult
iPhone App	[F] [T] First-Then Board	Sequencing	Preschool to Grade 2
iPhone App	Sorting Machine	Sequencing	Preschool to K
iPad App	123 Number Math Game	Sequencing	Preschool to K
iPad App	Number Blast! – Sequence Memory	Sequencing	Preschool to Grade 2
iPad App	Number Recall	Sequencing	Preschool to Grade 2
iPad App	What is the next integer	Sequencing	Preschool to Grade 3
iPad App	Number Track—Sequence Memory	Sequencing	Preschool to Grade 1
iPhone App	A Tracker Time Tracker	Managing Time	Preschool to adult
iPhone App	BeFocused	Managing Time	Preschool to adult

TECHNOLOGY TOOL CATEGORY (WEBSITE, SOFTWARE, APP)	NAME OF TECHNOLOGY	EXECUTIVE FUNCTION AREA ADDRESSED	AGE GROUP
iPad App	Flat Tomato	Managing Time	Grades 8 to adult
iPad App	Supermarket Mania Journey	Managing Time	Preschool to Grade 4
iPad App	Timer+	Managing Time	Preschool to adult
iPhone App	Any.do: To-do list	Planning	Grade 3 to adult
iPhone App	Calendars by Readdle	Planning	Grade 3 to adult
iPhone App	myHomework	Planning	Grade 1 to Grade 12
iPhone App	Planner Pro—Daily Calendar	Planning	Grade 3 to adult
iPhone App	TheHwApp	Planning	Grade 3 to adult
iPad App	Calendars by Readdle	Planning	Grade 3 to adult
iPad App	myHomework	Planning	Grade 1 to Grade 12
iPad App	Planner Pro—Daily Calendar	Planning	Grade 3 to adult
iPad App	Pocket Schedule Planner	Planning	Grade 3 to adult
iPad App	Swipes—to do & Task list, Planner	Planning	Grade 3 to adult

CASE STUDY: AMANDA

We will now return to the case study of Amanda (*see Appendix 1.1 for her full case study*)—an eight-year-old student in the third grade, previously introduced in Chapter 2—and apply the 7-Step Model in prioritizing, organizing, sequencing, managing time, and planning to her case.

The questions that need to be considered to determine the appropriate executive function interventions that will support Amanda's learning needs are the following:

1. What are Amanda's executive function needs? (The step 1 process will answer this question.)

2. What are the strategies that can be used to support Amanda's executive function needs? (The step 3 process will answer this question.)

3. How should the effectiveness of the selected strategies in supporting Amanda's executive function need to be measured? (The steps 4 and 5 processes will answer this question.)

4. Do the selected strategies work? (The step 6 process will answer this question.)

The following example shows how to address one of Amanda's goals for prioritizing, organizing, sequencing, managing time, and planning difficulties using the 7-Step Model. *The model is not a lock-step procedure but merely a template to guide your thinking. Your flexibility and creativity in using this model to meet your needs and the needs of your student are encouraged.*

The 7-Step Model

Step 1

Determine the student's EF deficits and note them in the Executive Function (EF) Planning Chart (table 3.2).

Assessment

As described in chapter 1, the assessment process is completed through reviewing the student's records, as well as through observations of the student, and interviews with the student, family members, and other and previous teachers. Formal and informal assessments may also be used to help determine deficits. (***See Sample Student Self-Assessment Tool in Appendix 1.15***).

Key Questions

1. **How are the student's strengths and difficulties exhibited in terms of executive functions?**
   After a thorough review of Amanda's records, including current test scores on standardized tests, report card grades, work samples, observations of Amanda in academic and social settings, and interviews with Amanda, Amanda's previous teachers, and her parents, the following strengths and needs in terms of prioritizing, organizing, sequencing, and managing time are identified:

Amanda's Strengths

- Amanda is very resilient as she works on assignments involving planning.
- She is motivated to improve her organizational skills.
- She has some "splinter skills" in the general area of sequencing (i.e., she remembers and follows a sequence of steps when dancing), but she does not generalize that to other areas of her life.
- She enjoys helping the teacher organize class materials for the day.
- She does well in science and enjoys participating in the activities.

Amanda's Difficulties

Amanda has difficulty with prioritizing tasks.

- She does not set priorities.
- She does not spend time studying for tests.
- She finds attending to more than one task at a time confusing.
- She gives her work a "quick look over" instead of focusing on checking each response.
- Amanda frequently checks the work of others to see what they are doing.

Amanda has difficulty with organization.

- She does not organize her materials.
- She rarely has her materials and glasses available and has trouble locating them when needed.
- Her papers are not organized in her binder.

Amanda has difficulty with sequencing.

- She often has difficulty following a sequence.

Amanda has difficulty with managing time.

- She does not have a good sense of time.
- She rushes through assignments and does not check her work.
- She rushes through her assignments and makes careless errors.
- She often does not hand in assignments or hands them in incomplete, saying she did not have time to finish.

Amanda has difficulty with planning.

- She does not plan.

Amanda also has difficulties with other Executive Function Skills as can be seen on the Executive Function Planning Chart below. *Blank templates, modifiable versions of materials, and strategy cards can be found at http://resources.corwin.com/ ExecutiveFunctioning.*

For the purpose of this chapter, the focus will be Amanda's executive function deficit in the area of prioritizing, organizing, sequencing, managing time, and planning.

2. **Is there an executive function deficit in prioritizing, organizing, sequencing, managing time, and planning?**
   Looking at the information presented in answer to question 1, it is established, in addition to other deficits, that there is an executive function deficit in prioritizing, organizing, sequencing, managing time, and planning.

3. **How does the difficulty in prioritizing, organizing, sequencing, managing time, and planning present?**
   The **Executive Function Planning Chart** specifies how Amanda's Prioritizing, Organizing, Sequencing, Managing Time, and Planning difficulties present. If Amanda were eligible for services, an IEP objective for this goal might read, Amanda will find her papers and materials in her binder on the first try with 95 percent accuracy using a strategy for organization.

TABLE 3.2 Executive Function (EF) Planning Chart

EXECUTIVE FUNCTION SKILL AREA	WHAT DOES THE DIFFICULTY LOOK LIKE FOR THIS STUDENT? (EXAMPLES)
Prioritizing, Organizing, Sequencing, Managing Time, and Planning	She cannot find materials, glasses, and assignments. She either rushes through an assignment or does not finish the task on time. Her papers are sloppy and disorganized.
Working Memory	She does not remember what she has read. She forgets math facts and/or how to spell words she knew the night before. She gets confused when following multistep directions.
Attending, Initiating, and Focusing	She needs several reminders to get started on a task or assignment. She loses concentration very easily.
Controlling Social/Emotional and Inhibiting Behaviors	She impulsively calls out in class. She makes inappropriate comments to peers and adults.
Communicating, Cognitive Flexibility/Shifting	She does not write coherently due to a lack of understanding language usage. Her writing lacks sequencing of concepts and supporting details. She may display inappropriate body language and facial expressions and/or have difficulty interpreting body language and facial expressions. She is extremely slow to move from one activity on to another. She finds it difficult to think about more than one thing at a time.

Step 2

Review the EF Planning Chart with the student, and start to develop a Game Plan.

As described in chapter 1, this will guide the skill training for this specific executive function area, Prioritizing, Organizing, Sequencing, Managing Time, and Planning. After reviewing the assessment results with Amanda and her parents, we completed the Executive Function Planning Chart in step 1. Once Amanda's areas of executive functioning weaknesses needing immediate attention are identified, you can begin to develop Amanda's Game Plan. This will give Amanda an opportunity to "buy in" to the process. This understanding and awareness will later lead to student self-advocacy and greater independence in Amanda's learning process. Amanda's Game Plan includes the student's strengths, difficulties, goals for improvement, strategies selected to enhance executive functioning through UDL, and appropriate strategies. *A blank Game Plan template may be found in Appendix 1.9a and blank templates, modifiable versions of materials, and strategy cards can be found at http:// resources.corwin.com/ExecutiveFunctioning.*

FIGURE 3.16 Amanda's Game Plan for the Executive Function Skill of Prioritizing, Organizing, Sequencing, Managing Time, and Planning

Student Name: <u>Amanda</u>

What I do best: I am very helpful to my teacher.

What I do best: I try very hard even when I get confused.

What I do best: I am really good at science and love doing science experiments.

THINGS I WOULD LIKE TO DO BETTER		THINGS I CAN DO TO HELP WITH MY DIFFICULTIES IN SCHOOL
Goal 1: I would like to be able to find my papers and other materials for class without having to search through everything.	→	**Strategy Name:** To be determined after completing step 3 **Technology I can use:** **Date Goal Met:**
Goal 2: I would like to remember where I place my eyeglasses so that I can find them easily.	→	**Strategy Name:** To be determined after completing step 3 **Technology I can use:** **Date Goal Met:**
Goal 3: I would like to have time to complete assignments.	→	**Strategy Name:** To be determined after completing step 3 **Technology I can use:** **Date Goal Met:**

Step 3

Considering UDL and metacognition, select an EF skill-building strategy and get commitment from the student. Add the strategy to the Game Plan.

What are the strategies that can be used to support Amanda's executive function needs? Think about how you would respond to the following questions:

- What are Amanda's learning needs and challenges in terms of UDL (Multiple Means of Representation, Multiple Means of Action and Expression, and Multiple Means of Engagement)? See table 3.3.
- What approaches and supports will be used to help Amanda access the lesson, given her prioritizing, organizing, sequencing, and managing time deficit? Examples include
  - allowing extra time to complete tasks
  - connecting prior knowledge
  - binder checks
  - using a multisensory approach (verbal directions with visual cues)
  - modeling and role play
  - scaffolding information taught
  - cueing and prompting
  - color-coding daily schedule and posting in binder or on desk
  - self-monitoring checklist
  - incorporating supportive technology
- What strategies will be taught to Amanda and added to her Game Plan?
  - Select from those described in the first part of the chapter, other resources, or those you have used previously.
  - Use the **Selecting a Strategy for the Student While Integrating UDL Chart**, table 3.3, as a tool to prompt your thinking in terms of selecting the appropriate strategy that matches Amanda's learning needs and challenges. Written completion of this chart is not required. A sample thought process for prioritizing, organizing, sequencing, managing time, and planning is provided below. *A blank chart may be found in Appendix 1.10 and blank templates, modifiable versions of materials, and strategy cards can be found at http://resources.corwin.com/ExecutiveFunctioning.*

TABLE 3.3 Selecting a Strategy for the Student While Integrating UDL Chart

Student: Amanda

Executive Function Deficit: Prioritizing, Organizing, Sequencing, Managing Time, and Planning

Game Plan Goal: Goal 1: I would like to be able to find my papers and other materials for class without having to search through everything.

MULTIPLE MEANS OF REPRESENTATION

Things for you to consider:

1. What information does the student already know?	2. What are the instructional goals for the student in relation to the executive function addressed?	3. What extended activities will be needed?	4. What enrichment activities can be implemented?	5. What will you need to incorporate when teaching the strategy?
She is aware that specific papers and other materials are needed daily to complete class work. She knows that she needs a system that will enable her to readily find the materials needed for each class.	*She needs to find her papers for the content taught in a specific task. Clear concise directives for organizing papers and other materials need to be given followed by wait time.*	*Use a multisensory approach for teaching binder organization. No more than two-step verbal directives for addressing the binder organization system. Verbal directions accompanied by a visual picture of the organization system and a teacher-created support such as a checklist to record completed steps.*	*Have Amanda practice reading information on teacher selected websites, newspaper ads, and posters, timing how long it takes to read each page and recording details on Post-it Notes.*	• *Connect prior knowledge, preteach prerequisite information.* • *Model the expected binder organization process for papers, strategy cards, and other materials.* • *Provide simple verbal directives and visual support.*

(Continued)

TABLE 3.3 (Continued)

MULTIPLE MEANS OF ACTION AND EXPRESSION

Things for you to consider:

1. How will you conduct preassessment, formative, and summative assessments for the student's learning?	**2. What platforms will be permitted for the student to demonstrate mastery?**
At the preassessment stage, the student will be given a verbal directive only for finding papers and other materials.	*Demonstrate mastery through the completion of graphic organizers, sequencing activities, talking about her answer, drawing pictorial representation of binder organization task and its completion. Checklist provided to monitor completed tasks when organizing binder.*
During the formative assessment stage, the student will be provided with simple verbal directives for finding specific papers and other materials, supported by a visual of the organization system and a checklist to mark off tasks as they are completed. The teacher will model the process the student will use. Using the binder organization strategy, the student will organize papers and other materials in a three-ring binder in a manner that will enable her to successfully find the appropriate materials with less than two errors.	
During the summative assessment, the accuracy of the student's performance in completing the task with 90 percent accuracy will determine whether outcomes are met.	

MULTIPLE MEANS OF ENGAGEMENT

Things for you to consider:

1. How will you teach the student in a manner that actively engages the student?

- *Engage student in creating goals that encourage success, using metacognition to self-monitor, and collecting data on effectiveness of strategy to help attain goals.*
- *Chunk information taught, check for understanding by allowing her to share the ideas she has for binder and book organization, provide verbal cues and visual checklist, provide extended time.*

TABLE 3.4 Student Implementation of Strategy With a Focus on Metacognition and UDL Principles

Student: Amanda

Executive Function Deficit: Prioritizing, Organizing, Sequencing, Managing Time, and Planning

Game Plan Goal: Goal 1: I would like to be able to find my papers and other materials for class without having to search through everything.

METACOGNITION—QUESTIONS THE STUDENT THINKS ABOUT AND RESPONDS TO

Things for you to consider:

1. What am I supposed to do?

Use the Binder Organization Strategy.

2. Why is this strategy important for me to use and how will it help me?

This strategy will help me to easily and quickly find my materials for class. If I can find my materials easily, then I will not feel upset because I will be able to not miss class time.

3. What are the steps of the strategy?

✓ *Use one binder with a cover that zips closed and a clear zipper pocket that clips into the binder to store pencils, erasers, highlighters, etc. for younger students.*

✓ *Clip strategy ring into binder.*

✓ *Use dividers for each subject.*

✓ *Make a homework section with three parts:*

1. *homework to be completed, materials or supplies needed, and due date;*
2. *homework partially completed;*
3. *homework completed that is ready to be handed in.*

4. Is there technology I can use?

● *Online Notebook (https://onlinenotebook.net)*

● *OneNote Class Notebook (https://onenote.com/classnotebook)*

● *SuperNote APP by Fitness22 LTD*

5. What should I think about when using this strategy?

I need to make sure that I place my materials in the correct section of my notebook.

If I need extra time to file my papers I need to nicely tell the teacher.

(Continued)

TABLE 3.4 (Continued)

Based on your Considerations of the Principles for this goal, what strategy would you select that aligns with the three Principles and Align with UDL and the Strategy Selected?

Name of Strategy: *Binder Organization Strategy*

This strategy is selected because

1. *Models the expected binder organization process that is to take place* **(Multiple Means of Representation).**

2. *Allows Amanda to demonstrate mastery and the effectiveness of the strategy through the use of metacognition and self-monitoring* **(Multiple Means of Action and Expression).**

3. *Provides an opportunity to organize binder through use of color-coding, visuals (which Amanda may help create), and checklists* **(Multiple Means of Engagement).**

- o Think about the components of **The Student Implementation of Strategy With a Focus on Metacognition and UDL Chart**, table 3.4. This chart should be completed with the student. It is a tool that helps the student to buy in to the strategy learning process. *A blank chart can be found in Appendix 1.11, and blank templates, modifiable versions of materials, and strategy cards can be found at http://resources.corwin.com/ ExecutiveFunctioning.*
- o Once you and the student have selected a strategy, add the strategy name to the "Things I can do to help with my difficulties in school" column of the Game Plan for an elementary student or the "Action" column of the Game Plan for a secondary student.

Below is Amanda's completed Game Plan, which lists her goals and the strategies she and her teacher have decided she will learn to strengthen her EF skills in the area of prioritizing, organizing, sequencing, managing time, and planning. Given her issues, additional strategies such as Big Rocks Little Rocks, Backward Mapping, Checklists, and supportive technology would be taught to Amanda to further strengthen this skill area.

Student Name: Amanda

> **What I do best:** I am very helpful to my teacher.

> **What I do best:** I try very hard even when I get confused.

> **What I do best:** I am really good at science and love doing science experiments.

THINGS I WOULD LIKE TO DO BETTER	THINGS I CAN DO TO HELP WITH MY DIFFICULTIES IN SCHOOL
Goal 1: I would like to be able to find my papers and other materials for class without having to search through everything.	**Strategy Name:** Binder Organization Strategy **Technology I can use:** 1. Online Notebook (https://onlinenotebook.net/) 2. OneNote Class Notebook(https://www.onenote.com/classnotebook) SuperNote APP by Fitness22 LTD **Date Goal Met:**
Goal 2: I would like to remember where I place my eyeglasses so that I can find them easily.	**Strategy Name:** Specific Location Strategy **Technology I can use:** Velcro Strip **Date Goal Met:**
Goal 3: I would like to have time to complete assignments.	**Strategy Name:** Time Needed Strategy **Technology I can use:** Timer **Date Goal Met:**

Step 4

Design and implement data collection tools to measure success in the use of the strategy, teach the selected strategy, and give the student a strategy card.

The following illustrates how step 4 would be applied to the Binder Organization Strategy which addresses goal 1.

The data from step 1 show the following:

We noticed that Amanda spends a lot of searching in her binder for her assignments and materials, which causes her to feel anxious. She frequently loses assignments and materials. There are times when she has completed an assignment but cannot find it in her binder to turn in for a grade. This results in Amanda receiving a poor grade.

We talked with Amanda about her difficulties and started to develop a Game Plan.

Amanda understands that many of her difficulties relate to **Prioritizing, Organizing, Sequencing, Managing Time, and Planning.** She wants to be able to find her school materials and glasses and would like to have time to complete her assignments.

The goals Amanda agreed to from step 2 are

Goal 1: I would like to be able to find my books and papers easily without having to search through everything.

Goal 2: I would like to remember where I place my eyeglasses so that I can find them easily.

Goal 3: I would like to have time to complete my assignments.

The Strategy you and Amanda selected in step 3 is

Binder Organization Strategy. Teach the Binder Organization Strategy to Amanda. Model the steps of the strategy and incorporate metacognition. Provide motivation for the strategy such as use of a reinforcement and gain a continued commitment by the student. Games such as Role Play, and Sequencing a List of the Steps involved in the strategy can be used to reinforce recall of how to use the strategy. Each game should require the student to explain the strategy and how it helps them.

Give the student the strategy card. Have the student practice the strategy using meta-cognition and referring to the strategy card as needed until he or she can use the strategy with automaticity. The strategy card summarizes the strategy and serves as a reminder of how to use it. It outlines the process and steps that need to be followed to successfully implement the strategy. To make the card, create or purchase a 3" x 5" or business-size card. Place the name of the strategy on the front of the card, along with visuals if that is helpful for the student. Place a description of how to use the strategy on the back of the card. It is helpful if this description is stated in the student's own words. Check the description for accuracy. Punch a hole in the top left of the card if you are placing the card on a strategy ring. This strategy ring will provide Amanda with an individualized portable reference system of strategies that support her EF skills in the area of prioritizing, organizing, sequencing, managing time, and planning.

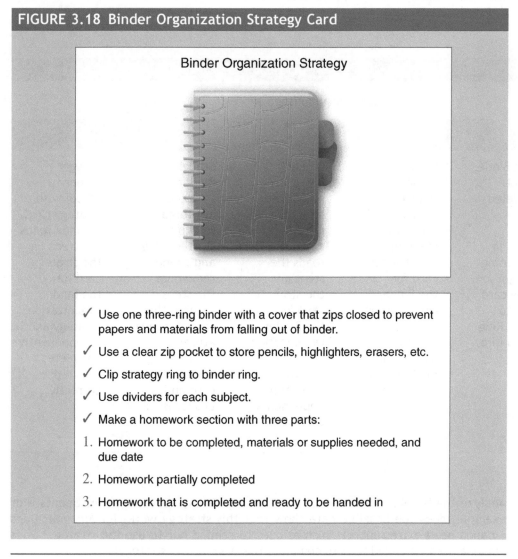

FIGURE 3.18 Binder Organization Strategy Card

Binder Organization Strategy

✓ Use one three-ring binder with a cover that zips closed to prevent papers and materials from falling out of binder.

✓ Use a clear zip pocket to store pencils, highlighters, erasers, etc.

✓ Clip strategy ring to binder ring.

✓ Use dividers for each subject.

✓ Make a homework section with three parts:

1. Homework to be completed, materials or supplies needed, and due date

2. Homework partially completed

3. Homework that is completed and ready to be handed in

IMAGE SOURCE: Pixabay.com/openclipart-vectors

As the student continues to practice the strategy, it is important to determine whether the strategy is appropriate for teaching the student the EF skill.

Design and collect data and revise as necessary.

Design the data tools, collect data on the success of the strategy, and revise as necessary. ***Blank templates, modifiable versions of materials, and strategy cards can be found at http://resources.corwin.com/ExecutiveFunctioning.***

This is the baseline phase of the data collection process. Once the baseline data has been collected, analyze the data and go back and make any necessary adjustments. For example, does the baseline data show that this strategy works for the student? Does the student need extra supports such as cues to remind her to use the strategy? Does the student need extended time to complete the steps of the strategy? After the student has been taught the strategy, it is important for you as the teacher to determine whether the strategy is appropriate for the student's needs and if the student is comfortable using the strategy. Not every strategy is appropriate for every student; therefore, it is important to evaluate if the selected strategy is suited to the student.

TABLE 3.5 Baseline Data Amanda's Usage of the Binder Organization Strategy				
☑ = tasks accomplished successfully				
MONDAY	**TUESDAY**	**WEDNESDAY**	**THURSDAY**	**FRIDAY**
☑ Brought Binder to school. We modeled Binder Strategy for Amanda incorporating metacognition. Strategy card is given to Amanda. Ring is placed into binder.	☑ Brought Binder to school. Amanda and I read the steps on the strategy card for the Binder Organization Strategy together as Amanda implements each step.	☑ Brought Binder to school with strategy ring. Amanda reads the steps on the strategy card for the Binder Organization Strategy together as Amanda implements each step.	☑ Brought Binder to school but forgot to clip in strategy ring and cannot remember the steps without the card. Amanda attempts the strategy without the card and is unsuccessful.	☑ Brought Binder to school with strategy ring. Amanda reads the steps on the strategy card for the Binder Organization Strategy and independently completes the steps correctly.

Analyze the baseline data and go back and make any necessary adjustments. For example, does the baseline data show that this strategy works for Amanda? Does Amanda need extra supports such as cues to remind her to use the strategy? Does Amanda need extended time to complete the steps of the strategy?

After Amanda has been taught the strategy it is important for you as the teacher to determine whether the strategy is appropriate for Amanda's needs and if Amanda is comfortable using the strategy. Not every strategy is appropriate for every student; therefore, it is important to evaluate if the selected strategy is suited for Amanda.

Step 5

Continue to collect data for the student's use of the strategy.

Determine the student's success in learning and generalizing the strategy, table 3.6. Considerations for Ongoing Data Analysis Chart, provides points you as the teacher need to consider as you continue to analyze the data addressing the student's correct use and generalization of the selected strategy. The teachers' responses to the questions considered in table 3.6 are posted below.

As explained in step 1, we need to determine whether Amanda has mastered the strategy which includes both using the strategy correctly and generalizing it of a variety of settings. Complete table 3.6 Considerations for Ongoing Data Analysis Chart for Amanda. *A blank chart template can be found in Appendix 1.12 and blank templates, modifiable versions of materials, and strategy cards can be found at http://resources.corwin.com/ExecutiveFunctioning.*

TABLE 3.6 Sample Considerations for Ongoing Data Analysis Chart

Student Name: *Amanda*

Strategy Used: *Binder Organization Strategy*

Please, write yes, no, or N/A for Not Applicable.

____*yes*____ 1. The strategy is cited in the student's Ongoing Data Analysis.

____*yes*____ 2. The student understands the goal of using the strategy.

____*yes*____ 3. The student can explain what the strategy is and why he or she is using it.

____*yes*____ 4. There is a means of collecting data to measure the student's progress.

____*yes*____ 5. The tools to measure the academic or socioemotional area that the executive function deficit is impacting are appropriate.

____*yes*____ 6. Daily feedback is provided for at least one week when the strategy began.

____*yes*____ 7. The student is provided with reinforcement and knows his or her standing.

____*yes*____ 8. Data are analyzed with the student and the revisions are made as needed.

____*yes*____ 9. The selected strategy is appropriate for the student's needs.

Comments:

Amanda enjoys using the Binder Organization Strategy. She stated that this strategy helps her find her materials and papers and it is easy to use. It also helps her to have a neater looking notebook.

She stated that she may need extra time to file her papers. This was discussed and it was decided that she would tell the teacher, in an appropriate manner, that she needed extra time to file.

She said she still forgets to file her homework in the correct place and then she cannot find it the next day to hand in. She said that practicing the strategy should help with this problem. She has agreed to continue using this strategy.

For the Binder Organization Strategy, the same data collection chart was used as used in baseline data collection.

TABLE 3.7 Amanda's Success Implementing the Binder Organization Strategy Use

☑ = tasks accomplished successfully

Amanda Week 1

MONDAY	TUESDAY	WEDNESDAY	THURSDAY	FRIDAY
☑ Brought binder to school with strategy ring clipped in	☑ Brought binder to school ☑ with strategy ring clipped in	☑ Brought binder to school with strategy ring clipped in	☑ Brought binder to school with strategy ring clipped in	☑ Brought binder to school with strategy ring clipped in
☑ Binder organized with separate section for each subject	☑ Binder organized with separate section for each subject	☑ Binder organized with separate section for each subject	☑ Binder organized with separate section for each subject	☑ Binder organized with separate section for each subject
☑ Assignments placed in correct subject section	☐ Assignments placed in correct subject section	☑ Assignments placed in correct subject section	☑ Assignments placed in correct subject section	☑ Assignments placed in correct subject section
☑ Completed homework assignments filed correctly	☐ Completed homework assignments filed correctly	☐ Completed homework assignments filed correctly	☑ Completed homework assignments filed correctly	☐ Completed homework assignments filed correctly
Comments: *teacher assisted*	**Comments:** *no cues or assistance provided*	**Comments:** *teacher provided cues and assistance*	**Comments:** *teacher provided cues and assistance*	**Comments:** *no cues or assistance provided*

Amanda Week 2

MONDAY	TUESDAY	WEDNESDAY	THURSDAY	FRIDAY
☑ Brought binder to school with strategy ring clipped in	☑ Brought binder to school with strategy ring clipped in	☑ Brought binder to school with strategy ring clipped in	☑ Brought binder to school with strategy ring clipped in	☑ Brought binder to school with strategy ring clipped in
☑ Binder organized with separate sections for each subject	☑ Binder organized with separate sections for each subject	☑ Binder organized with separate sections for each subject	☑ Binder organized with separate sections for each subject	☑ Binder organized with separate sections for each subject
☑ Assignments placed in correct subject section	☑ Assignments placed in correct subject section	☐ Assignments placed in correct subject section	☑ Assignments placed in correct subject section	☑ Assignments placed in correct subject section
☑ Completed homework assignments filed correctly	☑ Completed homework assignments filed correctly	☐ Completed homework assignments filed correctly	☑ Completed homework assignments filed correctly	☑ Completed homework assignments filed correctly
Comments: *teacher assisted*	**Comments:** *teacher cued*	**Comments:** *no assistance, teacher modeled correct behavior*	**Comments:** *no assistance*	**Comments:** *no assistance*

Reviewing this portion of the data collected, it appears that Amanda is correctly using the Binder Organization Strategy. Amanda brought her binder to school every day for 10 days. The sections in the binder were intact for the 10 days. Amanda placed her assignments in the correct section on 8 of 10 days. She filed her homework assignments correctly on 5 of 10 days. It appears the Binder Organization Strategy is most helpful to her at the end of the day. It is needed most to help her file completed homework correctly.

It is necessary to continually assess the use and generalization of the strategy. An assessment record keeping system is needed to track the student's progress in terms of the student's learning success and appropriate use of the strategy. Over time, students will be learning many strategies and it is important to assess the maintenance and use of these strategies.

Step 6

Analyze all the data collected and evaluate the student's success in using the strategy; update the Game Plan.

In analyzing Amanda's success in learning and generalizing the Binder Organization Strategy, and whether it has helped her, the overarching questions are

- Did she use the strategy in the noted area of executive function difficulty?
- Did she generalize, that is, use the strategy in different scenarios?
- Has the target executive function deficit improved since Amanda started using the strategy?

We can answer these questions by completing the Final Assessment of the Strategy. A final assessment of the strategy can be used to analyze all the data collected, evaluate Amanda's success and evaluate the effectiveness of the strategy. *A blank template for the* Sample Template for Final Assessment of the Strategy *can be found in Appendix 1.13 and blank templates, modifiable versions of materials, and strategy cards can be found at http://resources.corwin.com/ExecutiveFunctioning.*

Review the data recording tool and completed Final Assessment Template to determine the following:

- Does Amanda use the strategy in the noted area of executive function difficulty?
  - Yes, Amanda has mastered the strategy and feels the strategy has helped her.
- Does Amanda generalize?
  - Amanda would like to continue using this strategy and has started to use it in other classes and at home.
- Has the noted executive function deficit improved since the student started using the strategy?
  - Yes, it appears that Amanda's organization has improved. She independently places her work in the appropriate binder section.

Conclusion: Based on the data, Amanda is improving in organization using the Binder Organization Strategy. Amanda will continue to use this strategy, and she will use it independently.

Sample Template for Final Assessment of the Strategy

Date: 10/21/17

Name of Student: Amanda

Executive Function(s) Being Addressed: Organization

☑ **Intervention Implemented? (Describe the Strategy and How It Is Being Used)**

Binder Organization Strategy

- Use a three-ring binder with a zipper cover to store all papers and materials needed for class.
- Use dividers to create sections for each subject.
- Make a homework section with three parts:
    1. Homework to be completed, materials or supplies needed, and due date
    2. Homework partially completed
    3. Completed homework that is ready to be handed in

☑ **Strategy Used From:** 10/1/17 **To:** 10/15/17

☑ **UDL-EF Process Used:**

- Completed Executive Function Planning Chart
- Thought through Selecting a Strategy for the Student While Integrating UDL Chart
- Created with student a Strategy Implementation With a Focus on UDL and Metacognition Chart
- Field-tested the Binder Organization Strategy
- Created strategy card for Binder Organization Strategy and placed on Amanda's Strategy Ring
- Finalized Binder Organization Strategy and Selected this Strategy for Amanda
- Taught the strategy and kept data of usage
- Made revisions as necessary

☑ **Data for Measured Results:** Two weeks of data from step 5. (See completed Binder Organization Strategy Chart.)

☑ **Anecdotal Report of Results:**

- Amanda liked using the binder strategy and liked being able to find her assignments.
- She liked having everything organized in one binder.

☑ **Review of Results:**

- improved attitude regarding homework
- was able to maintain organization of binder
- continues to need support placing assignments in the correct section and filing completed homework assignments correctly

☑ **Summary Report on Game Plan Progress:** The Binder Organization Strategy has helped Amanda to attain **"Goal 1 with support:** "I would like to be able to find my papers and materials easily without having to search through everything." *Accomplished 10/14/2017*

(NOTE: Goals 2 and 3 on Amanda's Game Plan will be addressed at a later date once Amanda has mastered and generalized goal 1.)

Summary Report on Implications of Strategy Use on Academic Skills and Social Interactions: Amanda uses the Binder Organization Strategy with support. The strategy has helped to improve Amanda's attitude and preparedness.

Step 7

Revisit the Game Plan to determine whether the student's goals have been met. Once a goal is met, have the student write a Success Plan.

To determine whether Amanda's first goal has been met, look at the data for the entire period she has been using the strategy. Review the data with her and discuss with her the following key questions:

- Does she feel the use of the strategy is helping? Do the data support this perception?
  The data for goal 1 show that Amanda has been successful on goal 1 using the Binder Organization Strategy. (Goals 2 and 3 will be considered separately.)
- Does she feel it would be beneficial to continue to use this strategy?
  Amanda feels the strategy has helped her, and the data support this.
- Does she feel she is ready to move on to another goal for this executive function?
  Amanda says she feels ready to move on to another goal. She will continue to implement the Binder Organization Strategy.

After each goal on the student's Game Plan has been met, help her write a personal Success Plan to communicate what she plans to do to have a successful school year and self-advocate for the assistance she will need to help her on this journey toward success. This should identify the following:

- What I want to do next
- Difficulties I may have
- Strategies I can use to help myself
- What the teacher can do to help

Below is the sample template for Amanda's Prioritizing, Organizing, Sequencing, Managing Time, and Planning Goal 1 below. *A blank template for this chart is found in Appendix 1.14 and blank templates, modifiable versions of materials, and strategy cards can be found at http://resources.corwin.com/ExecutiveFunctioning.*

What I Want to Do Next

I would like to be able to find my papers and materials easily, without having to search through everything.

Difficulties I May Have

I have trouble finding papers and materials in my binder.

Strategies I Can Use to Help Myself

To help me find my papers and materials easily, I can use the Binder Organization Strategy. For this strategy, I need to have a binder that zips, a clear pencil case that clips into my binder, and colored dividers.

What the Teacher Can Do to Help

When I use the Binder Organization Strategy, the teacher might need to check my binder each Friday to make sure that I have filed things correctly. I might also need some extra time for filing things.

WHAT HAPPENS THEN?

When all three goals on the Game Plan are met, it is time to identify new challenges on which to focus. Few students experience difficulty in only one executive function. While Amanda will continue to work on strengthening her prioritizing, organizing, sequencing, managing time, and planning, there are other executive function area deficits to be addressed. The next step would be to return to the executive function planning chart to determine which EF deficits to address.

Summary

The ability to prioritize, organize, sequence, manage time, and plan is a lifelong skill set necessary for one to meet with success on a daily basis. For many students, the ability to efficiently and effectively use this skill set becomes a challenge. What further complicates this situation is the fact that the actions of prioritizing, organizing, sequencing, managing time, and planning become interrelated as one sees a task from start to fruition. We acknowledge that a deficit in prioritizing, organizing, sequencing, managing time, and planning looks different for each student, but most students with prioritizing, organizing, sequencing, managing time, and planning deficits have difficulty determining and prioritizing goals, forget to write down assignments, cannot locate materials needed to complete an assignment or task, cannot accurately sequence the steps necessary to complete a task, lose track of time and then rush to complete tasks, and do not plan for the time needed to complete long term projects. These difficulties and others have a negative impact on student achievement, behavior. and socioemotional well-being leading some into the Downward Spiral discussed in chapter 1. Supportive strategies both to improve and compensate for prioritizing, organizing, sequencing, managing time, and planning deficits are available for teachers and students who can work together toward student success. Checklist strategies, backward mapping strategies, and prioritizing strategies are just a few of those described in this chapter. Supportive technologies, some of which are listed in the chapter, are available to assist in the improvement of EF skills. Finally, the 7-Step Model is presented in this chapter for an elementary student presenting difficulty in prioritizing, organizing, sequencing, managing time, and planning, as well as other deficits. Through this example in prioritizing, organizing, sequencing, managing time, and planning, you can see how these steps come together working with an individual student. For those using the 7-Step Model Modified, it is helpful to see and select the parts of the model that will fit your particular situation. As teachers, you know your student best and we encourage you to use your knowledge, judgement and creativity, regardless of whether you are using the 7-Step Model or 7-Step Model Modified. You are the one to best determine what your student's(s') program will look like, keeping in mind that ongoing assessment, determination of what is needed, the consideration of UDL and metacognition in the choice of strategies, the implementation of strategies, and the commitment of the student are all vital components for a successful implementation of prioritizing, organizing, sequencing, managing time, and planning executive function skills training.

Practice

- Practice the 7-Step Model for prioritizing, organizing, sequencing, managing time, and planning using one of the case studies in the Appendix. Note that there is another case study for an elementary school student. As well, there are two case studies for students in secondary school. Carlos is the secondary student case study that we will focus on in chapters 4 and 5. You may use Fariha's case study (*see Appendix 1.4*) to practice the 7-Step Model for prioritizing, organizing, sequencing, managing time, and planning.

- Note any challenges and successes you experienced and review the content in chapter 1 for background information relating to this chapter.

- Practice the 7-Step Model for one of your students.

CHAPTER 4

Attending, Initiating, Focusing, and Supportive Strategies

Reader Outcomes

☑ You will be able to identify factors that suggest problems in the executive function skill of attending, initiating, and focusing.

☑ You will be able to identify how difficulties in attending, initiating, and focusing impact the student's behavior, social/emotional well-being, and academic success.

☑ You will be able to identify instructional strategies for teachers and learning strategies for students to use in addressing difficulty in attending, initiating, and focusing.

☑ You will be able to record student progress and make instructional changes based on the data.

WHAT IS ATTENDING, INITIATING, AND FOCUSING?

Attending, initiating, and focusing are all important executive functions, and often students will exhibit difficulty in all three. Dawson and Guare (2009) define attending as the capacity to keep paying attention to a situation or task in spite of distractibility, fatigue, or boredom (p. 16). According to Kaufman (2010), the ability to initiate is an "essential" executive function skill defined as "getting started on tasks and avoiding procrastination" (p. 5). Further, "students must marshal their cognitive energy and organize their thinking in the moment to make decisions about where and how to begin" (p. 6).

Moyes (2014) suggests that some teachers confuse initiation with motivation. She explains that the reason some children do not initiate an assignment may look like lack of motivation, but the student has an executive function deficit in initiation. Other executive function difficulties may also come into play such as working memory when a student cannot remember the goal of the work. She reminds us that when you want to teach a student to initiate, there needs to be explicit instruction with positive reinforcement for each step toward initiating. It is also important to determine whether the task is appropriate for the child's ability. Work refusal can have many causes, and ability to initiate is far different from the student not having the ability to do the assignment. It is important to look at the executive function of initiation for any student failing to start his or her work (pp. 83–92).

Lastly, focusing is defined by Meltzer (2010) as the ability to "clear a space" in the mind, and she says students cannot only be taught to clear that space but also be taught strategies that prompt their arousal for learning (p. 198).

Students with a deficit in the executive function area of attending, focusing, and initiating often fall victim to the Downward Spiral. As the student spirals downward, he or she may experience frustration, a decrease in self-esteem, avoidance behaviors, poor academic achievement, and an overall lack of willingness to strive for success. The impact on social/emotional wellbeing caused by this deficit continues into adulthood if not addressed as soon as the student begins exhibiting telltale behaviors. In adulthood, behaviors such as daydreaming during working, losing focus and becoming tangential during a conversation, procrastinating starting or completing tasks may be observed in people with a deficit in attending, focusing, and initiating, and may be incorrectly interpreted as a lack of interest, as laziness, or as incapability.

WHAT DOES A DIFFICULTY IN ATTENDING, INITIATING, AND FOCUSING LOOK LIKE?

Attending Behaviors

Students who have problems in attending may

- not seem aware of what is happening around him or her.
- not be attending to the task at hand.
- not be attending to what a speaker is saying.
- be easily distracted and stop attending.
- appear to be daydreaming constantly.
- appear tired in class even though the student has had plenty of sleep.

Initiating Behaviors

Students who have problems in initiating may

- shut down if not helped immediately.
- be slow in starting an assignment if started at all.

- look confused about what to do.

- become easily frustrated.

- complete the assignment when provided direction and support.

Focusing Behaviors

Students who have problems in focusing may

- have trouble focusing in on what is important.

- have trouble concentrating on the task at hand.

- have trouble finding errors in his or her work.

- rush through work without focusing on what is required.

- need to reread information several times.

- write in a matter that is tangential and often off topic.

HOW DOES A DIFFICULTY IN ATTENDING, INITIATING, AND FOCUSING IMPACT STUDENT ACHIEVEMENT?

Learning requires sustained attention to the task at hand. According to Tannock (2007), students who have difficulties attending often encounter roadblocks when it comes to reading and math achievement. There is new research written regarding specific reading and mathematics difficulties compounded by executive function issues, but most of that research centers on the nature of the effect rather than a cause. Some students have difficulty getting started on class work or homework, or initiating. When they do not get started on time, often they do not finish on time or at all. The inability to get started on time frequently leads to the Downward Spiral effect where the student finds that he or she is behind on most everything that day. The result is lower self-esteem and achievement. It is important that all adults working with the student are aware of what is happening. Students with focusing difficulties may begin an assignment and be on track, but as the student continues through the assignment, it is difficult to sustain attention. Often, the result is that the assignment does not get completed or it is completed with many "careless" errors in the last half portion of the work. Sustained attention is difficult to accommodate in the classroom. Teachers benefit from knowing approximately how long a student attends to an assignment. Are they quitting after five, ten, or fifteen minutes? Is the student focusing and concentrating as he or she checks his or her work or are there a lot of careless errors in work that is turned in. If so, that information is important for planning instruction and related activities. Also, focus on the right subject is important, but problem solving requires concentration too; so in addition to attention, both focus and concentration must be present for students to solve problems. Building sustained attention, focus, and concentration are all essential for student success. It is not enough to will the student to concentrate; we must initiate the student's attention and then keep him or her motivated to continue an assignment.

Some students who exhibit indicators of a deficit in the EF area of attending, initiating, and focusing, present as being unable to sustain attention for the duration of an assignment or make "careless" errors in the last portion of an assignment, have clinical Attention Deficit Disorder with Hyperactivity (ADHD). When this is the case, there are several people involved in monitoring the child's progress in attention and focusing. The team then may include a medical doctor, psychologist, or therapist. ADHD is diagnosed according to the parameters noted in the DSM-V, and, in some cases, medication is prescribed.

While ADHD is diagnosed with medical intervention, an attention executive function deficit can be recognized without medical intervention. "It is now understood that ADHD is more than a disorder of the three core symptoms in attention, impulsivity, and hyperactivity; it affects the executive function of the brain as well" (Rief, 2008, p.11). Students with this condition may be distractible due to difficulty attending to the intended focal point rather than distractors. However, it is important to note that not all students who have EF difficulties have ADHD. In addition many students with learning disabilities are also diagnosed with ADHD and present with executive function issues in attention.

SUPPORTIVE STRATEGIES WITH CARDS FOR ATTENDING, INITIATING, AND FOCUSING

The following are examples of supportive strategies to teach to students that can help them with goals related to the EF area of Attending, Initiating, and Focusing. It is important to note that all strategies will not work for all students. Step 3 in the 7-Step Model provides help in choosing appropriate strategies for students while considering UDL and metacognition, and step 4 will guide you through the teaching process. Steps 5, 6, and 7 address data tools for the assessment of strategy effectiveness, revision if needed, and the celebration of success with the strategy or strategies before moving on. *Blank templates, modifiable versions of materials, and strategy cards can be found at http://resources.corwin.com/ExecutiveFunctioning* .

POST-IT NOTE MODIFIED STRATEGY (SEE MORE ON THIS IN CHAPTER 2)

The Post-it Note Modified Strategy is designed to boost students' reading comprehension while helping them get started (use of the timer), helping them to attend to what they are reading until the end, and to focus on the important points to put on their Post-it Note concentrating to bring their focus to the important points.

TAKE A BREATHER STRATEGY (SEE MORE ON THIS STRATEGY IN CHAPTER 5)

This strategy has been found helpful when students are having trouble focusing. If not addressed, the student may become frustrated and give up on the project. Taking a short break from working to focus on breathing gives the student an opportunity to refresh mentally and physically before returning to the work at hand.

MOVEMENT HAS BEEN FOUND TO MAKE A DIFFERENCE IN ALL STUDENT'S LEARNING.

Teachers find that movement helps students to refocus and concentrate on learning. Movement may range from small movement within a seat to more intense movement like dancing. Sensory breaks are valuable to students, who may benefit from breaks such as moving in place on a sensory pillow. Breaks do not have to be disruptive; they can become a natural part of a student's day. Some students continue working while they are enjoying a sensory break.

PREWRITING STRATEGY FOR GETTING STARTED

When approaching a writing assignment, encourage the student to always set personal goals.

For the Student to Think About

- ☑ What is the goal of this writing assignment?
- ☑ How long do I have to complete it?
- ☑ What are the steps that I need to follow?
- ☑ What do I need to do first?
- ☑ Start writing.

FIGURE 4.1 Prewriting Strategy Card for Getting Started Upper Elementary to Secondary

Prewriting Strategy for Getting Started	☑ What is the goal of this writing assignment? ☑ How long do I have to complete it? ☑ What are the steps that I need to follow? ☑ What do I need to do first? ☑ Start writing.

IMAGE SOURCE: Pixabay.com/clker-free-vector-images

FIGURE 4.2 Modified Prewriting for Getting Started for Early Elementary

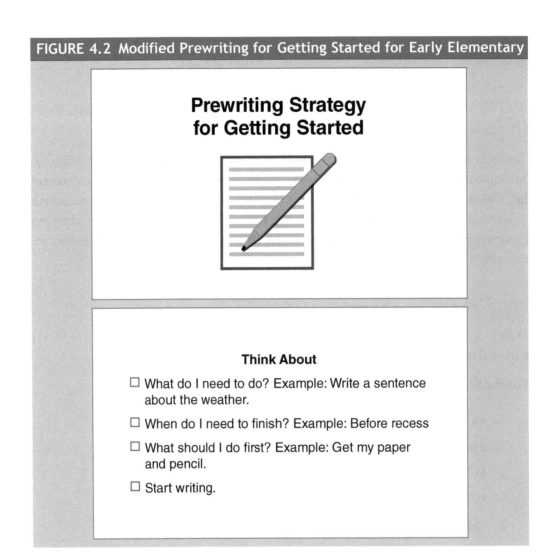

**Prewriting Strategy
for Getting Started**

Think About

☐ What do I need to do? Example: Write a sentence about the weather.

☐ When do I need to finish? Example: Before recess

☐ What should I do first? Example: Get my paper and pencil.

☐ Start writing.

IMAGE SOURCE: Pixabay.com/clker-free-vector-images

FOR THE TEACHER TO CONSIDER

Combining Working Memory, Attending, Initiation, and Focus

Some students find it difficult to retrieve ideas and words without starters. It may seem the student is not beginning because he or she is being difficult when the real reason is that the student is overwhelmed and shuts down instead of seeking help. Starters provided to students both through technology and written work can prove helpful. Brainstorming is a popular strategy, but when asked to brainstorm, students with working memory and initiating issues often do not know where to begin.

If a student is asked to brainstorm a subject for written work, help them list three ideas following an example provided.

Example:

Student X was assigned to write a paper on a famous person he or she admired. To provide a starter, you model three categories that have famous people:

1. Sports figures

2. Presidents

3. Musicians

The choice of three categories provides the student an anchor for his or her thinking. You then select one of the three categories and identify and list famous people in that category. Next, you select one of the people you listed. The next step would be for you to brainstorm aloud what you know about the person you selected while writing what you are brainstorming. Let the student know that you now have chosen your topic and are ready to start finding information about this famous person. Ask the student to follow this process.

COPS STRATEGY (SEE CHAPTER 6 FOR COMMUNICATION ACTIVITY ON COPS)

COPS stands for Capitalization, Organization, Punctuation, and Spelling. This strategy provides the student an opportunity to focus on each of the components in COPS to self-check his or her work for errors. Upon finding those errors, the student can correct them and hand in a corrected paper. Students with EF issues may need to use a modified version of COPS. In the modified version of COPS shown below for students who need prompts, we suggest scaffolding for them by using an individualized developmentally and age-appropriate guide. This version should be fluid in that new checkpoints will be added as the student learns additional writing skills. As the student continues to use COPS, many of the errors will be found in the initial scan. This expanded version of COPS is vital for some students and guides their search for errors.

Below is an example for a sixth grader based on his or her individual needs.

FIGURE 4.3 COPS Editing Checklist

First scan your paper for errors in general and make corrections. After scanning your paper and making corrections, use the checkpoints below to make certain that all of the areas listed were reviewed. Make the final corrections and submit your paper.

CAPITALIZATION

☐ Capitalized the beginning of all sentences

☐ Capitalized proper nouns

ORGANIZATION

☐ Organized by main idea

(Continued)

FIGURE 4.3 (*Continued*)

☐ Created paragraphs with a topic sentence, supporting details, and closing sentence or transition sentence to the next paragraph

☐ Created varied sentences (simple, compound, complex)

☐ Distinguished facts from opinions by providing evidence

☐ Used descriptors as appropriate

PUNCTUATION

☐ Placed commas correctly (series; states and places; commas with compound and or complex sentences; semicolons, etc.)

☐ Used the proper tense

☐ Used prepositions correctly

☐ Used pronouns that agree with the antecedent

☐ Formatted quotations and dialogue

☐ Used conjunctions correctly

☐ Completed sentences without run-ons

SPELLING

☐ Scanned for spelling errors correcting any words you know how to spell and marking any that do not look correct but that you do not know how to spell

☐ Used plural and possessive nouns correctly

☐ Corrected errors with frequently confused words

☐ Used technology, if available. Spell Check is useful but be aware of unique spellings for names, inappropriate word substitutions, homonyms, etc.

SELF-MONITORING STRATEGY

Students can self-monitor with checklists and to-do lists. They may need reinforcement to begin using them, but once they experience success, they usually agree to their use. It is important that the lists are not too long.

Time Needed Strategy for Time Management (See more on this strategy in chapter 3).

When given a specific amount of time and the ability to self-monitor, students can increase their attending, initiating, and focusing.

Example:

- **Assignment 1**—Read for 20 minutes using Post-it Note Modified Strategy.

- Think about what you read: 5 minutes.

- **Assignment 2**—Complete a page of addition of fractions: 15 minutes; Check backward and correct: 5 minutes.

- **Assignment 3**—Complete a one-paragraph character sketch; Web a plan for the character sketch: 5 minutes; Write: 10 minutes.

Attending, Initiating, and Focusing

You can use this checklist as a visual reminder to help:

☑ Start (initiate) a task.

☑ Attend to the task at hand.

☑ Focus on the process needed to complete the task.

☑ Check when I have started the assignment.

☑ Attend to the task at hand.

☑ Focus on the process needed to complete the task.

IMAGE SOURCE: Pixabay.com/clker-free-vector-images

SELF-CHECK CARD STRATEGY FOR ELEMENTARY STUDENTS

This strategy allows students to monitor their progress toward completion of an assignment by moving a bead on a pipe cleaner on an index card. The card is hole punched at each end, and a pipe cleaner with a bead strung on it is attached to the card. The increments stand for **Not Started Yet, Started Working, Doing My Work With No Problem,** and **Finished My Work.** The teacher can call for self-check, and students will move their bead to where they are in completion of the assignment. Students can also move their bead themselves as they move through the assignment. Teachers can assess who needs help getting started and who needs help while working.

DIRECTIONS TO STUDENTS ON THE USE OF THE SELF-CHECK CARD STRATEGY

Everyone wants to do well in school, and we all know that one way to do well is to work hard in class. We can help ourselves in class by paying attention to instruction and

FIGURE 4.5 Self-Check Card for Elementary Students

Self-Check Card Strategy

1. Put my bead at Not Started Yet.

2. Start my assignment and move my bead to Started Working.

3. When I am working with no problem, move my bead to Doing My Work.

4. When I finish, move my bead to Finished My Work.

explanation of the information we need to start and finish our work in a timely manner. Some days it is harder to focus on our work than others. It is helpful if we each keep ourselves alert and on task. This self-check card helps you keep track of how you are doing getting started, working on, and finishing your assignments.

You will have a card with a movable bead. When your teacher says self-check, move your bead to where you rate your work at that moment. This is your opinion of how you are doing.

Ask yourself this question: Where am I on this scale in terms of staying on task and finishing my assignment on time? Be truthful with yourself. Your teacher may walk around and look at how you self-rated. You are not being graded on where you put your bead.

What if you do not like your rating? Ask yourself what you can do to improve. Try to see if you can move up to the next higher rating by paying attention, getting started, and working until the task is finished on time. Ask your teacher for help if you are confused.

Teacher Testimonial from: Andi Anglin-Alonso

Special Educator, Resource

Grade(s) Taught: Elementary

Executive Function Addressed: Attending, Initiating, and Focusing

Strategy Name: Visual Schedule for Planning

Strategy Designed for: Whole Class

Break Pass Cards can be used to help students who are having difficulty focusing on their work.

Allow students to use these cards when they need a short break from concentrating on an assignment. They may need a short time away from the assignment only to return and refocus. Break Pass Cards are designed to look like credit cards. The cards are magnetic and laminated. Students keep them on the side of their desk. It is important that you explain that these are to be used at explicit times, so students will not take advantage of their use of the card.

FIGURE 4.6 Break Pass Strategy Card for Elementary Students

Keep your Break Pass Card on the side of your desk.

When you are feeling like you cannot concentrate anymore, put the card on top of your desk. Take a short break and think about something else for a minute or two.

Return your card to the side of your desk.

Resume working on your assignment.

IMAGE SOURCE: iStock.com/robertindiana

Teacher Testimonial from: Kim Hale

Grade Taught: 3rd

Executive Function Addressed: Attending, Initiating, and Focusing

Strategy Name: Self-Check Card Strategy

Strategy Designed for: Individual Student or Whole Class

Kim Hale

About half way through the school year, I observed that my third graders as a class were having difficulty starting their work as quickly as they had before. I informed them of a Self-Check Card Strategy that they might find helpful. The students agreed that they would like to try this strategy. I provided instruction on the strategy including modeling my use of the strategy. I then told the students that they would make their Self-Check Cards. The materials and written instructions were distributed; I explained and modeled making the card and then directed students to make theirs. Once the cards were made, I explained to the students that self-checking accurately is harder than it sounds. I had them identify different examples including not working at all, starting my work, doing my work with no problem, and finishing my work. I explained to them that I would be rating them periodically to determine whether my ratings were the same as theirs. The students starting using the strategy in class and I called out, "Self-Check" when I felt that some of them needed to focus on their work. The students as a whole used this strategy daily for about a month and then they were given a choice as to whether they needed to continue using it. A few students chose to discontinue and the others continued until they felt they no longer needed the card.

SLANT STRATEGY (ELLIS, 1991)

This is a strategy that can be used for attention and focus. Students are taught to take a learning position in their seat and direct their mind to the speaker and the topic being discussed. Teachers find they can call SLANT as a verbal cue for students as a class, or they can call it as a subtle cue for individual students. Once the students have mastered SLANT, they use metacognition to rehearse and use it in generalized settings.

SLANT STRATEGY CARDS

FIGURE 4.7 SLANT Strategy (Grades 8-12)

SLANT

SLANT Strategy

S - Sit up straight

L - Lean forward (writing position)

A - Activate your thinking

N - Note important points

T - Track the talker (keep your eyes on whomever is doing the informing)

SOURCE: Ellis, 1991.

FIGURE 4.8 Modified SLANT Strategy (Grades 2-7)

SLANT

SLANT Strategy

S - Sit up straight in your seat

L - Look at the speaker and listen to the speaker

A - Allow your mind to think only about the subject the teacher is discussing

N - Nod occasionally to let the speaker know you are getting the information

T - Track the teacher with your eyes

IMAGE SOURCE: Pixabay.com/openclipart-vectors

FIGURE 4.9 Modified SLANT Strategy (Grades Pre K-1)

SLANT

SLANT Strategy

S - Sit up straight where ever you are

L - Look at the teacher and listen to what the teacher says

A - Always pay attention to the teacher

N - Nod to the teacher to show that you are paying attention

T - Turn your head so you can always see the teacher

SOURCE: Pixabay.com/openclipart-vectors

Teacher Testimonial from: Kim Hale

Grade Taught: 3rd

Executive Function Addressed: Attending, Initiating, and Focusing

Strategy Name: SLANT Strategy

Strategy Designed for: Individual Student or Whole Class

I taught SLANT during the Morning Meeting at the beginning of the school year. We role played several examples of what SLANT does and does not look like. I placed a visual of SLANT on the wall of our classroom. I shared with students that I would be slanting my arm as a cue for them to use SLANT. We used it the entire school year on some occasions more than others. I really like this strategy because it is easy to implement and does not interfere with the instructional flow.

THE SHAKA STRATEGY

The SHAKA Strategy is a strategy for attending, initiating, and focusing used in classes the authors visited in Hawaii. It is an example of a culturally responsive strategy.

Teacher Testimonial from: Mychael Moe

Special Educator

Grade(s) Taught: Elementary and High School

Executive Function Addressed: Attending and Focusing

Strategy Name: SHAKA Strategy

Strategy Designed for: Whole Class

Mychael Moe

Purpose of the strategy: To promote positive behavior, get attention, and help with transitions.

This strategy is similar to SLANT, but is a modified local version used in some parts of Hawaii's Big Island. The teacher posts signs on walls and then introduces the strategy to the students. The teacher practices with students until the routine has been established. It does not disrupt the class because it is an attention-getting strategy. The strategy works best during transitions to get students settled and ready to learn. The SHAKA is accomplished by sticking up thumb and pinky fingers and holding down three middle fingers.

Step-by-Step Process:

1. Teacher posts poster with directions on wall.
2. Teacher says, "I want to see SHAKA."
3. Teacher says, "S." Students say, "Sit in learning position." Teacher says, "Show shaka." Students shaka.
4. Teacher says, "H." Students say, "Have your materials ready." Teacher says, "Show shaka." Students shaka.
5. Teacher says, "A." Students say, "Answer appropriately." Teacher says, "Show shaka.", Students shaka.
6. Teacher says, "K." Students say, "Keep on tracking." Teacher says, "Show shaka." Students shaka.
7. Teacher says, "A." Students say, "Always respect other students' turn." Teacher says, "Show shaka." Students shaka.

(Continued)

FIGURE 4.10 The SHAKA Strategy Card for Secondary Students

The Shaka Strategy

SOURCE: iStock.com/ylivdesign

1. Teacher will post poster with directions on wall.

2. Teacher says, "I want to see SHAKA."

3. Teacher says, "S." I say, "Sit in learning position." Teacher says, "Show shaka." I show shaka.

4. Teacher says, "H." I say, "Have your materials ready." Teacher says, "Show shaka." I show shaka.

5. Teacher says "A." I say, "Answer appropriately." Teacher says, "Show Shaka." I show shaka.

6. Teacher says "K." I say, "Keep on tracking." Teacher says, "Show shaka." I show shaka.

7. Teacher says, "A." I say, "Always respect other students' turn." Teacher says, "Show shaka." I show shaka.

Data on strategy: No hard data, but locally, students enjoy practicing a strategy with a local twist.

SUPPORTIVE TECHNOLOGIES

With the onset of technology, new instructional tools and supports are now available to meet the diverse learning needs of all students. Many of these tools integrate a UDL platform, are highly engaging and interactive, and may be used to reinforce instructional content or executive function skills. We use technology to compliment and support executive function skill training. Below are some of the technology tools we have found to be beneficial when teaching executive function skills and strategies.

TABLE 4.1 Supportive Technologies for Attending, Initiating, and Focusing

TECHNOLOGY TOOL CATEGORY (WEBSITE, SOFTWARE, APP)	NAME OF TECHNOLOGY	EXECUTIVE FUNCTION AREA ADDRESSED	AGE GROUP
Website	Center on the Developing Child Harvard University *https:// developingchild.harvard.edu/*	All areas	Most ages
Website	Child Mind Institute https:// childmind.org/	All areas	Most ages
Website	Common Sense Education https:// www.commonsense.org/	All areas	Most ages

TECHNOLOGY TOOL CATEGORY (WEBSITE, SOFTWARE, APP)	NAME OF TECHNOLOGY	EXECUTIVE FUNCTION AREA ADDRESSED	AGE GROUP
Website	Intervention Central: Response to Intervention—RTI Resources http://www.interventioncentral.org/	All areas	Most ages
Website	LD Online www.ldonline.org/	All areas	Most ages
Website	Understood.org https://www.understood.org/	All areas	Most ages
iPhone App	Digit Span-Train of Thought	Focus and attention	Upper Elementary to adult
iPhone App	Popplet	Initiating and attention	Middle and High School
iPhone App	Focus Bar	Focus	High School
iPad App	Math Attack Pro	Focus	Elementary
iPad App	Time Timer	Initiating and focus	Elementary
iPad App	Kazu Timer	Initiating and focus	Preschool to Grade 4
iPad App	Inspiration Maps	Initiating	K to Grade 12
iPad App	Sound Note	Attention and focus	Middle to High School
iPad App	Mole Story	Attention and focus	Grade 3 to adult

CASE STUDY: CARLOS

We will now look at the case study of Carlos (*see Appendix 1.2 for his full case study*), a fifteen-year-old student in the tenth grade with executive function deficits in several skill areas. In this chapter, the 7-Step Model for Executive Function Skills Training explained in chapter 1 will be applied to the area of attending, initiating, and focusing.

The questions that need to be considered to determine the appropriate executive function interventions that will support Carlos's learning needs are

1. What are Carlos's executive function needs? (The step 1 process will answer this question.)

2. What are the strategies that can be used to support Carlos's executive function needs? (The step 3 process will answer this question.)

3. How should the effectiveness of the selected strategies in supporting Carlos's executive function be measured? (The step 4 and step 5 processes will answer this question.)

4. Do the selected strategies work? (The step 6 process will answer this question.)

The following example shows how to address one of Carlos's goals for attention, initiating, and focusing using the 7-Step Model. *This model is not a lock-step procedure but merely a template to guide your thinking. Your flexibility and creativity in using this model to meet your needs and the needs of your student are encouraged.*

Step 1

Determine the student's EF deficits and note them in the Executive Function (EF) Planning Chart.

Assessment

As described in chapter 1, the assessment process is completed through reviewing the student's records as well as through observations of the student and interviews with the student, as well as his or her family members and other and previous teachers. Formal and informal assessments may also be used to help determine EF deficits. (**See Sample Student Self-Assessment Tool** *in Appendix 1.15.*)

Key Questions

1. **How are the student's strengths and difficulties exhibited in terms of executive functions in attending, initiating, and focusing behaviors?**

After a thorough review of Carlos's records, including current test scores on standardized tests; report card grades; work samples; observations of Carlos in academic, extracurricular activities, social settings; and interviews with him, Carlos's previous teachers and his parents, the following strengths and needs in terms of attending, initiating, and focusing are identified.

Carlos's Strengths

- Carlos has a good school attendance record.
- Carlos enjoys and excels at playing sports, especially football. He is a good analytical thinker when it comes to the design and implementation of football plays.
- Carlos is a good analytical thinker during group discussions in class but needs processing time to express these thoughts.
- Acceptance and being valued by his peers is important to Carlos.
- Carlos can focus and attend to video games for hours.

Carlos's Difficulties

Attention

- Finds it difficult to attend for a sustained period
- Daydreaming
- Gets distracted easily
- Finds attending to more than one task at a time confusing
- Rushes through his assignments and makes careless errors

Initiating

- Appears tired even though he has gotten enough sleep
- Has difficulty beginning assignments and completing them
- Does not begin a task when asked, especially when it comes to writing

Focusing

- Has difficulty focusing on the person talking
- Has difficulty proofreading his work
- Becomes easily frustrated
- Has trouble focusing on what is important
- Gives his work a "quick look over" instead of focusing on checking each response

Carlos also has difficulties in other areas of executive functioning as can be seen on the **Executive Function (EF) Planning Chart**. Below is a summary of all Carlos's executive function difficulties. The following **Executive Function (EF) Planning Chart** specifies how Carlos's Attending, Initiating, and Focusing difficulties present. *Blank templates, modifiable versions of materials, and strategy cards can be found at http://resources.corwin.com/ExecutiveFunctioning.*

TABLE 4.2 Executive Function Planning (EF) Chart

EXECUTIVE FUNCTION SKILL AREA	WHAT DOES THE DIFFICULTY LOOK LIKE FOR THIS STUDENT? (EXAMPLES)
Attending, Initiating, and Focusing	He needs several reminders to get started on a task or assignment. He loses concentration very easily. Gives his work a "quick look over" instead of focusing on checking each response. He has difficulty focusing on the person talking.
Working Memory	He has difficulty comprehending class readings. He has splinter skills in mathematics and has difficulty solving multistep problems. He gets confused when he has to remember what was said to him.
Prioritizing, Organizing, Sequencing, Managing Time, and Planning	He has difficulty organizing school materials and assignments, especially his backpack. He either rushes through an assignment or does not finish the task on time. His papers are sloppy and disorganized.

(Continued)

TABLE 4.2 (Continued)

EXECUTIVE FUNCTION SKILL AREA	WHAT DOES THE DIFFICULTY LOOK LIKE FOR THIS STUDENT? (EXAMPLES)
Controlling Social/Emotional and Inhibiting Behaviors	He is very chatty socially but sometimes refuses to participate in class discussions and seems to be daydreaming. He doodles instead of interacting during group work. He works hard to be liked by other students.
Communicating, Cognitive Flexibility/Shifting	He does not write coherently due to a lack of understanding language usage. His writing lacks sequencing of concepts and supporting details. He is extremely slow to move from one activity on to another. He finds it difficult to think about more than one thing at a time.

2. **Is there an executive function deficit in attending, initiating, and focusing?**
Looking at the information presented in answer to question 1, it is established that, in addition to other EF deficits, Carlos has an executive function deficit in attending, initiating, and focusing.

3. **How does the difficulty in attending, initiating, and focusing present?**
The Executive Function Planning Chart, table 4.2, specifies how Carlos's attending, initiating, and focusing difficulties present. An IEP objective for Carlos might be written as this: Given instruction in breathing strategies, Carlos will self-regulate by using the focusing strategies when he feels he is losing focus as measured by a self-check card and complete his work 80 percent of the time.

Step 2

Review the EF Planning Chart with the student and start to develop a Game Plan.

This will guide the skill training for this specific executive function area, Attending, Initiating, and Focusing. After you have the results of either formal or informal assessments, discuss the results with the student and his parents. Once Carlos's areas of executive functioning weaknesses needed for immediate attention are identified, you can begin to develop Carlos's Game Plan. This will give Carlos an opportunity to "buy in" to the process. It enables the student to understand his areas of strength and difficulty. This understanding and awareness will later lead to student self-advocacy and greater independence in Carlos's learning process. Carlos's Game Plan includes his strengths, difficulties, goals for improvement, and strategies selected to enhance executive functioning through UDL, and appropriate strategies. See chapter 1 for directions on starting a student Game Plan. *A blank template for the* Game Plan *can be found in Appendix 1.9b, and blank templates, modifiable versions of materials, and strategy cards can be found at http://resources.corwin.com/ExecutiveFunctioning.*

Student Game Plan for: Carlos

What I like to do and feel that I do well: I am great at football and want to play professional football someday. I am a good thinker and I am able to see many sides or solutions to things. I have great school attendance. I am the video game champion!

Goals for Improvement and Corresponding Actions

GOAL 1: I would like to pay attention to a speaker and take notes.	GOAL 2: I would like to be on time to school, class, and submitting assignments.	GOAL 3: I would like to check my work and correct it before handing it in.
Action 1: To be determined after completing step 3	**Action 2:** To be determined after completing step 3	**Action 3:** To be determined after completing step 3
Supporting Technology:	**Supporting Technology:**	**Supporting Technology:**
Date Goal Met:_____	Date Goal Met:_____	Date Goal Met:_____

Step 3

Considering UDL and metacognition, select an EF skill-building strategy and get commitment from the student. Add the strategy to the Game Plan.

What are the strategies that we can use to support Carlos's executive function needs? Think about how you would respond to the following questions:

- What are Carlos's learning needs and challenges in terms of UDL (Multiple Means of Representation, Multiple Means of Action and Representation, and Multiple Means of Engagement)? See table 4.3.
- What approaches and supports will be used to help Carlos access the lesson given his deficit in attending, initiating, and focusing? Examples include
  - using strategies to promote attending, initiating, and focusing.
  - modeling and role play appropriate strategies to help with attending, initiating, and focusing
  - teaching Carlos to use metacognition to think about the subject at hand, getting started, and solving problems
  - providing a self-check card and a self-monitoring checklist
  - chunking assignments
  - incorporating supportive technology
  - providing scaffolding
  - reinforcing appropriate time on task
- What strategies will be taught to Carlos and added to his Game Plan?
  - Select from those described in the first part of the chapter, other resources, or those you have used previously. Discuss the strategy options with Carlos and guide him to select strategies that are appropriate and agreeable to him.

Use the **Selecting a Strategy for the Student while Integrating UDL Chart**, table 4.3, as a tool to prompt your thinking in terms of selecting the appropriate strategy that matches Carlos's learning needs and challenges. Written completion of this chart is not necessary. *A blank chart can be found in Appendix 1.10, and blank templates, modifiable versions of materials, and strategy cards can be found at http:// resources.corwin.com/ExecutiveFunctioning.*

TABLE 4.3 Selecting a Strategy for the Student While Integrating UDL

Student: Carlos

Executive Function Deficit: Attending, Initiating, and Focusing

Game Plan Goal: Goal 1: I would like to pay attention to the speaker and take notes.

MULTIPLE MEANS OF REPRESENTATION

Things for you to consider:

1. What information does the student already know?

Carlos wants to be able to physically and mentally pay attention to the speaker and take notes on what is being discussed. He is interested in doing well, but he loses attention and focus.

2. What are the instructional goals for the student in relation to the executive function addressed?

Carlos should be able to attend to the speaker for short periods of time. He should be able to focus on what the speaker is saying and fill in a structured note pad.

He should be able to physically take an attentive pose.

3. What extended activities will be needed?

He will be taught using a multisensory approach that includes role play, prompts and cues, metacognition, and checklists.

4. What enrichment activities can be implemented?

Carlos will be asked to demonstrate how to appropriately respond to and take notes form speakers in a variety of settings.

5. What will you need to incorporate when teaching the strategy?

• *Connect prior knowledge, preteach prerequisite information.*

• *Model and role play the expected process for listening and taking structured notes.*

• *Multiple opportunities for practice.*

• *Technology such as videos to practice and reinforce the acceptable behaviors.*

(Continued)

TABLE 4.3 (Continued)

MULTIPLE MEANS OF ENGAGEMENT

Things for you to consider:

1. How will you conduct preassessment, formative, and summative assessments for the student's learning?

Carlos will be assessed during the preassessment stage in terms of how he attends to and tracks the speaker and how he takes structured notes during the talk.

During the formative stage, Carlos will be provided with prompts and cues that are appropriate for attending to the speaker and role play, and what it should look like. His success in attending, tracking, and taking will be analyzed to determine whether outcomes are met.

For the summative assessment, Carlos will have to physically attend to and track the speaker. He also will have to focus on what the speaker is saying to complete the structured notes.

2. What platforms will be permitted for the student to demonstrate mastery?

Demonstrate mastery through the ability to self-monitor supported by a strategy card provided to prompt and cue expected behaviors. When he meets the goal 1 criteria with 90 percent he will have mastered this goal.

MULTIPLE MEANS OF ENGAGEMENT

Things for you to consider:

1. How will you teach the student in a manner that actively engages the student?

Engage student in creating goals that encourage success, using metacognition to self-monitor, and collecting data on effectiveness of strategy to help attain goals.

Role play information taught, check for understanding by allowing him to share his structured notes and video tape appropriate listening behaviors, provide verbal cues, and a strategy card as a visual reminder.

TABLE 4.3 (Continued)

Based on your Considerations of the Principles for this goal, what strategy would you select that aligns with the three Principles and Align with UDL and the Strategy Selected?

Name of Strategy: *SLANT Strategy (Sit, Lean, Activate, Note, and Track)*

This strategy is selected because it

- *models the appropriate behaviors in a natural manner* **(Multiple Means of Representation).**
- *presents key concepts through demonstrations, visual prompts, cues from the teacher, color-coded checklists, and role play* **(Multiple Means of Representation).**
- *provides an opportunity to demonstrate mastery by role playing, videos, providing structured notes, and responding to prompts and cues in a realistic, natural setting* **(Multiple Means of Action and Expression).**
- *allows Carlos to demonstrate mastery and effectiveness of the strategy through metacognition and self-monitoring* **(Multiple Means of Engagement).**

Think about the components of **The Student Implementation of Strategy with a Focus on Metacognition and UDL Chart**, table 4.4. This chart should be completed with the student. It is a tool that helps the student to buy in to the strategy learning process. *A blank chart can be found in Appendix 1.11, and blank templates, modifiable versions of materials, and strategy cards can be found at http://resources .corwin.com/ExecutiveFunctioning.*

Once you and the student have selected a strategy, add the strategy name to the "Things I can do to help with my difficulties in school" column of the Game Plan for an elementary student or the "Action" column of the Game Plan for a secondary student.

Below is Carlos's completed Game Plan, which lists his goals and the strategies he and his teacher have decided he will learn to strengthen his EF skills in the area of Attending, Initiating, and Focusing. Given his issues, additional strategies such as Self-Monitoring Checklist Strategy, Time Needed Strategy, COPS, and supportive technology would be taught to Carlos to further strengthen this skill area. *A blank* **Game Plan** *template can be found in Appendix 1.9b, and blank templates, modifiable versions of materials, and strategy cards can be found at http://resources .corwin.com/ExecutiveFunctioning.*

TABLE 4.4 Student Implementation of Strategy With a Focus on Metacognition and UDL Principles

Student: Carlos

Executive Function Deficit: Attending, Initiating, and Focusing

Game Plan Goal: Goal 1: I would like to pay attention to the speaker and take notes.

Strategy Selected: SLANT Strategy (Sit, Lean, Activate, Note, and Track)

METACOGNITION—QUESTIONS THE STUDENT THINKS ABOUT AND RESPONDS TO

Things for you to consider:

1. What am I supposed to do?

*Use the **SLANT** (Sit, Lean, Activate, Note, and Track) Strategy*

2. Why is this strategy important for me to use and how will it help me?

This strategy will help me to better attend to the speaker and focus on what he or she is saying. Noting the information will help me to remember it.

3. What are the steps of the strategy?

SLANT (Sit, Lean, Activate, Note, and Track) Strategy

When listening to a speaker, I must

- *Sit up straight*
- *Lean a little forward*
- *Activate my thinking to the relevant subject*
- *Note what the speaker is saying*
- *Track the speaker as he or she moves about the room.*

4. Is there technology I can use?

- *Focus Bar (Common Sense Media iPhone App) (https://www.understood .org/en/tools/tech-finder)*
- *Vibrating reminder*
- *Videos of self*

5. What should I think about when using this strategy?

- *I need to make sure that I am continuing to do this during the entire time the speaker is talking.*
- *I need to think about how I look to the speaker. I want to make certain the speaker sees me as paying attention and taking notes on the subject at hand. I want to make certain I have structured notes to use to study from.*

FIGURE 4.12 Carlos's Completed Game Plan

Student Game Plan for: Carlos

What I like to do and feel that I do well: I am great at football and want to play professional football someday. I am a good thinker and I am able to see many sides or solutions to things. I have great school attendance. I am the video game champion!

Goals for Improvement and Corresponding Actions

GOAL 1: I would like to pay attention to a speaker and take notes.	GOAL 2: I would like to be on time to school, class, and submitting assignments.	GOAL 3: I would like to check my work and correct it before handing it in.
Action 1: I can use the **SLANT (Sit, Lean, Activate, Note, Track) Strategy**	**Action 2:** I can use the **Self-Monitoring Checklist Strategy** and **Time Needed Strategy**	**Action 3:** I can use the **COPS Strategy** with my modified help sheet.
Supporting Technology: • Videos • Vibrating Watch • Focus Box iPad App • Focus Bar iPad App	**Supporting Technology:** • Timer • Vibrating Watch • Popplet, iPhone App	**Supporting Technology:** • Tools for Grammar, Spelling, and Dictionary
Date Goal Met:__4/5/2018__	**Date Goal Met:**_____	**Date Goal Met:**_____

Step 4

Design and implement data collection tools to measure success in the use of the strategy, teach the strategy, and give the student a strategy card.

The following illustrates how step 4 would be applied to the SLANT Strategy, which addresses goal 1:

The data from step 1 show the following:

We noticed that Carlos did not seem to be attending to the teacher when he or she was talking to the class. He had difficulty beginning an assignment and continuing to attend to the assignment until he finished it. He also has difficulty focusing on the work to see his mistakes and correct them. This results in low grades.

We talked with Carlos about his strengths and difficulties and started to develop a Game Plan.

Carlos understands that his lack of participation in class impedes his academic performance. Carlos agreed that he was having trouble with attending, initiating, and focusing. From this information, we developed goals with Carlos that addressed these concerns. Keeping his grades high enough for football eligibility is very important to Carlos.

The goals Carlos agreed to from step 2 are

Goal 1: I would like to pay attention to the teacher and take notes.

Goal 2: I would like to be on time to school, class, and submitting assignments.

Goal 3: I would like to be able to check my work and correct it before handing it in.

The strategy you and Carlos selected in step 3 is

SLANT (Sit, Lean, Activate, Note, and Track) Strategy. Teach the strategy to Carlos. Model the steps of the strategy and incorporate metacognition. Provide motivation for the strategy such as use of a reinforcement and gain a continued commitment by the student. Role play the use of this strategy using various scenarios. Engage the student in sharing situations that often result in his attending to the speaker and taking structured notes. His strategy card can be used to reinforce recall of how to use the strategy. Each role-play scenario should require the student to explain the strategy and how it helps them.

Give the student the SLANT Strategy card. Have the student practice the strategy using metacognition and referring to the strategy card as needed until he can use the strategy with automaticity. The strategy card summarizes the strategy and serves as a reminder of how to use it. It outlines the process and steps that need to be followed to successfully implement the strategy. To make the card, create or purchase a business-size card. Place the name of the strategy on the front of the card, along with visuals if that is helpful for the student. Place a description of how to use the strategy on the back of the card. It is helpful if this description is stated in the student's own words. Check the description for accuracy. For the business-size strategy card, place it in a clear business card pocket folder for future reference. This will provide Carlos with an individualized portable reference system of strategies that support his EF skills in the area of Attending, Initiating, and Focusing.

FIGURE 4.13 SLANT Strategy Card (Grades 8–12)

	SLANT Strategy
SLANT	**S** - Sit up straight **L** - Lean forward (writing position) **A** - Activate your thinking **N** - Note important points **T** - Track the talker (keep your eyes on whomever is doing the informing)

SOURCE: Ellis, 1991.

As the student continues to practice the strategy, it is important to determine whether the strategy is appropriate for teaching the student the EF skill attending, initiating, and focusing.

Design and collect data and revise as necessary.

Design the data tools, collect data on the success of the strategy, and revise as necessary. ***Blank templates, modifiable versions of materials, and strategy cards can be found at http://resources.corwin.com/ExecutiveFunctioning.***

This is the baseline phase of the data collection process. Once the baseline data have been collected, analyze the data and go back and make any necessary adjustments. For example, does the baseline data show that this strategy works for the student? Does the student need extra supports such as cues to remind him or her to use the strategy? Does the student need extended time to complete the steps of the strategy? After the student has been taught the strategy, it is important for you as the teacher to determine whether the strategy is appropriate for the student's needs and if the student is comfortable using the strategy. Not every strategy is appropriate for every student; therefore, it is important to evaluate if the selected strategy is suited to the student and review and revise as necessary.

Analyze the baseline data and go back and make any necessary adjustments. For example, does the baseline data show that this strategy works for Carlos? Does Carlos need extra supports such as cues to remind him to use the strategy? Does Carlos need extended time to complete the steps of the strategy?

After Carlos has been taught the strategy, it is important for you as the teacher to determine whether the strategy is appropriate for his needs and if he is comfortable using the strategy. Not every strategy is appropriate for every student; therefore, it is important to evaluate if the selected strategy is suited for Carlos.

At the conclusion of the baseline data collection period, Carlos met with his teacher to review and discuss their data collection results. An analysis of the baseline data resulted in Carlos being surprised at the number of times he used the SLANT Strategy. He shared with the teacher that he was using it because it helped him pay attention to the speaker and learn what was being said. The vibrating-watch reminder was very helpful to remind him to SLANT again.

Student Collected Data In First Column

Teacher Added Data in the Second Column

Student Name: Carlos

Data Collected By: Student

Number of Times I Used SLANT In Class

	CLASS: *SOCIAL STUDIES*	CLASS:	CLASS:	COMMENTS FROM STUDENT
Monday Date: 11/11	Tallies: II Total: 2			
Tuesday Date: 11/12	Tallies: I Total: 1			
Wednesday Date: 11/13	Tallies: III Total: 3			I had trouble understanding and had to stop and start.
Thursday Date: 11/14	Tallies: IIII Total: 4			I had trouble understanding and had to stop and start.
Friday Date: 11/15				I was absent Friday for an away football game. On the four days I used SLANT, it helped me to stop and start when I was getting lost.

TABLE 4.5 (Continued)

Student Name: Carlos

Data Collected By: Student

Number of Times Inappropriate Comments are Made in Class

	CLASS: *SOCIAL STUDIES*	CLASS:	CLASS:	COMMENTS FROM STUDENT
Monday Date: 11/18	**Tallies:** III **Total:** 3			
Tuesday Date: 11/19	**Tallies:** IIII **Total:** 4			It helps me to start and stop.
Wednesday Date: 11/20	**Tallies:** I **Total:** 1			The teacher only spoke once, and we worked on our project the rest of class.
Thursday Date: 11/21	*Thanksgiving break*	*Thanksgiving break*	*Thanksgiving break*	
Friday Date: 11/22	*Thanksgiving break*	*Thanksgiving break*	*Thanksgiving break*	

TABLE 4.6 The Number of Reminders for Use of SLANT Strategy

Teacher Reported on 5-minute interval recording for 15-minute periods

Student Name: Carlos

Data Collected By: Teacher

Number of Reminders During Three 5-Minute Intervals

	CLASS: *ENGLISH*	CLASS:	CLASS:	COMMENTS FROM TEACHER
Monday Date: 11/11	Tallies: III Total: 3			Used it as soon as reminded
Tuesday Date: 11/12	Tallies: III Total: 3			Used it as soon as reminded
Wednesday Date: 11/13	Tallies: I Total: 1			Seems to be initiating using the strategy
Thursday Date: 11/14	Tallies: II Total: 2			Seemed to be struggling
Friday Date: 11/15				Student absent

TABLE 4.6 (Continued)

Student Name: Carlos

Data Collected By: Teacher

Number of Reminders During Three 5-Minute Intervals

	CLASS: *ENGLISH*	CLASS:	CLASS:	COMMENTS FROM TEACHER
Monday Date: 11/18	**Tallies:** II **Total:** 2			Used it as soon as reminded
Tuesday Date: 11/19	**Tallies:** II **Total:** 2			Used it as soon as reminded
Wednesday Date: 11/20	**Tallies:** I **Total:** 1			Seems to be initiating using the strategy
Thursday Date: 11/21				Thanksgiving break
Friday Date: 11/22				Thanksgiving break

Step 5

Continue to collect data for the student's use of the strategy.

Determine Carlos's success in learning and generalizing the strategy, table 4.7, Considerations for Ongoing Data Analysis Chart, provides points you as the teacher need to consider as you continue to analyze the data addressing the student's correct use of the generalization of the selected strategy. Once the baseline data has been collected and analyzed, and the decision has been made to use the strategy, there is need for further data collection to determine the successful use and generalization of the strategy. Table 4.7, Considerations for Ongoing Data Analysis Chart, provides points you as the teacher need to consider as you continue to analyze the data addressing the student's correct use and generalization of the selected strategy. Carlos's responses to the questions considered in table 4.7 are posted below. *A blank template of this chart is provided in Appendix 1.12, and blank templates, modifiable versions of materials, and strategy cards can be found at http://resources.corwin.com/ExecutiveFunctioning.*

Select or design a data recording and analysis plan to be used. For the SLANT Strategy, table 4.8 shows the data collection for Carlos's use of the SLANT Strategy. *Blank templates, modifiable versions of materials, and strategy cards can be found at http://resources.corwin.com/ExecutiveFunctioning.*

TABLE 4.7 Considerations for Ongoing Data Analysis Chart

Student Name: *Carlos*

Strategy Used: *SLANT Strategy*

Please write yes, no, or N/A for Not Applicable.

_____Yes_____ 1. The strategy is cited in the student's Ongoing Data Analysis.

_____Yes_____ 2. The student understands the goal of using the strategy.

_____Yes_____ 3. The student can explain what the strategy is and why he or she is using it.

_____Yes_____ 4. There is a means of collecting data to measure the student's progress.

_____Yes_____ 5. The tools to measure the academic or social/emotional area that the executive function deficit is impacting are appropriate.

_____Yes_____ 6. Daily feedback is provided for at least one week from when the strategy began.

_____Yes_____ 7. The student is provided with reinforcement and knows his or her standing.

_____Yes_____ 8. Data are analyzed with the student and the revisions are made as needed.

_____Yes_____ 9. The selected strategy is appropriate for the student's needs.

Comments:

Carlos likes using the SLANT Strategy. He likes how he can easily remember the steps to this strategy so that he does not require a visual reminder or cue that his peers can notice. He agrees this strategy helps him pay attention and focus on what the speaker is saying.

TABLE 4.8 The Number of Times Student Used SLANT Strategy Student

Student Name: Carlos

Data Collected By: Student

Number of Reminders During Three 5-Minute Intervals

	CLASS: *SOCIAL STUDIES*	CLASS:	CLASS:	COMMENTS FROM TEACHER
Monday Date: 11/25	**Tallies:** IIIII **Total:** 5			Trouble focusing
Tuesday Date: 11/26	**Tallies:** III **Total:** 3			
Wednesday Date: 11/27	**Tallies:** I **Total:** 1			
Thursday Date: 11/28	**Tallies:** II **Total:** 2			
Friday Date: 11/29	**Tallies:** II **Total:** 2			

(Continued)

TABLE 4.8 (Continued)

Student Name: Carlos

Data Collected By: Student

Number of Reminders During Three 5-Minute Intervals

	CLASS: *SOCIAL STUDIES*	CLASS:	CLASS:	COMMENTS FROM TEACHER
Monday Date: 12/2	Tallies: IIII Total: 4			Trouble focusing after the weekend
Tuesday Date: 12/3	Tallies: II Total: 2			
Wednesday Date: 12/4	Tallies: II Total: 2			
Thursday Date: 12/5	Tallies: II Total: 2			
Friday Date: 12/6	Tallies: II Total: 2			

Since Carlos enjoyed the baseline data collection process, it was decided to allow him to collect data on the usage of the SLANT Strategy during social studies class. Carlos collected data on his use of SLANT over a nine-day period (see table 4.8).

Reviewing all of this data, it appears that the SLANT Strategy is working for Carlos and that he should continue to use this strategy as part of his daily learning routine.

Step 6

Analyze all the data collected and evaluate the student's success in using the strategy; update the Game Plan.

In analyzing Carlos's success in learning and generalizing the SLANT Strategy (Ellis, 1991) and whether it has helped him, the overarching questions are

- Does the student use the strategy in the noted area of executive function difficulty?
- Does the student generalize, that is, use the strategy in different scenarios?
- Has the target executive function deficit improved since the student started using the strategy?

We can answer these questions by completing the **Final Assessment of The Strategy**. A final assessment of the strategy can be used to analyze all the data collected, evaluate Carlos's success, and evaluate the effectiveness of the strategy. *A blank template of the* Final Assessment of The Strategy *can be found in Appendix 1.13, and blank templates, modifiable versions of materials, and strategy cards can be found at http://resources.corwin.com/ExecutiveFunctioning.*

Review the data recording tool and completed Sample Template for Final Assessment of the Strategy to determine the following:

- Does the student use the strategy in the noted area of executive function difficulty?
  - Yes, Carlos consistently uses the strategy and feels the strategy has helped him. He understands that using the strategy makes him less anxious since he is following what everyone is saying and is able to take notes.
- Does the student generalize?
  - Carlos has started to use this strategy across settings. This decision was made by him because he recognized the positive results when he used the SLANT strategy.
- Has the noted executive function deficit improved since the student started using the strategy?
  - Yes, it appears that Carlos's ability to positively interact has improved since he has decreased incidents of feeling anxious about losing focus on what the speaker is saying.

Conclusion: Overall, based on the data, he has shown an increase in using the SLANT Strategy. It appears the SLANT Strategy is increasingly being used and working for Carlos. He will use it independently.

Sample Template for Final Assessment of the Strategy

Date: 12/10/16

Name of Student: Carlos

Executive Function(s) Being Addressed: Attending, Initiating, and Focusing

☑ **Intervention Implemented? (Describe the Strategy and How It Is Being Used)**

SLANT (Sit, Lean, Activate, Note, and Track) Strategy

When Carlos is sitting in class, he can use this strategy to help him attend and focus. When he feels he is losing focus, he can refocus by using SLANT to get back on track.

☑ **Strategy Used From:** 11/11/16   **To:** 12/10/16

☑ **UDL-EF Process Used:**

- Completed Executive Function Planning Chart
- Thought through Selecting a Strategy for the Student While Integrating UDL Chart
- Created with student a Strategy Implementation With a Focus on UDL and Metacognition Chart
- Field-tested the SLANT Strategy
- Created strategy card for SLANT Strategy and placed in Carlos's business card holder
- Finalized SLANT Strategy and Selected this Strategy for Carlos
- Taught the strategy and kept data of usage
- Made revisions as necessary

☑ **Data for Measured Results:** Nine days of data. See completed SLANT Strategy Charts and Bar Graph.

☑ **Anecdotal Report of Results:**

- Carlos liked using the SLANT Strategy. He found it easy to remember and the strategy process easy to implement.
- He stated that he now has better control of his attention and is able to complete structured notes.
- He suggested that he implement this strategy across settings.
- He likes it when teachers commend him for his attention and structured notes showing he has focused on what they were saying.

☑ **Review of Results:**

- Enjoyed collecting and after analyzing the data. This gave him an awareness of his attention and focus and an opportunity to assume responsibility for his learning.
- Consistently uses strategy and has recognized its success in helping him use metacognition and think about his attention and focus
- Continues to increase use of strategy across settings

☑ **Summary Report on Game Plan Progress:**

The SLANT Strategy has helped Carlos to achieve **Goal 1:** "I would like to be able to attend to the speaker and focus on what he or she is saying." *Accomplished 12/10/16.*

(**NOTE:** Goals 2 and 3 on Carlos's Game Plan will be addressed later once Carlos has mastered and generalized goal 1.)

Summary Report on Implications of Strategy Use on Attending, Initiating, and Focusing: Carlos uses the SLANT Strategy consistently in social studies class and has started to use this strategy across settings. The strategy has helped to improve Carlos's attitude toward school and his rapport with his social studies teacher has also improved.

Step 7

Revisit the Game Plan to determine whether the student's goals have been met. Once a goal has been met, have the student write a Success Plan.

The purpose of the Success Plan is to outline the steps the student will follow as he or she transitions to using the strategy independently, as well as generalizing the strategy to other settings. The Success Plan assists the student in advocating for his or her needs.

To determine whether Carlos's first goal has been met, look at the data for the entire period he has been using the strategy. Review the data with him and discuss with him the following key questions:

- Does he feel the use of the strategy is helping? Do the data support this perception?
  - Carlos feels the SLANT Strategy is helping, and the data collected for nine days supports this.
- Does he feel it would be beneficial to continue use of this strategy?
  - Carlos would like to continue to use this strategy. He likes that when he controls when he attends to the speaker and focuses on what the speaker says, he is able to complete his structured notes. (Goals 2 and 3 will be considered separately.)
- Does he feel ready to move on to another goal for this executive function?
  - Carlos feels ready to work on goal 2 while he continues to work on generalizing goal 1 across settings.

After each goal on the student's Game Plan has been met, help him write a personal Success Plan to communicate what he plans to do to have a successful school year and self-advocate for the assistance he will need to help him on this journey toward success. This should identify to the following:

- What I want to do next
- Difficulties I may have
- Strategies I can use to help myself
- What the teacher can do to help

Below is the sample template for Carlos's Attending, Initiating, and Focusing, goal 1. *A template for this chart is found in Appendix 1.14 and blank templates, modifiable versions of materials, and strategy cards can be found at http://resources.corwin.com/ExecutiveFunctioning.*

FIGURE 4.14 Sample Success Plan for Carlos (Attending, Initiating, and Focusing, Goal 1)

What I Want to Do Next

I would like to be able to control paying attention to the speaker and focusing on what is being said.

Difficulties I May Have

- *I may start out paying attention and focusing on what the speaker is saying but lose attention later.*
- *I will have difficulty taking notes without a structured notes template to fill in as the speaker talks.*

Strategies I Can Use to Help Myself

- *To help me pay attention and focus on what the speaker is saying, I will need to use the SLANT Strategy.*
- *I will use my vibrating-watch timer.*

What the Teacher Can Do to Help

- *The teacher might need to provide key words for my structured notes page.*
- *The teacher might need to cue me if you notice I look like I am not using SLANT.*
- *I may need you to look over my notes to make certain I have all the information.*

WHAT HAPPENS THEN?

When all three goals on the Game Plan are met, it is time to identify new challenges on which to focus. The completion of the Game Plan is also a time to identify new challenges to work on. Few students experience difficulties in only one executive function. While Carlos will continue to work on strengthening his Attending, Initiating, and Focusing strategies, he and his teacher have decided he will also learn to strengthen his EF skills in other executive function areas.

Summary

The ability to attend, initiate, and focus is a lifelong skill set necessary for one to meet with success on a daily basis. For many students, the ability to efficiently and effectively use this skill set becomes a challenge. What further complicates this situation is the fact that the actions of attending, initiating, and focusing become interrelated as one sees a task from start to fruition. We acknowledge that a deficit in attending, initiating, and focusing looks different for each student, but most students with attending, initiating, and focusing deficits have difficulty attending to and sustaining their attention, getting started, focusing in on a specific point, participating in class discussions, and remaining on task. These difficulties and others have a negative impact on student achievement, behavior, and social/emotional well-being leading some into the Downward Spiral discussed in chapter 1. Supportive strategies both to improve and compensate for attending, initiating, and focusing deficits are available for teachers and students who work together toward student success. Checklist strategies to help attention and initiation, and strategies that help the student focus on a speaker are just a few of those described in this chapter. Supportive technologies, some of which are listed in the chapter, are available to assist in the improvement of EF skills. Finally, the 7-Step Model is presented in this chapter for a secondary student presenting difficulty in attending, initiating, and focusing, as well as other deficits. Through this example in attending, initiating, and focusing, you can see how these steps come together working with an individual student. For those using the 7-Step Model Modified, it is helpful to see and select the parts of the model that will fit your particular situation. As teachers, you know your student best and we encourage you to use your knowledge, judgement and creativity, regardless of whether you are using the 7-Step Model or 7-Step Model Modified. You are the one to best determine what your student's(s') program will look like, keeping in mind that ongoing assessment, determination of what is needed, the consideration of UDL and metacognition in the choice of strategies, the implementation of strategies, and the commitment of the student are all vital components for a successful implementation of attending, initiating, and focusing executive function skills training.

Practice

- Practice the 7-Step Model for attending, initiating, and focusing using one of the case studies in the Appendix. Note that there is another the case study for a secondary student, Emily. *(See Appendix 1.3.)* Carlos is the secondary student case study that we will focus upon in chapters 4 and 5. You may use Emily's case study to practice the 7-Step Model for prioritizing, organizing, sequencing, managing time, and planning.

- Note any challenges and successes you experienced and review the content in chapter 1 for background information relating to this chapter.

- Practice the 7-Step Model for one of your students.

CHAPTER 5

Social/Emotional and Inhibiting and Supportive Strategies

Reader Outcomes

☑ You will be able to identify factors that suggest problems in regulating the executive function area of social/emotional and inhibiting.

☑ You will be able to identify how difficulties in regulating social/emotional and inhibiting impact the student's behavior, social/emotional well-being, and academic success.

☑ You will be able to identify instructional strategies for teachers and learning strategies for students to use in addressing difficulty in social/emotional and inhibiting.

☑ You will be able to record student progress and make instructional changes based on the data.

WHAT IS SOCIAL/EMOTIONAL AND INHIBITING?

Social/emotional and lack of impulse control can lead students into the Downward Spiral at any point in their educational years. Students who have executive function difficulties in these areas are at risk for a variety of academic and behavioral consequences. Social/emotional behaviors are complex as illustrated in terms of the definition. Dawson and Guare (2009) define emotional control as "the ability to manage emotions to achieve goals, complete tasks, or control and direct behavior" (p. 16).

Kaufman (2010) specifies that "social/emotional behaviors are complex in terms of self-awareness, self-management, social awareness, and relationship management, [and] are all largely synonymous with social emotional regulation elements of executive function" (p. 205).

Meltzer (2010) stated, "The skill sets involved in emotional regulation include the ability to recognize and label one's own emotions, and as children mature to understand one's emotional triggers, manage the intensity of one's emotions, and knowing when and how to express one's emotions in various social contexts" (pp. 178–179).

Self-regulation, also known as response inhibition is vital in the development of appropriate social/emotional behaviors (Medina, 2018). It encompasses the self-control of one's impulses leading to a positive outcome. In this chapter, you will learn how your student monitors his or her social and emotional behavior. We define social/emotional behaviors as fluid, adaptable behaviors that allow someone to interact with his or her environment in an appropriate manner. These behaviors continue to develop throughout one's lifetime.

Some students who have difficulty in social/emotional and inhibiting executive functioning may have had a Functional Behavior Assessment (FBA) and may have a Behavior Intervention Plan (BIP). In many cases, the BIP will include strategies that also help students' executive function deficits. It is important that the BIP take precedence when working on these executive function skills. Since many students who have social/emotional issues also lack self-confidence, it is important to include self-confidence strategies in addressing this area. It is often difficult for these same students to self-advocate, because they often do not know what supports they need.

Diamond and Lee (2012) found that programs addressing executive function skill training improve executive functioning with young children. Two such programs are PATHS (Promoting Alternative Thinking Strategies) and CSRP (Chicago School Readiness Project). The PATHS program teaches children to stop, take a deep breath, state the problem and verbalize their feelings (metacognition), and determine a positive course of action. Much like the PATHS program, we address strategies in this book that teach children of all ages to inhibit reactive behaviors through metacognition, incorporate wait time as a positive plan of action is determined, and then execute the positive plan of action.

One's behavior and social/emotional well-being are impacted by deficits in social/emotional and inhibiting behaviors. Diamond and Lee (2011) suggest that control of one's social/emotional state and the ability to control inhibiting behaviors are core executive function skills. Children with deficits in the area of social/emotional and inhibiting tend to be less persistent, display more impulsive behaviors, have worse health, and in the long term, earn less and commit more crimes.

Pandey et al. (2018) conducted a meta-analysis of self-regulation interventions in children and adolescents ranging in age from birth to nineteen. A review of forty-nine studies, conducted from 1977 to 2017, led to the conclusion that the teaching of self-regulation skills universally resulted in positive outcomes in the areas of mental health, behavioral problems, social skills, and academic achievement. As well, there was a decrease in school suspensions and substance abuse.

Kaufman (2010) describes students with social/emotional difficulties as being reactive. They react more intensely to events and do not let the consequences deter their response. Although some students' executive function skill problems occur without any other disorders, many students with executive function difficulties also have other disorders.

Those most common include attention deficit hyperactivity disorder (ADHD), learning disabilities (LD), and autism spectrum disorder (ASD); however, there are other disorders that manifest themselves in the social/emotional area that include executive function skill deficits (Cooper-Kahn & Dietzel, 2008). For instance, some students who have executive function difficulties also have diagnosed disorders such as anxiety disorders. In this case, both the anxiety disorder and executive function issues need to be addressed. Sensory processing disorder, or even some sensory processing issues, may cause emotional difficulties in that the student may experience under sensitivity and react by invading others' personal space, for instance. Others may avoid the student as a result. If a student has over sensitivity, for example, he or she may exhibit exaggerated fears and anxiety over being touched leading to social issues. Some students crave touch, and that can create problems also.

WHAT DOES A DIFFICULTY IN SOCIAL/ EMOTIONAL AND INHIBITING LOOK LIKE?

Social/Emotional Behaviors

Students who have problems with social/emotional behaviors may

- not adjust emotions to the classroom culture,
- have an awareness that emotional behavior is inappropriate but be unable to control it and may often be remorseful.
- experience poor relationships with peers and adults.
- be depressed and unable to function.
- be the victim of others who treat him or her unkindly.

Inhibiting Behaviors

Students who have problems with inhibiting behaviors may

- react before thinking.
- constantly apologize for inappropriate behaviors.
- engage in off-task conversations and responses.
- not check work.
- not check to see if task or goal is attained.
- blurt out in class.
- say things that hurt or embarrass others.
- talk back to the teacher.
- be physical or aggressive with others.
- bully.
- be too shy to interact with others.

HOW DOES A DIFFICULTY IN SOCIAL/ EMOTIONAL AND INHIBITING IMPACT STUDENT ACHIEVEMENT?

The ability to control and shift emotions is critical for an effective classroom environment that supports learning (Meltzer, 2010). It is important to note that students with executive function deficits in this area find it very difficult to control their impulses. It is important that students with impulse control issues have external structure and support to help them improve. Self-regulation can be taught, but instruction must be purposeful and ongoing. As the student faces challenges, self-regulation can be applied to current situations.

Later in life, if this executive function area is not addressed, these unacceptable behaviors may persist in social and workplace settings. Here, the unacceptable behaviors of interrupting others while speaking, constantly changing plans for dinner or gatherings, expressing thoughts without filtering them first, or rushing to complete a work task and not attending to detail thus resulting in a product not meeting company standards. These could lead to difficulty making and keeping friends and getting along in the workplace. This may result in failure to gain a job or even loss of a job.

Durlak, Weissberg, Dymnicki, Taylor, and Schellinger (2011) conducted a meta-analysis of 213 studies that incorporated over 270,000 students and addressed social emotional learning and the impact it had on academic achievement. Of the 213 studies, 120 of them were conducted at the elementary level. The study revealed that students receiving social/emotional skill training showed an 11 percent gain in academics, appropriate behaviors, and ability to handle stress.

In terms of academic impact, social/emotional well-being affects student attendance, attention to the task at hand, willingness to persevere in the learning process, and falling behind the other students in terms of achievement. In terms of behavioral impact, the behaviors of students with difficulties in the social/emotional area often are perceived as misbehaving or not cooperating when in fact, the students are finding it difficult to regulate their social/emotional behaviors. It important to provide a frequent schedule of positive reinforcement as students learn to inhibit behaviors. As the student learns to inhibit unacceptable behaviors, the reinforcement schedule is gradually faded. Absence of attention to Social/Emotional and Inhibition skills may result in the student's entry into the Downward Spiral described in chapter 1.

SUPPORTIVE STRATEGIES WITH CARDS FOR SOCIAL/EMOTIONAL AND INHIBITING

The following are examples of supportive strategies to teach to students that can help them with goals related to the EF area of Social/Emotional and Inhibiting. It is important to note that all strategies will not work for all students. Step 3 in the 7-Step Model provides help in choosing appropriate strategies for students while considering UDL and metacognition, and step 4 will guide you through the teaching process. Steps 5, 6, and 7 address data tools for the assessment of strategy effectiveness, revision if needed, and the celebration of success with the strategy or strategies before moving on. ***Blank templates, modifiable versions of materials, and strategy cards can be found at http://resources.corwin.com/ExecutiveFunctioning.***

DRAGON QUILT STRATEGY

The Dragon Quilt is a strategy that supports a student's ability to be flexible. When a student encounters a situation that is "dragging them down," he or she writes a summary of this situation on a slip of paper and then clips the paper onto a quilt square. Quilt squares are made available to each student, and they keep them in their binder. Once the paper has been placed on the quilt, students are instructed to "move on and leave the dragging down" situation on the quilt. They can revisit the situation later when they are better prepared to deal with it.

Note: If quilt squares are not available, a picture of a dragon pasted on a piece of paper that has a place to write the issue that is dragging the student down may be used. Clips or Velcro can be used to secure the "issue" to the dragon picture.

Below is a sample strategy card for the Dragon Quilt Strategy.

FIGURE 5.1 Dragon Quilt Strategy Card for Elementary Students

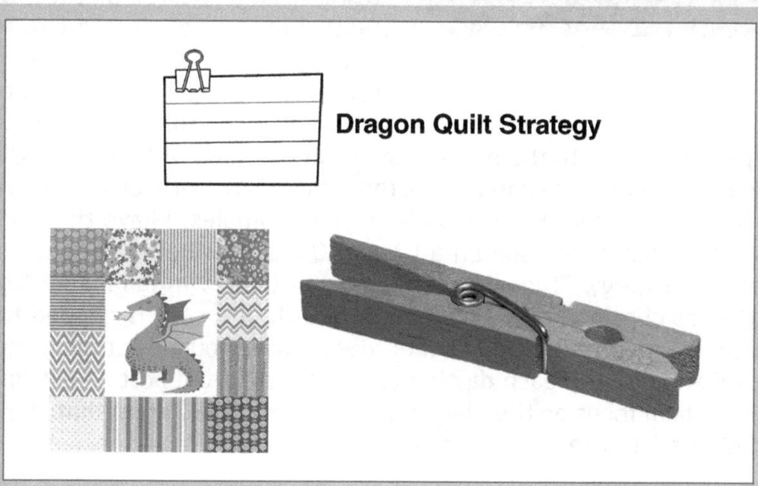

Dragon Quilt Strategy

1. When something is bothering or exciting me, I will write it down on a card and clip it to my dragon quilt.

2. Then, I will stop thinking about it so that I can complete my work.

3. I will revisit the card on my dragon quilt later when I have time to think about what is bothering or exciting me.

Teacher Testimonial from: Jennifer Ventura

Grade Taught: 1st

Executive Function Addressed: Social/Emotional

Strategy Name: Dragon Quilt Strategy

Strategy Designed for: Individual Student or Whole Class

Jenny Ventura

I have found the Dragon Quilt Strategy included in this book to be a good tool for my first-grade students to use when they cannot focus on their work because something is bothering or exciting to them. I have used this strategy for my entire class or for individual students. At the beginning of the school year, during our Morning Meeting routine, I tell my students about how they can use the Dragon Quilt Strategy when something is bothering them or is so exciting they can't do their work. Using a large poster of the Dragon Quilt, I model how to use this strategy. When modeling this strategy, I use examples of things that bother me and things that excite me. As I model these examples, I share with them how I can clear my mind of these thoughts so I can do my schoolwork. I state that I can look at the things I have written on my Dragon Quilt when I have free time. After I show and discuss my examples, I have the students share possible examples they might see on a Dragon Quilt. This helps the student to further "buy in" to the strategy. Students are then given their own laminated Dragon Quilt poster, one clothes clip, and one 3" x 5" index card. The card is clipped to the poster, and the poster is taped to the side of their desk. I have found that by giving the student only one card and one clip each day limits the student from posting extraneous information and helps them focus on the "big" issues. As well, I tell them that they can talk with me or another adult later about the issues they post.

WHAT'S ON MY MIND STRATEGY

Although secondary students can perseverate on issues that are "dragging them down," the Dragon Quilt Strategy is not developmentally appropriate. The What's On My Mind Strategy is a modified version of the Dragon Quilt Strategy that is designed for older students. With this strategy, the student records a few words on a small Post-it Note and places the note in an inconspicuous location of his or her choice. This issue of concern may then be revisited at a more appropriate time.

FIGURE 5.2 What's On My Mind Strategy Card for Secondary Students

What's On My Mind Strategy

1. When something is bothering me, I will write it down on a Post-it Note and place the note where it belongs.

2. I will stop thinking about it so that I am not distracted and can complete my work.

3. I will revisit the issue on the Post-it Note at an appropriate time when I can think about it.

Teacher Testimonial from: Elisabeth Halici

Grade: Middle School

Executive Function Addressed: Social/Emotional and Inhibiting

Activity Name: Think It, Become It Strategy

Strategy Designed for: Whole Class

As positivity is an extremely important part of my classroom, I started a **Think It, Become It Activity** board. This is a board that is utilized by students to write positive notes about each other. Students are able to write whatever is on their mind about our classroom at any time of the day. At the beginning of the year, I tell them about this board and model how to use it. Initially, I write, read and post notes such as, "Jim, thank you for helping Sam with his science experiment today. That was very kind of you." Some of the quotes this year stated, "Thank you Mrs. Halici for helping me with the math problem instead of giving up on me"; "Thanks M. for sitting beside me at lunch today." An example of the board is illustrated below.

FIGURE 5.3 Think It, Become It Activity

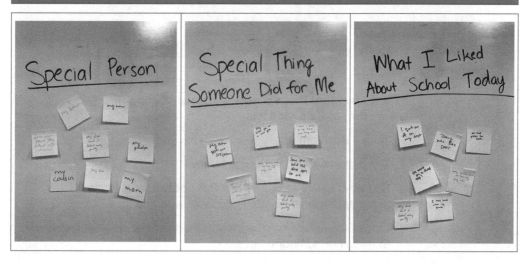

SOCIAL STORIES

Social stories are helpful to students who have social/emotional executive function deficits (Crozier & Sileo, 2005). Carol Gray (2000, 2002) originally developed social stories to use with children diagnosed with autism spectrum disorder (ASD). The stories are written about the student while stressing the student's strengths but also including behaviors with which the student has difficulty. The student participates as much as possible in the writing of the story. These stories have become such popular interventions that they are now used successfully with students who are not on the spectrum (Crozier & Sileo, 2005). Additional information can be found at the Gray Center website (http://thegraycenter.org/social-stories/carol-gray).

RAP STRATEGY

RAP (Respect And Perform) is a strategy designed for students to use when interacting with authority figures. The purpose of this strategy is to teach students how to perform an appropriate reaction to a situation where the student may feel spoken to harshly,

FIGURE 5.4 RAP Strategy Card for Elementary

RAP Strategy (Respect And Perform)

When I feel that that someone speaks to me unfairly or in a way that upsets me I will

1. Take a deep breath

2. Think about what I am going to say

3. Say what I want to say so it is **Respectful, and Perform** it using appropriate words, body language and tone of voice

4. Once I am away from the person I will vent my real feelings to myself or someone I trust.

FIGURE 5.5 RAP Strategy Card for Secondary Students

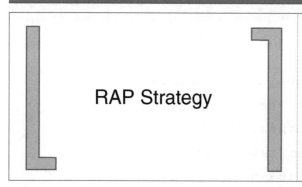

When I feel that I am spoken to harshly, verbally attacked, or judged unfairly, I will

1. Put my personal feelings aside
2. Think about what I am going to say
3. Deliver what I am going to say so it is **Respectful, And Perform** it using appropriate words, body language, and tone of voice
4. Once I am away from the person, I will vent my real feelings to myself or someone I trust.

verbally attacked, or judged unfairly. The student is taught to put personal feelings aside for the moment and respond to an upsetting, accusatory, or uncomfortable situation with respect by thinking about and delivering a response that is performed with the appropriate use of verbal and body language and tone of voice. Once the situation has been addressed, and the authority figure is no longer present, the student may vent personal feelings quietly to himself or herself or to someone he or she trusts. This strategy is taught through role playing various realistic scenarios encountered at school and work environments.

SELF-MONITORING CHUNKING STRATEGY

The Self-Monitoring Chunking Strategy is an important tool for students to gradually take charge of changing or maintaining a behavior. A source of anxiety for some students is completing their assignments. This strategy helps the student to divide or chunk an assignment into steps for completion thus concentrating on one step at a time rather than becoming overwhelmed by the whole. The student checks each completed step before moving to the next step. These can be custom made for a student or you may choose to use commercial items. The important point about self-monitoring is that ultimately the student will take more and more responsibility for monitoring himself or herself in various situations. This is just one example.

STA STRATEGY (STOP, THINK, ACT)

The STA strategy supports the student's ability to inhibit behaviors such as impulsivity, off-task conversations and inappropriate reactions. The first step to learning this strategy is for students to identify situations that trigger inappropriate reactions such as impulsivity. Students then role play these situations using the three components of the STA Strategy.

FIGURE 5.6 Self-Monitoring Chunking Strategy Card for Elementary Students

Self-Monitoring Chunking Strategy

☑ Step 1 for assignment

☑ Step 2 for assignment

☑ Step 3 for assignment

☑ Did I take my time?

☑ Did I check my work?

When I have an assignment to complete, I will

- break the assignment into tasks.
- check off the tasks as I complete them.
- take my time when completing the tasks and check my work.

FIGURE 5.7 Self-Monitoring Chunking Strategy Card for Secondary Students

Self-Monitoring Chunking Strategy

When I have an assignment to complete, I will

1. break the assignment into tasks.
2. estimate the time needed to complete each task and allocate that time.
3. check off the tasks as I complete them.
4. take my time when completing the tasks.
5. check my work and make any necessary revisions.

FIGURE 5.8 STA (Stop, Think, Act) Strategy Card for Elementary Students

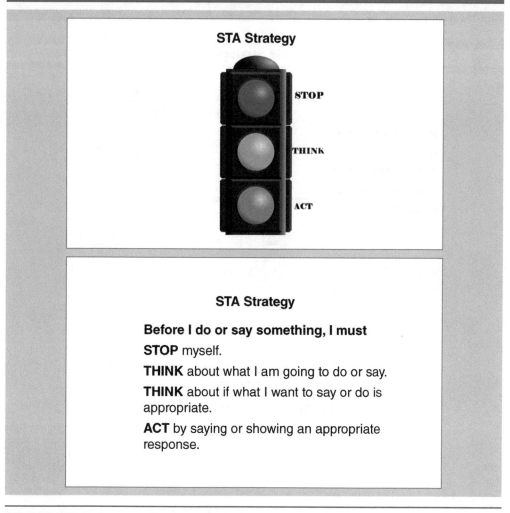

STA Strategy

STOP

THINK

ACT

STA Strategy

Before I do or say something, I must

STOP myself.

THINK about what I am going to do or say.

THINK about if what I want to say or do is appropriate.

ACT by saying or showing an appropriate response.

IMAGE SOURCE: Pixabay.com/clker-free-vector-images

FIGURE 5.9 STA (Stop, Think, Act) Strategy Card for Secondary Students

STA (Stop, Think, Act) Strategy

Before I say or do something I need to

STOP myself from reacting immediately.

THINK of an appropriate way to express what I need to say or do.

ACT on the appropriate response that I have thought about.

PAW STRATEGY

PAW (Put your hand in the air, Act appropriately, Wait quietly to be chosen to speak)

PAW is a strategy for elementary school students. This strategy supports the student's ability to share ideas in class in an appropriate manner. Role playing is essential for students to learn to use this skill instead of calling out.

PAW Strategy

Place my hand in the air,

Act appropriately,

Wait for permission to speak.

1. When I am in class and have an answer or comment to share, I will use the PAW Strategy.

2. I use PAW Strategy so that I give my peers a chance to share their ideas.

IMAGE SOURCE: iStock.com/annasunny

Teacher Testimonial from: Kim Hale

Elementary School Teacher

Executive Function Addressed: Social/Emotional and Behavior

Strategy Name: PAW Strategy

Strategy Designed for: Individual Student

During the first week of school, when we develop our class rules and identify and discuss class expectations, I share with my students that we need to be courteous to our classmates. One important way to show courtesy while working in a large group is to raise their hand and wait for their turn to speak. By third grade, the majority of my students already know and exhibit this courtesy, but once in a while I have a student who has difficulty waiting for his or her turn and continually "calls out" responses in class. I have had students who struggled with waiting for their turn to talk so I taught them the PAW Strategy. First, I met with the student and discussed the fact that he or she was not waiting their turn to talk and they agreed. They told me that they were calling out because they wanted to share their answer. I told them that I had a strategy that might help them not to call out as much. After discussing the PAW Strategy with them, they decided to try it. We practiced the strategy during class with me cueing by raising my hand each time I asked the class a question. Once they had an opportunity for practice, they used the strategy independently without cues. Each student kept his or her own data. Daily, they created a small card that they kept at their desk. Each time they raised their hand and did not call out, they would mark a tally on the card. They were permitted to mark the tally when they raised their hand and did not speak unless called upon. I frequently checked their data recording for validity and accuracy. One student successfully used this strategy from mid-October to early December. The only reinforcement he desired was to share his data with me daily. During that time, he recorded 1,296 times that he raised his hand and waited to be recognized instead of calling out. He shared that he did not need to record the number of times he raised his hand and waited any longer. I found there were few calling out incidences during the second semester.

SWT (STOP, WAIT, TALK) STRATEGY

SWT is a strategy that helps the student to self-regulate responses or thoughts that pop into his or her head. This strategy supports the student's ability to think before speaking and possibly choosing different words or deciding not to speak at all.

FIGURE 5.11 SWT (Stop, Wait, Talk) Strategy Card for Elementary Students

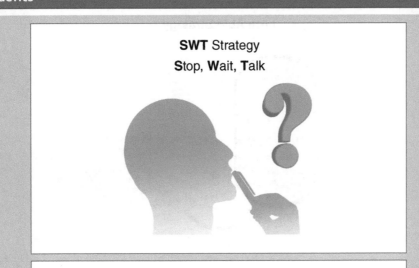

SWT Strategy
Stop, **W**ait, **T**alk

SWT Strategy

Before I say something I must

STOP

WAIT and Think about what I am going to say and how it will affect others

TALK to others in a kind, appropriate way.

IMAGE SOURCE: Pixabay.com/geralt

FIGURE 5.12 SWT (Stop, Wait, Talk) Strategy Card for Secondary Students

SWT (Stop, Wait, Talk) Strategy

Before I say something I must

STOP

WAIT and Think about what I am going to say and how it will affect others

TALK to others in a kind, appropriate way.

I AM ABLE STRATEGY

The I Am Able Strategy supports the elementary student's ability to initiate through the promotion of self-confidence and self-regulation. This potentially evidence-based strategy is particularly successful with students who are unwilling to take academic and social interaction risks. A decorated container serves as a visual reminder of challenges

FIGURE 5.13 I Am Able Strategy Card for Elementary Students

I Am Able Strategy

1. On a paper strip, I will write a task that is hard for me.
2. I will work on completing the task.
3. Once I complete the task, I can put the strip of paper in the can.
4. I can look at the strips in the can and think about all the hard things I was able to do.

SOURCES: Pixabay.com/clker-free-vector-images and Pixabay.com/stux

the student needs to address. The student decorates the can to his or her liking. Each time the student encounters a challenging academic or social situation, he or she writes this challenge on a strip of paper and places the strip on his or her desk. Once the student has successfully met this challenge, the strip of paper is then placed in the can to serve as a reminder of the student's accomplishment.

TAKE A BREATHER STRATEGY

This calming strategy provides a process an elementary or secondary student can follow to calm himself or herself without bringing undue attention to the situation. Often by diverting the student's attention from the explosive situation to following a process, he or she can get through the situation without saying or doing something regrettable.

FIGURE 5.14 Take a Breather Strategy Card for Elementary Students

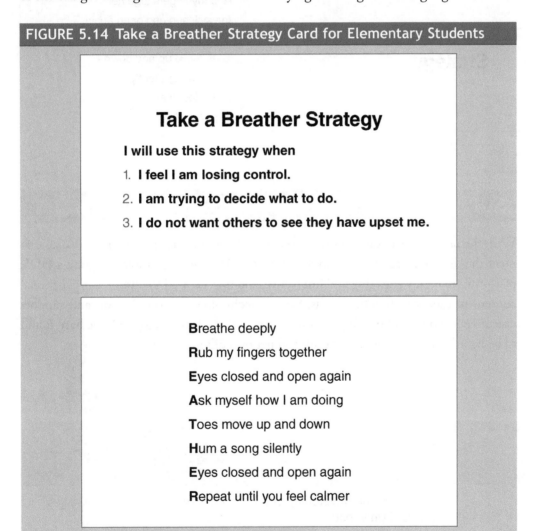

The Take a Breather Strategy involves the following sequence of steps:

1. Breathe deeply

2. Rub my fingers together

3. Eyes closed and open back up

4. Ask myself how I am doing

5. Toes move up and down

6. Hum a song silently

7. Eyes closed and open back up

8. Repeat until you feel calmer

**Take a Breather
Strategy**

Breathe deeply
Rub my fingers together
Eyes closed and open again
Ask myself how I am doing
Toes move up and down
Hum a song silently
Eyes closed and open again
Repeat until you feel calmer

SUPPORTIVE TECHNOLOGIES

With the onset of technology, new instructional tools and supports are now available to meet the diverse learning needs of all students. Many of these tools integrate a UDL platform, are highly engaging and interactive, and may be used to reinforce instructional content or executive function skills. We use technology to complement and support executive function skill training. Below are some of the technology tools we have found to be beneficial when teaching executive function skills and strategies.

TABLE 5.1 Sample Supportive Technologies

TECHNOLOGY TOOL CATEGORY (WEBSITE, SOFTWARE, APP)	NAME OF TECHNOLOGY	EXECUTIVE FUNCTION AREA ADDRESSED	AGE GROUP
Website	Center on the Developing Child Harvard University https://developingchild.harvard.edu/	All areas	Most ages
Website	Child Mind Institute https://childmind.org/	All areas	Most ages
Website	Common Sense Education https://www.commonsense.org/	All areas	Most ages

TECHNOLOGY TOOL CATEGORY (WEBSITE, SOFTWARE, APP)	NAME OF TECHNOLOGY	EXECUTIVE FUNCTION AREA ADDRESSED	AGE GROUP
Website	Intervention Central Response to Intervention — RTI Resources http://www.interventioncentral.org/	All areas	Most ages
Website	LD Online www.ldonline.org/	All areas	Most ages
Website	Understood.org https://www.understood.org/	All areas	Most ages
iPhone App	Choiceworks	Social/Emotional	Preschool to Grade 2
iPhone App	Social Stories	Social/Emotional	All ages
iPad App	Emotions	Social/Emotional	Preschool to Grade 6
iPad App	EQ Game	Social/Emotional	Preschool to Grade 8
iPad App	Feelings IAP	Social/Emotional	Preschool to Grade 4
iPad App	My W Days (Lite)	Social/Emotional	K to Grade 12
iPad App	RecoEmo	Social/Emotional	Preschool to Grade 4
iPad App	iMimic	Inhibiting	Grade 3 to adult
iPhone App	Impulse	Inhibiting	Grade 1 to adult
iPhone App	Impulse Break	Inhibiting	Grade 3 to adult
iPhone App	Impulse GP	Inhibiting	Grade 3 to adult

(*Continued*)

TABLE 5.1 (Continued)

TECHNOLOGY TOOL CATEGORY (WEBSITE, SOFTWARE, APP)	NAME OF TECHNOLOGY	EXECUTIVE FUNCTION AREA ADDRESSED	AGE GROUP
iPhone App	Memorise	Inhibiting	Grade 3 to adult
iPad App	Flash Tap Free	Inhibiting	K to adult
iPad App	Impulse	Inhibiting	Grade 1 to adult
iPad App	Impulse Break	Inhibiting	Grade 3 to adult
iPad App	Impulse GP	Inhibiting	Grade 3 to adult

CASE STUDY: CARLOS

We now look again at the case study of Carlos, (*see Appendix 1.2 for his full case study*), a fifteen-year-old student in the tenth grade with executive function deficits in several skill areas. In this chapter, the 7-Step Model for Executive Function Skills Training explained in chapter 1 will be applied to the area of social/emotional and inhibiting behaviors.

The questions that need to be considered to determine the appropriate executive function interventions that will support Carlos's learning needs are the following:

1. What are Carlos's executive function needs? (The step 1 process will answer this question.)

2. What are the strategies that can be used to support Carlos's executive function needs? (The step 3 process will answer this question.)

3. How does the effectiveness of the selected strategies in supporting Carlos's executive function need to be measured? (The step 4 and step 5 processes will answer this question.)

4. Do the selected strategies work? (The step 6 process will answer this question.)

The following example shows how to address one of Carlos's goals for social/emotional and inhibiting behavior difficulties using the 7-Step Model. *This model is not a lock-step procedure but merely a template to guide your thinking. Your flexibility and creativity in using this model to meet your needs and the needs of your student are encouraged.*

Step 1

Determine the student's EF deficits and note them in the Executive Planning Chart.

Assessment

As described in chapter 1, the assessment process is completed through reviewing the student's records, as well as through observations of the student, and interviews with the student, as well as his or her family members and other and previous teachers. Formal and informal assessments may also be used to help determine EF deficits. *See a blank template for the* **Sample Student Self-Assessment Tool** *in Appendix 1.15, and blank templates, modifiable versions of materials, and strategy cards can be found at http:// resources.corwin.com/ExecutiveFunctioning.*

Key Questions

1. **How are the student's strengths and difficulties exhibited in terms of executive functions (in this case social/emotional and inhibiting behaviors)?**
   After a thorough review of Carlos's records, including current test scores on standardized tests, report card grades, work samples, observations of Carlos in academic, extracurricular activities, social settings, and interviews with Carlos, Carlos's previous teachers, and his parents, the following strengths and needs in terms of social/emotional and inhibiting behaviors are identified:

Carlos's Strengths

- Carlos has a good school attendance record.
- Carlos enjoys and excels at playing sports, especially football. He is a good analytical thinker when it comes to the design and implementation of football plays.
- Carlos is a good analytical thinker during group discussions in class but needs processing time to express these thoughts.
- Acceptance and being valued by his peers is important to Carlos.
- Carlos has the ability to focus and attend to video games for hours.
- Carlos recognizes his difficulties and would like to do better with his school and home responsibilities.

Carlos's Difficulties

Carlos has social/emotional behavior difficulties.

- When struggling with a reading or writing assignment, Carlos quickly goes into a downward spiral and becomes frustrated, angry or shuts down. Sometimes he places his head on his desk and states he does not feel well.
- Carlos enters his classes that are co-taught with a general educator and special educator late because he does not want his football teammates to know that he receives special education services.

Carlos has inhibiting behavior difficulties.

- Carlos has difficulty verbally expressing himself which often is exhibited through his inappropriate comments. Carlos often acts before he thinks about the consequences of his comments or actions.
- When unable to complete a task, Carlos employs avoidance and deflecting techniques such as acting like the class clown, changing the topic, or engaging his peers in an off task conversation.
- Once he completes a task, he openly announces his progress to the class.
- While teachers and peers talk, Carlos frequently makes sighing noises and starts to daydream or doodles on a piece of paper.

Carlos also has difficulties in other areas of executive functioning as can be seen on the Executive Function (EF) Planning Chart. Below is a summary of all of Carlos's executive function difficulties. The following Executive Function Planning Chart specifies how Carlos's Social/Emotional and Inhibiting difficulties present. ***Blank templates, modifiable versions of materials, and strategy cards can be found at http://resources.corwin.com/ExecutiveFunctioning.***

TABLE 5.2 Executive Function (EF) Planning CHART

EXECUTIVE FUNCTION SKILL AREA	WHAT DOES THE DIFFICULTY LOOK LIKE FOR THIS STUDENT? (EXAMPLES)
Controlling Social/ Emotional and Inhibiting Behaviors	He is very chatty socially but sometimes refuses to participate in class discussions and seems to be daydreaming. He doodles instead of interacting during group work. He works hard to be liked by other students.
Working Memory	He has difficulty comprehending class readings. He has splinter skills in mathematics and has difficulty solving multistep problems. He gets confused when he has to remember what was said to him.
Prioritizing, Organizing, Sequencing, Managing Time, and Planning	He has difficulty organizing school materials and assignments, especially his backpack. He either rushes through an assignment or does not finish the task on time. His papers are sloppy and disorganized.
Attending, Initiating, and Focusing	He needs several reminders to get started on a task or assignment. He loses concentration very easily. Gives his work a "quick look over" instead of focusing on checking each response. Has difficulty focusing on the person talking.
Communicating, Cognitive Flexibility/ Shifting	He does not write coherently due to a lack of understanding language usage. His writing lacks sequencing of concepts and supporting details. He is extremely slow to move from one activity on to another. He finds it difficult to think about more than one thing at a time.

THE EXECUTIVE FUNCTION GUIDEBOOK

This chapter will focus on Carlos's executive function deficit in the area of Social/ Emotional and Inhibiting.

2. **Is there an executive function deficit in social/emotional and inhibiting?**
   Looking at the information presented in answer to question 1, it is established that, in addition to other EF deficits, Carlos has an executive function deficit in the area of social/emotional and inhibiting.

3. **How does the difficulty in social/emotional and inhibiting present?**
   The Executive Function (EF) Planning Chart (table 5.2) specifies how Carlos's social/emotional and inhibiting difficulties present. An IEP objective for Carlos might be written as Carlos will express himself appropriately on the first try with 90 percent accuracy.

Step 2

Review the EF Planning Chart with the student and start to develop a Game Plan.

This will guide the skill training for this specific executive function area, Social/ Emotional and Inhibiting. After you have the results of either formal or informal

---

FIGURE 5.16 Carlos's Game Plan Chart for the Executive Functions of Social/ Emotional and Inhibiting Behaviors

Student Game Plan for: Carlos

What I like to do and feel that I do well: I am great at football and want to play professional football someday. I am a good thinker and I am able to see many sides or solutions to things. I have great school attendance. I am the video game champion!

Goals for Improvement and Corresponding Actions

GOAL 1: I would like to be able to control when I speak and what I say when in class and talking with my friends.	GOAL 2: I would like to control my emotions and display appropriate behavior when I feel overwhelmed.	GOAL 3: I would like to appropriately react to situations that I find uncomfortable or a challenge.
Action 1: To be determined after completing step 3	**Action 2:** To be determined after completing step 3	**Action 3:** To be determined after completing step 3
Supporting Technology:	**Supporting Technology:**	**Supporting Technology:**
Date Goal Met:_____	**Date Goal Met:**_____	**Date Goal Met:**_____

---

assessments, discuss the results with the student and his parents. Once Carlos's areas of executive functioning weaknesses needed for immediate attention are identified, you can begin to develop Carlos's Game Plan. This will give Carlos an opportunity to "buy in" to the process. It enables the student to understand his areas of strength and difficulty. This understanding and awareness will later lead to student self-advocacy and greater independence in Carlos's learning process. Carlos's Game Plan includes his strengths, difficulties, goals for improvement, and strategies selected to enhance executive functioning through UDL and appropriate strategies. See chapter 1 for directions on starting a student Game Plan. *A blank* **Game Plan** *is provided in Appendix 1.9b and blank templates, modifiable versions of materials, and strategy cards can be found at http://resources.corwin.com/ExecutiveFunctioning.*

Step 3

Considering UDL and metacognition, select an EF skill-building strategy and get commitment from the student. Add the strategy to the Game Plan.

What are the strategies that we can use to support Carlos's executive function needs?

Think about how you would respond to the following questions:

- What are Carlos's learning needs and challenges in terms of UDL (Multiple Means of Representation, Multiple Means of Action and Expression, and Multiple Means of Engagement)? See table 5.2.
- What approaches and supports will be used to help Carlos access the lesson given his deficits in the skill area of Social/Emotional and Inhibiting?

  Examples include

  - modeling and role play appropriate social interactions,
  - modeling and role play appropriate body language,
  - teaching Carlos to use metacognition to think about, express, and reinforce appropriate social behaviors,
  - using metacognition to think about the consequences of actions taken,
  - using strategies to promote appropriate social/emotional and inhibiting behaviors,
  - providing a self-monitoring checklist,
  - scaffolding acceptable behaviors through cueing and prompting,
  - incorporating supportive technology,
  - reinforcing appropriate responses.

- What strategies will be taught to Carlos and added to his Game Plan?

  - Select from those described in the first part of the chapter, other resources, or those you have used previously. Discuss the strategy options with Carlos and guide him to select strategies that are appropriate and agreeable to him.
  - Use the **Selecting a Strategy for the Student While Integrating UDL Chart**, table 5.3, as a tool to prompt your thinking in terms of selecting the appropriate strategy that matches Carlos's learning needs and challenges. Written completion of this chart is not necessary. *A blank chart can be found in Appendix 1.10 and blank templates, modifiable versions of materials, and strategy cards can be found at http://resources.corwin.com/ExecutiveFunctioning.*

TABLE 5.3 Selecting a Strategy for the Student While Integrating UDL

Student: Carlos

Executive Function Deficit: Social/Emotional and Inhibiting

Game Plan Goal: Goal 1: I would like to be able to control when I speak and what I say when in class and talking with my friends.

MULTIPLE MEANS OF REPRESENTATION

Things for you to consider:

1. What information does the student already know?	2. What are the instructional goals for the student in relation to the executive function addressed?	3. What extended activities will be needed?	4. What enrichment activities can be implemented?	5. What will you need to incorporate when teaching the strategy?
Carlos wants to be a part of the classroom environment. Carlos wants to be accepted by his teachers and peers and hold appropriate conversations.	*Carlos should be able to control his impulse to speak and appropriately converse in the classroom setting and with his teachers and peers.*	*He will be taught using a multisensory approach that includes, role play, prompts and cues, metacognition, and checklists.*	*Carlos will be asked to demonstrate how to appropriately respond to and converse with peers and adults in a variety of settings.*	• *Connect prior knowledge, preteach prerequisite information.* • *Model and role play the expected process for responding to and conversing with adults and peers.* • *Provide multiple opportunities for practice.* • *Suggest technology to practice and reinforce the acceptable behaviors.*

MULTIPLE MEANS OF ACTION AND EXPRESSION

Things for you to consider:

1. How will you conduct preassessment, formative, and summative assessments for the student's learning?	2. What platforms will be permitted for the student to demonstrate mastery?
Carlos will be assessed during the preassessment stage in terms of how he converses during class and with peers (i.e., waiting to be called upon and then answering questions asked by the teacher, making inappropriate comments during instructional time, conversing with peers). *During the formative stage, Carlos will be provided with prompts and cues that are appropriate for conversations in the classroom and with peers, role play, and cues from the teacher. His success in controlling what he says in class and with peers and teachers and when he says it will be analyzed to determine whether outcomes are met.* *For the summative assessment, Carlos will have to appropriately converse within all classroom settings and with peers including waiting to be recognized before answering.*	*Demonstrate mastery through the ability to self-monitor supported by a strategy card provided to prompt and cue expected behaviors. When he meets the goal 1 criteria with 90 percent accuracy he will have mastered this goal.*

MULTIPLE MEANS OF ENGAGEMENT

Things for you to consider:

1. How will you teach the student in a manner that actively engages the student?

Engage student in creating goals that encourage success, using metacognition to self-monitor, and collecting data on effectiveness of strategy to help attain goals.

Role play information taught, check for understanding by allowing him to share his structured notes and video tape appropriate listening behaviors, provide verbal cues and a strategy card as a visual reminder.

(Continued)

TABLE 5.3 (Continued)

Based on your Considerations of the Principles for this goal, what strategy would you select that aligns with the three Principles and Align with UDL and the Strategy Selected?

Name of Strategy: *SWT Strategy (Stop, Wait, Talk)*

This strategy is selected because

1. Models the appropriate behaviors in a natural manner *(Multiple Means of Representation)*
2. Presents key concepts through demonstrations, visual prompts, cues from the teacher, color-coded checklists and role play *(Multiple Means of Representation)*
3. Provides an opportunity to demonstrate mastery by role playing, using discussion, using color-coded checklists, and responding to prompts and cues in a realistic, natural setting *(Multiple Means of Action and Expression)*
4. Allows Carlos to demonstrate mastery and effectiveness of the strategy through metacognition and self-monitoring *(Multiple Means of Engagement)*

- ○ Think about the components of **The Student Implementation of Strategy With a Focus on Metacognition and UDL Chart**, table 5.4. This chart should be completed with the student. It is a tool that helps the student to buy in to the strategy learning process. *A blank chart can be found in Appendix 1.11 and blank templates, modifiable versions of materials, and strategy cards can be found at http://resources.corwin.com/ExecutiveFunctioning.*
- ○ Once you and the student have selected a strategy, add the strategy name to the "Things I can do to help with my difficulties in school" column of the Game Plan for an elementary student or the "Action" column of the Game Plan for a secondary student.

Below is Carlos's completed Game Plan, which lists his goals and the strategies he and his teacher have decided he will learn to strengthen his EF skills in the area of Social/Emotional and Inhibiting behaviors.

TABLE 5.4 Student Implementation of Strategy With a Focus on Metacognition and UDL Principles

Student: Carlos

Executive Function Deficit: Social/Emotional and Inhibiting

Game Plan Goal: Goal 1: I would like to be able to control when I speak and what I say when in class and talking with my friends.

Strategy Selected: SWT (Stop, Wait, Talk) Strategy

METACOGNITION—QUESTIONS THE STUDENT THINKS ABOUT AND RESPONDS TO

Things for you to consider:

1. What am I supposed to do?	2. Why is this strategy important for me to use and how will it help me?	3. What are the steps of the strategy?
Use the SWT (Stop, Wait, Talk) Strategy.	*This strategy will help me to better control what I say by waiting and thinking about what pops into my head before blurting it out to my friends or during class. Waiting will help me to decide whether the comment I thought of is appropriate to share and, if appropriate, how and when I should share my thoughts.*	*SWT (Stop, Wait, Talk) Strategy* *Before I say something I must* • *STOP* • *WAIT and THINK about what I am going to say and how it will affect others, and* • *TALK to others in a kind, appropriate way.*

4. Is there technology I can use?

- *Yes You Can! (Common Sense Media: Mental Health Awareness for Mind, Mood & Wellbeing, iPhone App; https://www .understood.org/en/tools/tech-finder/find-tech/2018/01/17/18/17/mental-health-awareness-for-mind-mood-amp-wellbeing)*

- *ConversationBuilderTeen (Common Sense Media iPhone App; https:// www.understood.org/en/tools/tech-finder/find-tech/2016/03/02/19/04/ conversationbuilderteen)*

- *EQ Game—iPad App*

- *Flash Tap—iPad App*

- *Impulse GP—iPad App*

- *Mind Impulse—iPad App*

5. What should I think about when using this strategy?

- *I need to make sure that I consider the feelings of others, and the appropriate time and way to express my thoughts.*

- *I need to think about and carefully choose the words I share and share them at the right time.*

FIGURE 5.17 Carlos's Completed Game Plan

Student Game Plan for: Carlos

What I like to do and feel that I do well: I am great at football and want to play professional football someday. I am a good thinker and I am able to see many sides or solutions to things. I have great school attendance. I am the video game champion!

Goals for Improvement and Corresponding Actions

GOAL 1: I would like to be able to control when I speak and what I say when in class and talking with my friends.	GOAL 2: I would like to control my emotions and display appropriate behavior when I feel overwhelmed.	GOAL 3: I would like to appropriately react to situations that I find uncomfortable or a challenge.
Action 1: I can use the **SWT (Stop, Wait, Talk) Strategy**	**Action 2:** I can use the **Take a Breather Strategy**	**Action 3:** I can use the **STA (Stop, Think, Act) Strategy**
Supporting Technology: • Yes You Can! (Common Sense Media: Mental Health Awareness for Mind, Mood & Wellbeing, iPhone App; https://www.understood.org/en/tools/tech-finder/find-tech/2018/01/17/18/17/mental-health-awareness-for-mind-mood--amp-wellbeing) • ConversationBuilderTeen (Common Sense Media, iPhone App; https://www.understood.org/en/tools/tech-finder/find-tech/2016/03/02/19/04/conversationbuilderteen) • EQ Game—iPad App • Flash Tap—iPad App • Impulse GP—iPad App • Mind Impulse—iPad App **Date Goal Met:** 4/5/2018	**Supporting Technology:** Classroom clock or personal watch to time 2 minutes before responding. **Date Goal Met:**_____	**Supporting Technology:** Classroom clock or personal watch to time 2 minutes before responding. **Date Goal Met:**_____

Step 4

Design and implement data collection tools to measures success in the use of the selected strategy, teach the strategy, and give the student a strategy card.

The following illustrates how step 4 would be applied to the SWT (Stop, Wait, Talk) Strategy, which addresses Goal 1:

The data from step 1 show:

> We observed that Carlos does not filter what he says and often makes inappropriate comments or acts as the class clown which is disruptive to his peers and teachers. When he becomes angry or frustrated, he shuts out his environment by placing his head on his desk. These deflecting and avoiding behaviors result in Carlos not performing well academically or socially.

We talked with Carlos about his strengths and difficulties and started to develop a Game Plan.

Carlos understands that his inappropriate comments and behaviors in class impede his academic performance and appropriate social interactions with his friends. Carlos agreed that he was having trouble with participating in class. From this information, we developed goals with Carlos that addressed these concerns. Keeping his grades high enough for football eligibility is very important to Carlos.

The goals Carlos agreed to from step 2 are

Goal 1: I would like to be able to control when I speak and what I say when in class and talking with my friends.

Goal 2: I would like to control my emotions and display appropriate behavior when I feel overwhelmed.

Goal 3: I would like to appropriately react to situations that I find uncomfortable or a challenge.

The Strategy you and Carlos selected in step 3 is

SWT Strategy (Stop, Wait, Talk). Teach the SWT Strategy to Carlos. Model the steps of the strategy and incorporate metacognition. Provide motivation for the strategy such as use of a reinforcement and gain a continued commitment by the student.

Role play the use of this strategy using various scenarios. Engage the student in sharing situations that often result in his saying inappropriate things that he later regrets and role play the use of the SWT strategy under these circumstances. A strategy card can be used to reinforce recall of how to use the strategy. Each role play scenario should require the student to explain the strategy and how it helps him.

Give the student the SWT strategy card. Have the student practice the strategy using metacognition and referring to the strategy card as needed until he can use the strategy with automaticity. The strategy card summarizes the strategy and serves as a reminder of how to use it. It outlines the process and steps that need to be followed to successfully implement the strategy. To make the card, create or purchase a 3" x 5" business-size card. Place the name of the strategy on the front of the card, along with visuals if that is helpful for the student. Place a description of how to use the strategy on the back of the card. It is helpful if this description is stated in the student's own words. Check the description for accuracy. For the business-size strategy card, place the card in a clear business card pocket folder for future reference. This will provide Carlos with an individualized portable reference system of strategies that support his EF skills in the area of Social/Emotional and Inhibiting.

After Carlos has been taught the strategy, it is important for you as the teacher to determine whether the strategy is appropriate for his needs and if he is comfortable using the strategy. Not every strategy is appropriate for every student; therefore, it is important to evaluate if the selected strategy is suited for Carlos.

FIGURE 5.18 SWT (Stop, Wait, Talk) Strategy Card for Secondary Students

SWT (Stop, Wait, Talk) Strategy

Before I say something I must
STOP
WAIT and Think about what I am going to say and how it will affect others
TALK to others in a kind, appropriate way

As the student continues to practice the strategy, it is important to determine whether the strategy is appropriate for teaching the student the EF skill Social/Emotional and Inhibiting.

Design and collect data and revise as necessary.

Design the data tools, collect data on the success of the strategy, and revise as necessary. *Blank templates, modifiable versions of materials, and strategy cards can be found at http://resources.corwin.com/ExecutiveFunctioning.* This is the baseline phase of the data collection process. Once the baseline data has been collected, analyze the data and go back and make any necessary adjustments. For example, does the baseline data show that this strategy works for the student? Does the student need extra supports such as cues to remind her to use the strategy? Does the student need extended time to complete the steps of the strategy? After the student has been taught the strategy, it is important for you as the teacher to determine whether the strategy is appropriate for the student's needs and if the student is comfortable using the strategy. Not every strategy is appropriate for every student; therefore, it is important to evaluate if the selected strategy is suited to the student and make revisions as necessary.

TABLE 5.5 The Number of Carlos's Inappropriate Comments Baseline Data—Student Collected Data

<u>Student Name:</u> Carlos

<u>Data Collected By:</u> Student

Number of Times Inappropriate Comments Are Made in Class

	CLASS: *ENGLISH*	CLASS:	CLASS:	COMMENTS FROM STUDENT
Monday Date: 3/19	**Tallies:** IIIIII **Total:** 6			**English Class:** I was not aware that I said something inappropriate 6 times.
Tuesday Date: 3/20	**Tallies:** IIII **Total:** 4			
Wednesday Date: 3/21	**Tallies:** IIIIIII **Total:** 7			**English Class:** The class was too difficult.
Thursday Date: 3/22	**Tallies:** IIIII **Total:** 5			**English Class:** I can't help myself.

TABLE 5.6 The Number of Carlos's Inappropriate Comments Baseline Data—Teacher Collected Data

<u>Student Name:</u> Carlos

<u>Data Collected By:</u> Student

Number of Times Inappropriate Comments Are Made in Class

	CLASS: *ENGLISH*	CLASS:	CLASS:	COMMENTS FROM TEACHER
Monday Date: 3/19	**Tallies:** IIIIIIII **Total:** 8			**English Class:** Carlos's inappropriate comments required me to repeat information for the class 4 times this class period.
Tuesday Date: 3/20	**Tallies:** IIIII **Total:** 5			**English Class:** Better behavior than yesterday but still too many disruptions.
Wednesday Date: 3/21	**Tallies:** IIIIIIIII **Total:** 9			**English Class:** Carlos placed his head on his desk as soon as he was told that writing would be involved with today's class.
Thursday Date: 3/22	**Tallies:** IIIIIII **Total:** 7			**English Class:** Carlos called out inappropriate remarks 3 times today. He attempted to engage his peers seated around him in appropriate conversations 4 times this class

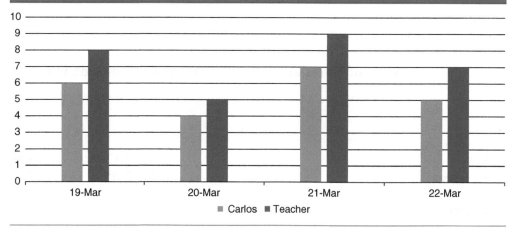

Analyze the baseline data and now you can respond to the following questions: Does the baseline data show that this strategy works for Carlos? Does Carlos need extra supports such as cues to remind him to use the strategy? Does Carlos need extended time to complete the steps of the strategy?

Carlos met with his teacher to review and discuss their data collection results. An analysis of the baseline data resulted in Carlos being surprised at the number of times he made inappropriate comments. He shared with the teacher that he did not realize the frequency of his inappropriate comments. When noting that the teacher data showed a higher frequency of inappropriate comments, Carlos stated that he was sometimes unaware of the fact that he had made an inappropriate comment. The SWT (Stop, Wait, Talk) Strategy was introduced to Carlos and he agreed to try this strategy.

Step 5

Continue to collect data for the student's use of the strategy.

Determine Carlos's success in learning and generalizing the strategy, table 5.7, Considerations for Ongoing Data Analysis Chart, provides points you as the teacher need to consider as you continue to analyze the data addressing the student's correct use of the generalization of the selected strategy. Once the baseline data has been collected and analyzed, and the decision has been made to use the strategy, there is need for further data collection to determine the successful use and generalization of the strategy. Table 5.7, Considerations for Ongoing Data Analysis Chart, provides points you as the teacher need to consider as you continue to analyze the data addressing the student's correct use and generalization of the selected strategy. Carlos's responses to the questions considered in table 5.7 are posted below. *A blank template of this chart is provided in Appendix 1.12 and blank templates, modifiable versions of materials, and strategy cards can be found at http://resources .corwin.com/ExecutiveFunctioning.*

TABLE 5.7 Considerations for Ongoing Data Analysis Chart

Student Name: *Carlos*

Strategy Used: *SWT Strategy*

Please, write yes, no, or N/A for Not Applicable.

___Yes___	1. The strategy is cited in the student's Ongoing Data Analysis.
___Yes___	2. The student understands the goal of using the strategy.
___Yes___	3. The student can explain what the strategy is and why he or she is using it.
___Yes___	4. There is a means of collecting data to measure the student's progress.
___Yes___	5. The tools to measure the academic or social/emotional area that the executive function deficit is impacting are appropriate.
___Yes___	6. Daily feedback is provided for at least one week when the strategy began.
___Yes___	7. The student is provided with reinforcement and knows his or her standing.
___Yes___	8. Data are analyzed with the student and the revisions are made as needed.
___Yes___	9. The selected strategy is appropriate for the student's needs.

Comments:

Carlos likes using the SWT Strategy. He likes how he can easily remember the steps to this strategy so that he does not have to have a visual reminder or cue that his peers can notice. He agrees this strategy helps him control what he says and he wants to practice this strategy until it becomes.

Select or design a data recording and analysis plan to be used or use the same data and analysis plan used for gathering baseline data. For the SWT Strategy, table 5.8 shows the data collection for Carlos's use of the SWT Strategy. **Blank templates, modifiable versions of materials, and strategy cards can be found at** http://resources.corwin.com/ExecutiveFunctioning Since Carlos enjoyed the baseline data collection process, it was decided to allow him to collect data on the usage of the SWT Strategy during English class. Carlos collected data on his use of SWT over a nine-day period (table 5.8).

Select or design a data recording and analysis plan to be used. For the SWT Strategy, table 5.8 shows the data collection for Carlos's use of the SWT Strategy. A blank template of the table is provided in the Appendix. Since Carlos enjoyed the baseline data collection process, it was decided to allow him to collect data on the usage of the SWT Strategy during English Class. Carlos collected data on his use of SWT over a nine day period.

TABLE 5.8 The Number of Times I Used the SWT Strategy—Student Collected Data

Student Name: Carlos

Data Collected By: Student

Number of Times I Used SWT Strategy in Class

	CLASS: *English*	CLASS:	CLASS:	COMMENTS FROM STUDENT
Monday Date: 3/26	**Tallies:** I **Total:** 1			**English Class:** I still forget to use the strategy but the teacher looks at me when I make an inappropriate comment. This lets me know that I need to use SWT.
Tuesday Date: 3/27	**Tallies:** II **Total:** 2			**English Class:** Better day. I remembered to use SWT **more.**
Wednesday Date: 3/28	**Tallies:** IIII **Total:** 4			
Thursday Date: 3/29	**Tallies:** IIII **Total:** 4			**English Class:** I am more aware of when I need to use the SWT strategy. Teacher told me I did a nice job.
Friday Date: 3/30	**Tallies:** IIIIII **Total:** 6			**English Class:** Great day!
Monday Date: 4/02	**Tallies:** III **Total:** 3			**English Class:** Kept forgetting to use SWT.
Tuesday Date: 4/03	**Tallies:** IIIII **Total:** 5			
Wednesday Date: 4/04	**Tallies:** IIIIII **Total:** 6			
Thursday Date: 4/05	**Tallies:** IIIII **Total:** 5			**English Class:** SWT is helping me. I am going to use this strategy in my other classes.

Reviewing all of this data, it appears that the SWT Strategy is working for Carlos and that he should continue to use this strategy as part of his daily interaction with others repertoire.

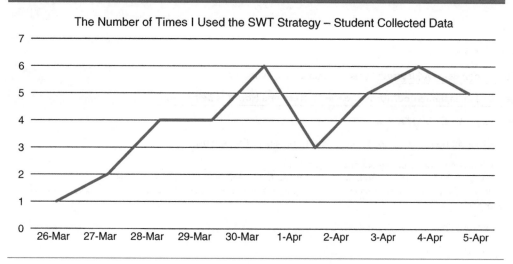

FIGURE 5.20 Carlos's Use of the SWT Strategy During English Class From 3/26 Through 4/05

The Number of Times I Used the SWT Strategy – Student Collected Data

Step 6

Analyze all the data collected and evaluate the student's success in using the strategy; update the Game Plan.

In analyzing Carlos's success in learning and generalizing the SWT Strategy and whether it has helped him, the overarching questions are

- Does the student use the strategy in the noted area of executive function difficulty?
- Does the student generalize, that is, use the strategy in different scenarios?
- Has the target executive function deficit improved since the student started using the strategy?

We can answer these questions by completing the **Final Assessment of The Strategy.** A final assessment of the strategy can be used to analyze all the data collected, evaluate Carlos's success and evaluate the effectiveness of the strategy. *A blank* **Final Assessment of the Strategy** *template can be found in Appendix 1.13, and blank templates, modifiable versions of materials, and strategy cards can be found at http://resources.corwin.com/ExecutiveFunctioning.*

Review the data recording tool and completed Sample Template for Final Assessment of the Strategy to determine the following:

- Does the student use the strategy in the noted area of executive function difficulty?
  - ○ Yes, Carlos consistently uses the strategy and feels the strategy has helped him. He understands that using the strategy makes everyone more comfortable that he is not blurting out the answers or unrelated comments.
- Does the student generalize?
  - ○ Carlos has started to use this strategy across settings. This decision was made by him because he recognized the positive results when he used the SWT strategy.

Sample Template for Final Assessment of the Strategy

Date: 4/10/18

Name of Student: Carlos

Executive Function(s) Being Addressed: Social/Emotional and Inhibiting

☑ **Intervention Implemented? (Describe the Strategy and How It Is Being Used.)**

SWT (Stop, Wait, Talk) Strategy

When a thought pops into Carlos's head, prior to speaking, Carlos must

- **STOP** himself from blurting out the thought and
- **WAIT** so that he can think about what he is going to say and how it will affect others.
- If deciding what he wants to say will have a positive effect on others, he will **TALK** to others in a kind, appropriate way.

☑ **Strategy Used From:** 3/26/18 **To:** 4/5/18

☑ **UDL-EF Process Used:**

- Completed Executive Function Planning Chart
- Thought through Selecting a Strategy for the Student While Integrating UDL Chart
- Created with student a Strategy Implementation With a Focus on UDL and Metacognition Chart
- Field-tested the SWT Strategy
- Created strategy card for SWT Strategy and placed in the business card holder
- Finalized SWT Strategy and Selected this Strategy for Carlos
- Taught the strategy and kept data of usage
- Made revisions as necessary

☑ **Data for Measured Results:** Nine days of data. See completed SWT Strategy Charts and Bar Graph.

☑ **Anecdotal Report of Results:**

- Carlos liked using the SWT Strategy. He found the strategy easy to remember and implement.
- He stated that he now has better control and does not blurt out whatever pops into his head.
- He suggested that he implement this strategy across settings.

☑ **Review of Results:**

- Enjoyed collecting and analyzing the data. This give him an awareness of his behavior and an opportunity to assume responsibility for his behavior.
- Consistently uses strategy and has recognized its success in helping him use metacognition and think about what he wants to say, if he should make the comment, and how he should say the comment.
- Continues to increase use of strategy across settings

☑ **Summary Report on Game Plan Progress:**

The SWT Strategy has helped Carlos to achieve **goal 1:**

"I would like to be able to control when I speak and what I say when in class and talking with my friends." *Accomplished 4/5/2018*

(NOTE: Goals 2 and 3 on Carlos's Game Plan will be addressed later once Carlos has mastered and generalized goal 1.)

Summary Report on Implications of Strategy Use on Academic Skills and Social Interactions: Carlos uses the SWT Strategy consistently in English class and has started to use this strategy across settings. The strategy has helped to improve Carlos's verbal and social interactions with his friends and teachers.

- Has the noted executive function deficit improved since the student started using the strategy?
  - Yes, it appears that Carlos's ability to positively verbally interact has improved since he has decreased incidents of blurting out and making inappropriate comments.

Conclusion: Based on the data, Carlos shows an increase in the number of times he correctly used the SWT Strategy over the course of nine days. Carlos continues to successfully use the SWT Strategy. Overall, he has shown an increase in using the SWT Strategy over a nine-day time frame. It appears the SWT Strategy is increasingly being used and working for Carlos.

Step 7

Revisit the Game Plan to determine whether the student's goals have been met. Once a goal is met, have the student write a Success Plan.

The purpose of the Success Plan is to outline the steps the student will follow as he or she transitions to using the strategy independently, as well as generalizing the strategy to other settings. The Success Plan assists the student in advocating for his or her needs.

To determine whether Carlos's first goal has been met, look at the data for the entire period he has been using the strategy. Review the data with him and discuss with him the following key questions:

- Does he feel the use of the strategy is helping?
  - Carlos feels the SWT Strategy is helping, and the data collected for nine days support this.
- Does he feel it would be beneficial to continue to use this strategy?
  - Carlos would like to continue to use this strategy. He likes that when he controls what he says and how he delivers his thoughts, his friends and teachers respond positively.
- Does he feel ready to move on to another goal for this executive function?
  - Carlos feels ready to work on goal 2 while he continues to work on generalizing goal 1 across settings.

After each goal on the student's Game Plan has been met, help him write a personal Success Plan to communicate what he plans to do to have a successful school year and self-advocate for the assistance he will need to help him on this journey toward success. This should identify the following:

- What I want to do next
- Difficulties I may have
- Strategies I can use to help myself
- What the teacher can do to help

A blank chart can be found in Appendix 1.14, and blank templates, modifiable versions of materials, and strategy cards can be found at http://resources .corwin.com/ExecutiveFunctioning.

What I Want to Do Next

I would like to be able to control when I speak and what I say when in class and talking with my friends.

Difficulties I May Have

I say things that pop into my head during class without thinking how what I say might affect others. I also get excited and blurt out answers or inappropriate comments.

Strategies I Can Use to Help Myself

To help think about what I say and how I say it, I will use the SWT Strategy. For this strategy, I need to Stop before I say something, Wait and Think about what I want to say, when to say it, and how it will affect others.

What the Teacher Can Do to Help

The teacher might need to cue me to use the SWT Strategy if I am having an "off day."

WHAT HAPPENS THEN?

When all three goals on the Game Plan are met, it is time to identify new challenges on which to focus. Few students experience difficulties in only one executive function. While Carlos will continue to work on strengthening his Social/Emotional and Inhibiting strategies, he and his teacher have decided he will also learn to strengthen his EF skills in other executive function areas.

Summary

The ability to regulate social/emotional behaviors is a lifelong skill set necessary for one to meet with success on a daily basis. For many students, the ability to efficiently and effectively use this skill set becomes a challenge. What further complicates this situation is the fact that the actions and social/emotional behaviors become interrelated as one sees a task from start to fruition. We acknowledge that a deficit in social/emotional behaviors looks different for each student, but most students with social/emotional behaviors deficits have difficulty with controlling impulses, making appropriate comments to peers and adults, controlling worries and fears, and having a positive self-concept. These difficulties and others have a negative impact on student achievement, behavior, and social/emotional well-being leading some into the Downward Spiral discussed in chapter 1. Supportive strategies both to improve and compensate for social/emotional behavior deficits are available for teachers and students who work together toward student success. Self-regulating strategies that help students to moderate social/emotional behaviors are described in this chapter. Supportive technologies, some of which are listed in the chapter, are available to assist in the improvement of EF skills. Finally, the 7-Step Model is presented in this chapter for a secondary student presenting difficulty in social/emotional behaviors, as well as other deficits. Through this example in social/emotional behaviors, you can see how these steps come together working with an individual student. For those using the 7-Step Model Modified, it is helpful to see and select the parts of the model that will fit your particular situation. As teachers, you know your student best and we encourage you to use your knowledge, judgement, and creativity, regardless of whether you are using the 7-Step Model or 7-Step Model Modified. You are the one to best determine what your student's(s') program will look like, keeping in mind that ongoing assessment, determination of what is needed, the consideration of UDL and metacognition in the choice of strategies, the implementation of strategies, and the commitment of the student are all vital components for a successful implementation of self-regulation of social/emotional behaviors executive function skills training.

Practice

- Practice the 7-Step Model for social/emotional and inhibiting using one of the case studies in the Appendix. Note that there is another the case study for a secondary student. You may use Emily's case study (Appendix 1.3) to practice the 7-Step Model for social/emotional behaviors.

- Note any challenges and successes you experienced and review the content in chapter 1 for background information relating to this chapter.

- Practice the 7-Step Model for one of your students.

CHAPTER 6

Communicating and Cognitive Flexibility/ Shifting and Supportive Strategies

Reader Outcomes

☑ You will be able to identify factors that suggest problems in the executive function skill of communicating and cognitive flexibility/shifting.

☑ You will be able to identify how difficulties in communicating and cognitive flexibility/shifting impact the student's behavior, social/ emotional well-being, and academic success.

☑ You will be able to identify instructional strategies for teachers and learning strategies for students to use in addressing difficulty in communicating and cognitive flexibility/shifting.

☑ You will be able to record student progress and make instructional changes based on the data.

WHAT IS COMMUNICATING AND COGNITIVE FLEXIBILITY/SHIFTING?

Communicating is multifaceted in that it encompasses both verbal (spoken) and written components. Approximately 8 to 9 percent of children struggle with a communication disorder (American Speech, Language and Hearing Association, 2014). As a teacher, it is important for you to understand the two components of communicating, the verbal and the written.

The first component verbal communication includes

- expressive language—the ability to share his or her thoughts and feelings through speech;

- receptive language—the ability to understand what others are saying and;

- social (pragmatic) language—the ability to have appropriate social conversation with others and accurately interpret the statements delivered by others (Understood, n.d.e). Social pragmatic language also involves the tone of voice, facial expression, hand gestures, and body language used when communicating (Women's and Children's Health Network, 2018).

"There are multiple causes for verbal communication problems. Those causes include physical factors (e.g., structural problems of the mouth, throat, and nose), syndromes or disabilities that cause delays in development (e.g., autism, hearing impairment, intellectual disability), acquired brain injury (e.g., damage to the parts of the brain that deal with communication), and communication problems (e.g., limited opportunities to talk with others)." (Women's and Children's Health Network, 2018)

The second component of communication involves written communication. Written communication is defined as " the process of communicating using printed symbols in the form of letters or visual characters, which make up words. Words are formulated into sentences; these sentences are organized into larger paragraphs and often into different discourse genres (narrative, expository, persuasive, poetic, etc.)" (American Speech, Language and Hearing Association, n.d.c). Written language includes two major processes that require students to use executive function skills. These processes include the following:

A student should

- **perform the writing process by thinking about** and **planning** what is to be written so that it will meet the specific audience needs or convey an accurate message, followed by the **organizing** of these thoughts in a logical, **sequential** manner, drafting these thoughts on paper, reflecting on what has been written, revising what has been written, and editing what has been written; and

- **compose the writing product by** selecting the correct words, creating correct sentence structure, and using accurate spelling, grammar, and punctuation (American Speech, Language and Hearing Association, https://www.asha.org/Practice-Portal/Clinical-Topics/Written-Language-Disorders/).

In summary, both verbal and written communication are complex processes that interrelate. There are multiple factors identified that impact the development of both processes. To further complicate the communication processes is the ability to employ cognitive flexibility/shifting to problem solve and switch gears.

Medina (2018) identifies cognitive flexibility/shifting as "the ability to adapt to changing circumstances in a tractable manner. This includes perspective switching—the ability to see objective problems (or subjective people) from multiple perspectives or points of view" (p. 19).

Rosen emphasizes the importance of cognitive flexibility/shifting in that it is one of the three main executive functions of the brain's command center. The other two main executive functions are working memory and inhibitory control. Cognitive flexibility/shifting allows us to shift gears and solve problems (Rosen, n.d.). The ability to problem solve and see things from a different perspective affects the communication process and one's actions as well.

WHAT DOES A DIFFICULTY IN COMMUNICATING AND COGNITIVE FLEXIBILITY/SHIFTING LOOK LIKE?

Communicating—Verbal

Students who have problems with verbal communication

- have a limited vocabulary that is not age appropriate.
- not use verbal language to make wants and needs known.
- talk in phrases or very short sentences.
- have difficulty verbally expressing feelings.
- may not understand what is being meant by the speaker.

Communicating—Written

Students who have problems with written communication may

- not write clearly and succinctly.
- have visual-spatial relationship difficulties.
- have difficulty communicating ideas in writing.
- have difficulty initiating a writing activity.
- demonstrate difficulty putting their thoughts on paper.
- find writing frustrating.
- have difficulty with grammar and the mechanics of writing.

Cognitive Flexibility/Shifting

Students who have problems with cognitive flexibility/shifting may

- find it difficult to change activities.

- find it difficult to multitask.

- become confused or upset when asked to change locations.

- tend to perseverate on routines and objects.

- find it difficult to shift from one thought to another when reading, writing, or solving a mathematics problem.

HOW DOES A DIFFICULTY IN COMMUNICATING AND COGNITIVE FLEXIBILITY/SHIFTING IMPACT STUDENT ACHIEVEMENT?

Communication is an important part of a child's development. The ability to effectively use communication skills crosses all areas of executive functioning. Academic proficiency is developed through a student's abilities and skills. Communication skills involve listening, reading, writing, and speaking. All these skills are managed through executive functioning. Students with communication difficulties struggle since communication is the basis for all learning (Newhall, 2012). Hulme and Snowling (2014) emphasize that the relationship between spoken and written communication and reading is strong.

In terms of communication, students need to be able to retrieve stored information from working memory accurately. Social/emotional control and self-monitoring often require a student to appropriately verbalize needs and feelings. When this is difficult, the student may act out behaviorally or become less communicative or noncommunicative with others. It is difficult to make and maintain relationships with other students when the communication is not effective. The executive function of planning and organizing in both receptive and expressive language requires the ability to process and produce written and verbal communication to successfully complete tasks and meet deadlines. Students with communication problems are often working with other professionals such as speech and language pathologists. Students with communication difficulties have, from an early age, a lack of the opportunity to let others know their wishes, what they know, how they feel, and how to get what they need. This often puts them in a Downward Spiral as explained in chapter 1. When they receive early intervention, they are less likely to enter the Downward Spiral. Some students will use assistive technology, and others will use technology available to the whole class.

The actual words used comprise only 5 percent of the of the communication process. Another 45 percent of effective communication incorporates one's tone of voice, inflection and other elements of voice, and 50 percent encompasses body language, eye contact, body movements, and facial expression (Business Dictionary, 2018). As a teacher, you need to consider and think about the role nonverbal communication plays when interacting with your students; as well, your students need to be aware of this element and its impact on the communication process.

Adults with communication issues may find it difficult to make and maintain friends. Job interviews present a major challenge as it is difficult for a person with these issues to make a good impression. The person interviewing may be qualified for the position but may not project that set of skills needed for the position. As a communicator, some of the adults with these issues are unable to clearly convey ideas through verbal or written communication. An individual with a communication deficit may be misunderstood by the recipient due to the words selected or tone of the communication. Some adults with communication deficits do not read body language and tend to make serious social errors.

According to Cooper-Kahn and Foster (2013) shifting is "the ability to 'change gears' to move freely from one situation to another, and to think flexibly in order to respond appropriately to a new or unexpected situation" (p. 11). All these situations require preparation for the student to accept and acclimate to these changes. Without the skill necessary to make smooth transitions, students may find themselves always behind in starting and ending activities. When activities are not completed, the student has not had the opportunity to participate in all the learning opportunities available to him or her. This often results in lower school academic achievement.

The inability to use cognitive flexibility/shifting skills can have a serious impact on learning. Cognitive flexibility/shifting often causes the student to unlearn a familiar process. Amanda Morin (n.d.) identifies six ways in which the executive function skill of cognitive flexibility/shifting impacts student learning. A student who does not have the skill of cognitive flexibility/shifting may have the following problems:

1. Have difficulty understanding that there is more than one way to complete a specific task. As the student gets older, this problem may impede the taking on of new responsibilities and jobs.

2. Have difficulty comprehending what is read and not grasp the key information and supporting details. Also, there might be difficulty in understanding the perspectives of others. This makes it a challenge for the student to understand the perspectives of characters in a story. Finally, the student may interpret a passage literally and have difficulty understanding the use of homophones and idioms.

3. Find writing a challenge due to the flexibility required by the process. The student may have difficulty in choosing a topic and providing the details of supporting ideas, using the correct choice of words, and using correct grammar and punctuation.

4. Experience learning the rules of language a challenge in terms of tense usage and rule exceptions. The student may also find it difficult to learn a foreign language since the letters can have different sounds and the sentence structure might differ from English.

5. Have difficulty in math due to a lack of understanding of key phrases such as "How many in all?" or may not understand that there can be more than one way to solve a problem.

6. Find homework and studying a challenge in that it requires the student to switch between subjects. As well, the student might have it difficult to determine what information is important and what is not when studying for a test.

Communicating and cognitive flexibility/shifting deficits can be improved through the learning and use of supportive executive function strategies. We have found students who improve their cognitive flexibility and ability to shift are more comfortable with the demands of the school environment and the learning process. In a safe, supportive environment instead of fearing the consequences from making a mistake, students can experience learning from mistakes. They are willing to take risks, try different ways of problem solving, and are able to accept changes in schedules and events.

SUPPORTIVE STRATEGIES WITH CARDS FOR COMMUNICATING AND COGNITIVE FLEXIBILITY/ SHIFTING

The following are examples of supportive strategies to teach to students that can help them with goals related to the EF area of communicating and cognitive flexibility/ shifting. It is important to note that all strategies will not work for all students. Step 3 in the 7-Step Model provides help in choosing appropriate strategies for students while considering UDL and metacognition, and step 4 will guide you through the teaching process. Steps 5, 6, and 7 address data tools for the assessment of strategy effectiveness, revision if needed, and the celebration of success with the strategy or strategies before moving on. *Blank templates, modifiable versions of materials, and strategy cards can be found at http://resources.corwin.com/ExecutiveFunctioning.*

VERBAL COMMUNICATION STRATEGIES

Dreamweaver Strategy

The Dreamweaver Strategy is an activity that encourages students to verbally share information about themselves with others and is applicable for students with verbal communication difficulties.

All About Me Strategy

The All About Me Strategy is a social communication strategy that provides students with an opportunity to describe themselves. Students can share information, verbally or in writing, about the areas in which they excel, what they like to think about, what subject they like, and what bothers them.

This strategy is a good tool to be used as an ice breaker or as a template for using appropriate pragmatics when conversing. The strategy can be adapted for use by various age groups.

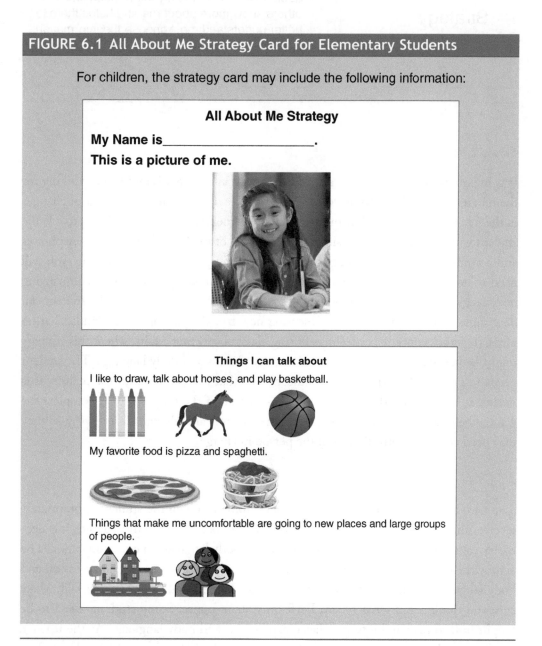

FIGURE 6.1 All About Me Strategy Card for Elementary Students

For children, the strategy card may include the following information:

All About Me Strategy

My Name is_____.
This is a picture of me.

Things I can talk about

I like to draw, talk about horses, and play basketball.

My favorite food is pizza and spaghetti.

Things that make me uncomfortable are going to new places and large groups of people.

SOURCES: iStock.com/asiseeit; Pixabay.com/openclipart-vectors; Pixabay.com/clker-free-vector-images; and Pixabay.com/ricinator

FIGURE 6.2 All About Me Strategy Card for Secondary Students

All About Me
Strategy

All About Me Strategy
This is my opportunity to share information about myself. Sharing my information lets others know more about me and helps them to better understand me. I choose the information that I wish to share.

Say the Message Strategy

It is important for students to learn how to let you know what is and is not working for them in terms of understanding content taught, rules that need to be followed, or changes in the school environment. The purpose of the Say the Message Strategy is to provide the student with a model for expressing what is and is not working. Appropriate key phrases and accompanying body language are practiced through role playing. Initially, you will need to determine the situations where the appropriate key phrases and accompanying body language are needed and model the expected behaviors. Eventually, the student can determine other situations such as meeting new friends; playing with friends; sharing ideas, thoughts, concerns, or feelings during class; or greeting adults, where this strategy might be needed and practice the expected key phrases and body language. The student needs to practice this type of communication so that it is delivered in the manner it is meant. It is important that discussion or instruction of the proper way to complete the wanted behavior precedes the role play. Some students are reluctant to role play, so they may need personal motivation from the person in charge.

LLUMP the Message Strategy

The LLUMP the Message Strategy uses an acronym to help the student appropriately receive, understand, and react to a message. As described earlier in this chapter, it is necessary to teach some students the importance of body language in communication. The acronym LLUMP stands for **L**isten to the message, **L**ook at the facial expression and body language of the person saying the message, **U**nderstand what is being said, **M**ake sure you think about what to say, **P**erform your response. Some students need to be taught how to read and interpret facial expressions and body language. As the teacher, you need to determine which facial expressions and body language stances the student will likely have to interpret such as happy, confused, sad, or worried. The next step is to have the student learn and interpret these facial expressions and body language stances. You then practice through role play the key phrases, accompanying facial expressions and body language, and responses he or she can perform when receiving a message. It is important that you model both inappropriate and appropriate ways to perform the response to the message so that the student is able to experience the difference.

FIGURE 6.3 Say the Message Strategy Card for Elementary Students

Say the Message Strategy

I need to tell you something.

When things are working well for me, I need to share this with my teacher. Key Phrases and body language:

- Smile and say, "I understand.", "This is easy.", "This helps me a lot."

When things are not working well for me, I need to share this with my teacher. Key Phrases and body language:

- Look at my teacher and calmly say, "I do not understand.", "I do not like doing this.", "This is too hard.", "Can you please help me?", "I need help."

IMAGE SOURCE: iStock.com.shironosov

FIGURE 6.4 Say the Message Strategy Card for Secondary Students

Say the Message Strategy

Say the Message

When things are working well for me, I need to share this with my teacher. Key Phrases and body language:

- Smile and say, "I understand.", "This is easy.", "This helps me a lot."

When things are not working well for me, I need to share this with my teacher. Key Phrases and body language:

- Look serious or concerned and calmly say, "I do not understand.", "I do not like doing this.", "This is hard", "Can you please help me?", "I need help."

FIGURE 6.5 LLUMP Strategy Card for Elementary Students

LLUMP Strategy

When someone speaks to me I need to

- **L**isten to the person
- **L**ook at the face and body language of the person to decide if they are happy, worried, upset, etc.
- **U**nderstand what is being said
- **M**ake sure I think about my response
- **P**erform my response

IMAGE SOURCE: iStock.com/ridofranz

FIGURE 6.6 LLUMP Strategy Card for Secondary Students

LLUMP Strategy

- **L**isten to the person
- **L**ook at the face and body language of the person to decide if he or she is happy, worried, upset, etc.
- **U**nderstand what is being said
- **M**ake sure I think about my response
- **P**erform my response

Self-Advocacy Story Strategy

Students who have difficulty communicating often find it difficult to advocate for themselves. For example, they might feel that a rule might be unfair but they do not know how to explain this feeling. They may withdraw, act out, or remain passive in a situation that could be resolved through self-advocacy. Self-advocacy allows the student to share in an appropriate manner what they do well, what they have difficulty with, and what assistance they might need to be successful. The Game Plan and Success Plan are tools where the student can self-advocate. Students need opportunities to practice self-advocating and the Self-Advocacy Story Strategy allows them to practice this important skill. The student's picture is included as part of the story as well as a self-made drawing. For secondary students, it is appropriate to have them identify the things they wish to share in a bulleted list instead of using a poem structure.

FIGURE 6.7 Self-Advocacy Story Strategy Activity for Elementary Students

Kristy: My Self-Advocacy Story

Hello, my name is Kristyne but my friends call me Kristy. I am in the 4th grade.

Something special about me is that I am the Oreo Cookie Stacking Champion of Upstate New York. I played Sarah in our school play, *Guys and Dolls*.

My favorite color is blue. I can do many things well. Some of these things are singing, gymnastics, roller blading, drawing, and reading.

Math problems, writing, and following directions that have lots for me to do are hard for me. I do not like these things because they make me feel not smart.

It helps me in class when I see and hear information. It also helps if the important parts of the information are in highlighted in blue. When my teacher gives simple two-step directions, it makes it easier for me to remember what I have to do. Sometimes I need the teacher or an elbow buddy to remind me what I need to do for my work or to check my work and make sure that I am doing it right. Sometimes I need extra time to finish my work.

My favorite things are singing and reading. I learn the words to new songs quickly and sing them all day.

IMAGE SOURCE: iStock.com/wavebreakmedia

FIGURE 6.8 Self-Advocacy Story Strategy Card for Elementary Students

Self-Advocacy Story Strategy

I want people to know

- my name,
- something special about me,
- things I do well,
- things I find difficult,
- how I learn best,
- some of my favorite things to do.

IMAGE SOURCE: iStock.com/tuktukdesign

FIGURE 6.9 Self-Advocacy Strategy Card for Secondary Students

Self-Advocacy Strategy

I want people to know

- my name,
- something special about me,
- things I do well,
- things I find difficult,
- how I learn best,
- some of my favorite things to do.

WRITTEN COMMUNICATION STRATEGIES

Written communication can be impacted by difficulties in the executive function area of communication, and it is important to note that difficulties in many of the executive functions can lead to poor written communication. For instance, planning and organization of what is being written, remembering thoughts, prioritizing, and sequencing play an important role in communicating with others through writing. The elements of sentence structure, grammar, and punctuation are also important. The following are some strategies used to assist students as they develop notetaking and writing skills.

Simply Note It Strategy

The Simply Note It Strategy is designed to make note taking easier. This strategy can be used for note taking while reading or listening to a lecture. Students vertically divide an 8½" x 11" sheet of notebook paper into two columns, one two-thirds of the sheet and the other one-third. The columns are labeled Important Points as the first section on the left, and Questions I Have as the second section on the right.

FIGURE 6.10 Simply Note It Strategy Card for Elementary Students

Simply Note It Strategy

Important Points:	Questions I have:
- in 1776, colonists wanted to not be ruled by King George.	1. Who wrote this letter?
- Wrote a letter called "Declaration of Independence" (Declaration means: say or write something)	

I can use this strategy when taking notes.

• I need a piece of notebook paper and a pen or pencil.

• Fold the notebook paper into two parts vertically.

• Label columns.

• Take notes using bullets in first column.

• Write my questions in the second column and get answers.

IMAGE SOURCE: Openclipart-vectors

FIGURE 6.11 Simply Note It Strategy Card for Secondary Students

Simply Note It Strategy

I can use this strategy when taking notes.

- I need a piece of notebook paper and a pen or pencil.
- Fold the notebook paper into 2 long columns with the first one used for notes and the second used for questions.
- Label columns.
- Take notes using bullets in the first column.
- Write questions in the second column and get answers.

SOURCE: **COPS Writing Strategy Play** (LD@school, https://www.ldatschool.ca/the-cops-editing-strategy/)

The COPS writing strategy is presented in chapter 4. This strategy is based on having the student proofread the written document and edit it.

Teacher Testimonial from: Shannon Sullivan

Grade: Middle School

Executive Function Addressed: Written Communication

Strategy Name: COPS Skit

Strategy Designed for: Whole Class

I use the COPS Skit (Retrieved and copied from Pegasus@UCF, pegasus.cc.ucf.edu/~scec1050/cops.pdf) to review the purpose and steps of the COPS strategy. The students enjoy performing the skit below.

FIGURE 6.12 COPS Writing Strategy Skit (Pegasus@UCF, pegasus.cc.ucf.edu/~scec1050/cops.pdf)

COPS Skit

A Skit for a Writing Strategy (Pegasus@UCF, pegasus.cc.ucf.edu/~scec1050/cops.pdf)

Courtesy of the University of Central Florida/Cocoa Campus Student Council for Exceptional Children #1050, (2002). Authored by Dan Ezell, Colleen Klein, Terri Decker, Jennifer Golden, Linda Lanza, Linda Meints, Rose Ann Roth, Theresa Murphy, and Carolynne Spaulding.

Officer #1:	"Hi boys and girls, I'm Officer #1 and this is Officer #2."
Officer #2:	"We're the cops from Communication Station."
Officer #1:	"Your teacher has been looking for a way to help teach you good writing skills, so she called the cops."
Officer #2:	"Yes, and writing is one way of communicating. Instead of speaking words, you are writing words."

Officer #1:	"Cops do a lot of communicating. We do a lot of speaking and we do a lot of writing. As a matter of fact, any job you may choose when you grow up will require writing skills, because every job has some writing involved."
Student #1:	"Are you going to write us a ticket?"
Officer #2:	"You'll get a ticket all right, but not the kind of ticket you're thinking of.

We're going to give you all a ticket with the C.O.P.S. strategy on it so that you can become good writers. |
Officer #1:	You see, cops is spelled "cops" and the letters c, o, p, and s each stand for an important item that all good papers need to have. The c stands for capitalization, o is for organization, p is for punctuation, and s stands for spelling. So, when you have to complete a writing assignment, call the cops!"
Officer #2:	"Let's go over them. The letter c stands for capitalization. Does every sentence start with a capital letter? Are all proper nouns capitalized? That is what you will look for after you finish an assignment. What does the letter c stand for everyone?"
All Students:	"Capitalization"
Officer #1:	"The letter o stands for organization. Are your paragraphs indented, is there space between your words, and is it neat? If your paper is organized, it makes it easier to read. What does the o stand for?"
All Students:	"Organization"
Officer #2:	"The letter p stands for punctuation. There are many types of punctuation that help the reader to make sense of what you are trying to say. Commas, question marks, exclamation points, and quotations are just a few. What does the p stand for?"
All Students:	"Punctuation"
Officer #1:	"And finally, the s stands for spelling. That's why your spelling tests are so important. What does the s stand for?"
All Students:	"Spelling"
Officer #2:	"So, anytime your teacher has you write an essay, a letter, or another type of assignment, just call the C.O.P.S."
Officer #1:	"Yes, and it's easy to remember. Did you notice that the first three words rhyme? They all end with "ation." Capitalization, organization, punctuation, and then there is spelling. Let's go over them one more time together, ready?"
Both Officers and all Students:	"Capitalization, organization, punctuation, and spelling."
Student #2:	"Have you ever arrested anyone?"
Officer #2:	Well yes, but I don't think your teacher will have you arrested for writing a bad paper. But, if you use the C.O.P.S. strategy, I bet you'll get a better grade!"

(Continued)

Officer #1:	"That's right! And because we think it is so important to learn good writing skills, we have written a rap song to help everyone remember this strategy. We'll demonstrate it and then you all can join in. Are you ready?"
All Students:	"Yes."
Officer #2:	"We are the cops from Communication Station."
Officer #1:	"To teach a strategy to the education nation."
Officer #2:	"You need this information for a writing situation."
Officer #1:	"So here's a demonstration to the C.O.P.S. creation."
Both Officers:	"C, C, Capitalization"
Both Officers:	"O, O, Organization"
Both Officers:	"P, P, Punctuation"
Both Officers:	"S is the last thing, Spelling"
Officer #2:	"So, if you're ready, we'll sing the next verse and you join in on the chorus.
Officer #1:	"Now that we've given you all the information."
Officer #2:	"We hope that you use it as a foundation."
Officer #1:	"Writing good papers is an inspiration."
Officer #2:	"When you get an "A," it's a celebration."
Both Officers and all Students:	"All together now, C, C, Capitalization, etc."
Officer #1:	"Excellent job! I think you are all on your way to becoming wonderful writers!"
Officer #2:	"Let's do a little review. Who would like to tell us why we use the C.O.P.S. strategy?"
Student #3:	"We use it so we can become better writers."
Officer #1:	"Who can tell us when we use the C.O.P.S. strategy?"
Student #4:	"We use it anytime we have to write a paper."
Officer #1:	"Perfect! You were really paying attention. The C.O.P.S. strategy is a writing strategy. What does the c stand for?"
Student #1:	"Capitalization, I have to make sure that all my sentences begin with a capital letter."
Officer #2:	"Good job, here's your ticket to writing success!"
Officer #1:	"What does the o stand for?"
Student #2:	"The o stands for organization. I want to make sure that my paragraphs are indented, that there is spaces between my words, and that it is neat."
Officer #2:	"That's right, here's your ticket to success!"

Officer #1:	"Tell us what the p stands for."
Student #3:	"It stands for punctuation. I need to make sure all my sentences have periods, commas, and if I quote somebody that I use quotation marks."
Officer #2:	"You've got it, here's your ticket to success!"
Officer #1:	"Linda, what does the last letter, s, stand for?"
Student #4:	"That would be spelling. If I don't know how to spell a word I should look it up in the dictionary."
Officer #2:	"Correct, here is your ticket to success!"
Officer #1:	"Congratulations class, you have all learned a very important writing strategy."
Officer #2:	"That's right, don't forget that when you have to write a paper in school, just call the cops!"
Officer #1:	"Wonderful job boys and girls, give yourselves a hand!"

Prewriting Strategy

The Prewriting Strategy for Getting Started and the Modified Prewriting Strategy can be used in conjunction with any of the above writing strategies. The purpose of these strategies is to help the student think about and plan for the writing assignment to be completed. Through our years of working with students, we have found that many students have difficulty with the logistics of the writing process because of a lack of understanding or vision of the steps needed to complete the assignment and what the end product should look like. These prewriting strategies provide the student with a framework for thinking about and planning for what the writing assignment requires and meeting this criteria. Please refer to chapter 2 for details about these strategies. This strategy is a modification of a prewriting strategy for early elementary students presented in chapter 2.

Think About

- What do I need to do? Example: Write a sentence about the weather.

- When do I need to finish? Example: Before recess.

- What should I do first? Example: Get my paper and pencil.

- Next? Example: Write the sentence.

- Next? Example: Check the sentence to see if I like it.

- Next? Example: Hand in my paper when the teacher collects it.

IMAGE SOURCE: Pixabay.com/clker-free-vector-images

COGNITIVE FLEXIBILITY/SHIFTING STRATEGIES

The following are strategies that we use to prepare students for change.

Why Change Can Be a Good Activity

The book *Who Moved My Cheese?* (Johnson, 1999) can be used to teach students to transition with less anxiety. This can be accomplished by studying the reactions and actions of the mice and people in this book. This popular book with adults is also available in both an elementary and a teen version (2002 & 2003). Students can enjoy the book by reading it, listening to it being read, or being told as a story. A discussion about the story can be meaningful for all students but especially for those who are hesitant to try new activities. Students also enjoy acting out the story of the mice. It is important that all the students have an opportunity to play a mouse that accepted change and to play a mouse who did not prepare for change. Older students enjoy writing a screenplay for the book in addition to acting or directing the scenario.

Teacher Testimonial from: Nadya Chacon

Grade: 1st

Executive Function Addressed: Cognitive Flexibility/Shifting

Strategy Name: Who Moved My Cheese

Strategy Designed for: Whole Class

Nadya Chacon reading the book, Who Moved My Cheese? by Spencer Johnson

I work in a school setting that has a high rate of transiency which impacts my students in terms of being flexible and accepting change with regard to a new living environment, new schools, and new friends. During our class meetings, I often discuss the importance of being flexible after I have explained what flexible means and how change, although it may be difficult at first, can work out for the better. I also have a hand movement (a waving motion) for "flexible" when I encourage the students to make changes. One of my favorite activities is to read to my first graders the elementary version of the book, *Who Moved My Cheese?* by Spencer Johnson. I provide props for the students to wear (cheese hats, mouse ears, signs with the characters names) as I read the story. As I read, we discuss the various situations that the characters encounter and how these situations are addressed. At the end of the story, the students divide into groups and each group identifies a time that required flexibility. They then decide what they must do to be flexible (wave) for that situation and share this information with the entire class.

Dreamweaver

Dreamweaver is an activity that encourages students to share information about themselves with others. This strategy was introduced earlier in this chapter. This strategy is also helpful in practicing transitioning from topic to topic. After each student has had an opportunity to share about the first topic, the teacher can start another round of sharing with a different topic. Another way to transition topics is to cue a new topic by changing the color of yarn. The students then view the dreamweaver they have constructed together.

Timed-Cue Strategy

The student is provided with a vibrating watch or timer. The teacher cues the class that activities will change in 5 minutes. The student who has difficulty transitioning for example, sets the timer or vibrating watch for 4 minutes, 30 seconds. The student is then able to view the amount of remaining time with 30 extra seconds to close what they are doing. At the end of 5 minutes, the student stops work and prepares for the next activity.

FIGURE 6.14 Timed-Cue Strategy Card for Elementary Students

1. The teacher cues me the amount of remaining time until the next activity begins.

2. I set my timer or vibrating watch for that amount of time plus a few seconds for closing out of what I am doing now.

3. Once the timer or vibrating watch goes off, I stop what I am doing and prepare for the next activity.

SOURCES: iStock.com/mizar_21984; iStock.com/victor_brave; and iStock.com/saiko3p

FIGURE 6.15 Timed-Cue Strategy Card for Secondary Students

Timed-Cue Strategy

1. **The teacher cues me amount of remaining time until the next activity begins.**

2. **I set my timer or vibrating watch for that amount of time plus a few seconds for closing out of what I am doing now.**

3. **Once the timer or vibrating watch goes off, I stop what I am doing and prepare for the next activity.**

Mr. Potato Head Activity

(Idea retrieved from Jonathan Brown, https://trello.com/c/yboWRH5d/18-mr-potato-head, modified by Sharpe & Strosnider, 2013)

The Mr. Potato Head Activity involves the executive function categories of communication and cognitive flexibility/shifting. Participants are divided into one of two roles, the observer/recorder and the assembler. The rules to implement this activity are listed below. The observers record the actions and comments of the assemblers. For example, they might write down comments made by the assemblers as they try to put together the Mr. Potato Head. Also, the observers/recorders might record who within the assembly group takes the lead and begins to direct the assembly process, which assemblers take a more passive role in the assembly process, how well the assemblers communicate with each other, and finally the ability for the assemblers to transition between conversation and directions to complete the task. The observer/recorder worksheet is below.

Directions

Group Size: 10 people (5 assemblers and 5 observers/recorders)
Age Range: Grades 3 to secondary

Set Up/Preparation

1. Before the activity starts, place the Mr. Potato Head pieces in an opaque bag (like a brown paper bag). Don't allow anyone to see the contents of the bag.

2. Gather the group of 5 people to be the assemblers; provide each assembler with a blindfold.

3. Gather a group of 5 people to be the observers/recorders; provide an Observer/Recorder Worksheet and pencil to each.

Rules

1. Ask the assemblers to sit themselves next to each other. This can be done seated at a round table or on the floor. Then have the observers/recorders position themselves together.

2. Ask the assemblers to put on their blindfolds.

3. Distribute an Observer/Recorder Worksheet and pencil to each observer/recorder. Give them time to read the worksheet.

4. Place the opaque bag with the Mr. Potato Head parts near the blindfolded assemblers and ask them to put the object together so that each part is in the correct place.

5. Have the observers/recorders complete their Observer/Recorder Worksheet as the assemblers work.

---

6. Once the assemblers are finished, have them remove their blindfolds to see the completed product.

7. Have the assemblers share with the entire group the easy parts of their role and the challenging parts of their role.

8. Have the observers/recorders share their information.

9. Discuss the ways communication and the ability to make change influenced the process of assembling the Mr. Potato Head.

Observer/Recorder Worksheet

Directions: Please record your observations, <u>without using the names of the assemblers</u>, to the following:

1. What are some of the statements made by the assemblers as they put together the object?

2. What are some of the gestures and body language displayed by the assemblers?

3. Did leaders surface among the assemblers as they worked toward achieving the end product? What behaviors made them leaders (e.g., Did they speak a lot, did their tone become firmer, did they communicate using commands, etc.?)

SUPPORTIVE TECHNOLOGIES

With the onset of technology, new instructional tools and supports are now available to meet the diverse learning needs of all students. We use technology to compliment and support executive function skills training. Many of these tools integrate a UDL platform, are highly engaging and interactive, and may be used to reinforce instructional content or executive function skills. Below are some of the technology tools we have found to be beneficial when teaching executive function skills and strategies.

TABLE 6.1 Sample Supportive Technologies

TECHNOLOGY TOOL CATEGORY (WEBSITE, SOFTWARE, APP)	NAME OF TECHNOLOGY	EXECUTIVE FUNCTION AREA ADDRESSED	AGE GROUP
Website	Center on the Developing Child Harvard University https://developingchild .harvard.edu/	All areas	Most ages
Website	Child Mind Institute https://childmind.org/	All areas	Most ages
Website	Common Sense Education https://www.commonsense .org/	All areas	
Website	Intervention Central Response to Intervention — RTI Resources http://www .interventioncentral.org/	All areas	Most ages
Website	LD Online www.ldonline.org/	All areas	Most ages
Website	Understood.org https://www.understood.org/	All areas	Most ages
Software	Inspiration, http://www .inspiration.com/	Communication— Written	Grade 7 to adult
Software	Kidspiration www.inspiration .com/Kidspiration	Communication— Written	K to Grade 6
Software	Merit Software https://www .meritsoftware.com/ software/process_writing.php	Communication— Written	Grade 7 to adult
Software	Odyssey Writer https://www .time4learning.com/writing-software.shtml#prewriting	Communication— Written	Grade 3 to adult

(Continued)

TABLE 6.1 (Continued)

TECHNOLOGY TOOL CATEGORY (WEBSITE, SOFTWARE, APP)	NAME OF TECHNOLOGY	EXECUTIVE FUNCTION AREA ADDRESSED	AGE GROUP
iPhone App	I feel, I speak	Communication	Preschool to Grade 2
iPhone App	Emilia's	Communication	Preschool to Grade 2
iPhone App	Social Stories	Communication and Cognitive Flexibility/Shifting	All ages
iPhone App	Sono Flex Lite	Communication and Cognitive Flexibility/Shifting	All ages
iPhone App	Super Voice	Communication and Cognitive Flexibility/Shifting	All ages
iPhone App	Voice Thread	Communication and Cognitive Flexibility/Shifting	All ages
iPad App	Glogster	Communication	Grade 3 to adult
iPad App	Mindmeister	Communication	Grade 3 to adult
iPad App	Lino	Communication	Grade 3 to adult
iPad App	Podcasts	Communication	Grade 5 to adult
iPad App	ShowMe	Communication and Cognitive Flexibility/Shifting	K to adult
iPad App	Social Stories	Communication and Cognitive Flexibility/Shifting	K to adult
iPad App	Sono Flex Lite	Communication and Cognitive Flexibility/Shifting	All ages
iPad App	Whiteboard	Communication and Cognitive Flexibility/Shifting	K to adult

THE EXECUTIVE FUNCTION GUIDEBOOK

CASE STUDY: AMANDA

We will now return to the case study of Amanda (*see Appendix 1.1 for her full case study*), an eight-year-old student in the third grade, previously introduced in chapters 2 and 3. In this chapter, the 7-Step Model for Executive Function Skills Training explained in chapter 1 will be applied to the executive function area of communication and cognitive flexibility/shifting.

The questions that need to be considered to determine the appropriate executive function interventions that will support Amanda's learning needs are the following:

1. What are Amanda's executive function needs? (The step 1 process will answer this question.)

2. What are the strategies that can be used to support Amanda's executive function needs? (The step 3 process will answer this question.)

3. How does the effectiveness of the selected strategies in supporting Amanda's executive function need to be measured? (The steps 4 and 5 processes will answer this question.)

4. Do the selected strategies work? (The step 6 process will answer this question.)

The following example shows how to address one of Amanda's goals for communication and cognitive flexibility/shifting difficulties using the 7-Step Model. *The model is not a lock-step procedure but merely a template to guide your thinking. Your flexibility and creativity in using this model to meet your needs and the needs of your student are encouraged.*

Step 1

Determine the student's EF deficits and note them in the Executive Function (EF) Planning Chart.

Assessment

As described in chapter 1, the assessment process is completed through reviewing the student's records as well as through observations of the student and interviews with the student, as well as his or her family members and other and previous teachers. Formal and informal assessments may also be used to help determine EF deficits. **See Sample Student Self-Assessment Tool *in Appendix 1.15, and blank templates, modifiable versions of materials, and strategy cards can be found at http:// resources.corwin.com/ExecutiveFunctioning*.**

Key Questions

1. **How are the student's strengths and difficulties exhibited in terms of executive functions?**
   After a thorough review of Amanda's records, including current test scores

on standardized tests, report card grades, work samples, observations of Amanda in academic and social settings, and interviews with her, Amanda's previous teachers, and her parents, the following strengths and needs in terms of communication and cognitive flexibility/shifting are identified.

Amanda's Strengths

- Amanda is very resilient as she works on assignments involving planning.
- She is motivated to improve her organizational skills.
- She has some "splinter skills" in the general area of sequencing (i.e., she remembers and follows a sequence of steps when dancing), but she does not generalize that to other areas of her life.
- She enjoys helping the teacher organize class materials for the day.
- She does well in science and enjoys participating in the activities.

Amanda's Difficulties

Amanda has difficulty with communication.

- Amanda prefers communicating with adults unless she is directing her peers.
- She finds it difficult to communicate in a two-way conversation when listening and taking turns talking is required.
- She avoids word problems partially because she cannot read and comprehend the problem and partially because she has difficulty remembering what she has read.
- Amanda has basic phonics skills and knows basic sight words, but she tends to lose focus and stare at the page instead of actively reading it.
- When she does read, she spends a lot of time looking for answers to comprehension questions and ends up rereading material she already read. She tires and asks that someone read the material to her.
- Amanda makes many careless errors in most written work, and her handwriting is difficult to read.
- She has difficulty spelling words and uses inventive spelling for many words.
- She does not want to use the word processor, because it takes her so long to find the letters on the keyboard. She becomes anxious when asked to use the word processor, even if it is for math drill and practice.
- Amanda has some great ideas when asked what she will be writing about, but she does not organize her thoughts in any way before she begins writing. Therefore, she forgets her train of thought and ends up rambling on and stopping abruptly. She does not check over her work before handing it in, causing her to lose points for careless errors.
- In addition, Amanda's teacher reports that Amanda calls out in class, disturbs her classmates, and seeks the attention of the teacher and classmates throughout the day with inappropriate comments.
- Amanda has difficulty reading and interpreting verbal and nonverbal social cues such as facial expressions and body language.

Amanda has difficulty with cognitive flexibility/shifting.

- Amanda tends to disrupt things at home by exhibiting tantrums when she does not get her way or needs to change her schedule.
- It is difficult for Amanda to make decisions about what to do next, so she procrastinates doing anything.

- She has difficulty with transitioning between classes and to begin a whole new train of thought.
- She is not flexible with change in the classroom routine.
- When she is involved in something she enjoys, she seems to perseverate and have great trouble changing to another activity.

Amanda also has difficulties with other executive function skills as can be seen on the Executive Function Planning Chart below. ***Blank templates, modifiable versions of materials, and strategy cards can be found at http://resources.corwin.com/ ExecutiveFunctioning.***

For the purpose of this chapter, the focus will be Amanda's executive function deficit in the area of communicating and cognitive flexibility/shifting.

2. **Is there an executive function deficit in communication and cognitive flexibility/shifting?**
   Looking at the information presented in answer to question 1, it is

TABLE 6.2 Executive Function (EF) Planning Chart

EXECUTIVE FUNCTION SKILL AREA	WHAT DOES THE DIFFICULTY LOOK LIKE FOR THIS STUDENT? (EXAMPLES)
Communicating, Cognitive Flexibility/Shifting	She does not write coherently due to a lack of understanding language usage. Her writing lacks sequencing of concepts and supporting details. She may display inappropriate body language and facial expressions and/or have difficulty interpreting body language and facial expressions. She is extremely slow to move from one activity on to another. She finds it difficult to think about more than one thing at a time.
Prioritizing, Organizing, Sequencing, Managing Time, and Planning	She cannot find materials, glasses, and assignments. She either rushes through an assignment or does not finish the task on time. Her papers are sloppy and disorganized.
Working Memory	She does not remember what she has read. She forgets math facts and/or how to spell words she knew the night before. She gets confused when following multistep directions.
Attending, Initiating, and Focusing	She needs several reminders to get started on a task or assignment. She loses concentration very easily.
Controlling Social/Emotional and Inhibiting Behaviors	She impulsively calls out in class. She makes inappropriate comments to peers and adults.

established, in addition to other EF deficits, that there is an executive function deficit in communication and cognitive flexibility/shifting.

3. **How does the difficulty in communication and cognitive flexibility/shifting present?**
   The **Executive Function Planning Chart** specifies how Amanda's communication and cognitive flexibility/shifting difficulties present (see table 6.2).

If Amanda were eligible for services, an IEP objective for this goal addressing communication and cognitive flexibility/shifting might be written as Amanda will start a writing assignment on the first try with 80 percent accuracy using a strategy for organization.

Step 2

Review the EF Planning Chart with the student and start to develop a Game Plan.

As described in Chapter 1, this will guide the skill training for this specific executive function area of communication and cognitive flexibility/shifting. After reviewing the assessment results with Amanda and her parents, we completed the Executive Function Planning Chart in step 1. Once Amanda's areas of executive functioning weaknesses needing immediate attention are identified, you can begin to develop Amanda's Game Plan. This will give Amanda an opportunity to "buy into" the process. This understanding and awareness will later lead to student self-advocacy and greater independence in Amanda's learning process. Amanda's Game Plan includes her strengths, difficulties, goals for improvement, and strategies selected to enhance executive functioning through UDL and appropriate strategies. (See chapter 1 for directions on starting a student Game Plan.) *A blank* **Game Plan** *template can be found in Appendix 1.9a, and blank templates, modifiable versions of materials, and strategy cards can be found at http://resources.corwin.com/ ExecutiveFunctioning.*

Student Name: <u>Amanda</u>

What I do best: I am very helpful to my teacher.

What I do best: I try very hard even when I get confused.

What I do best: I am really good at science and love doing science experiments.

THINGS I WOULD LIKE TO DO BETTER	THINGS I CAN DO TO HELP WITH MY DIFFICULTIES IN SCHOOL
Goal 1: I would like to be able to correctly start a writing assignment at the same time my classmates start the same assignment.	**Strategy Name:** To be determined after completing step 3 **Technology I can use:** **Date Goal Met:**
Goal 2: I would like to understand and correctly interpret the body language and social cues of my friends.	**Strategy Name:** To be determined after completing step 3 **Technology I can use:** **Date Goal Met:**
Goal 3: I would like to be able to easily switch between activities and conversations.	**Strategy Name:** To be determined after completing step 3 **Technology I can use:** **Date Goal Met:**

Step 3

Considering UDL and metacognition, select an EF skill-building strategy and get commitment from the student. Add the strategy to the Game Plan.

What are the strategies that we can use to support Amanda's executive functioning needs?

Think about how you would respond to the following questions:

- What are Amanda's learning needs in terms of UDL (Multiple Means of Representation, Multiple Means of Action and Expression, and Multiple Means of Engagement)?
- What approaches and supports could be used to help Amanda access the lesson given her deficit in the skill area of communication and cognitive flexibility/shifting? Examples include
  - allowing extra time to complete tasks,
  - connecting prior knowledge,
  - pictures of body language and corresponding meanings,
  - using a multisensory approach (verbal directions with visual cues),
  - modeling and role play,
  - scaffolding information taught,
  - cueing and prompting,
  - self-monitoring checklists, and
  - incorporating supportive technology.
- What strategies should be added to Amanda's Game Plan?
  - Select from those described in the first part of the chapter, other resources, or those you have used previously.
  - Use the **Selecting a Strategy for the Student While Integrating UDL Chart**, table 6.3, as a tool to prompt your thinking in terms of selecting the appropriate strategy that matches Amanda's learning needs and challenges. Written completion of this chart is not necessary. ***Blank templates, modifiable versions of materials, and strategy cards can be found at http://resources.corwin.com/ ExecutiveFunctioning.*** A sample thought process for communication and cognitive flexibility/shifting is provided below.
  - Think about the components of **The Student Implementation of Strategy With a Focus on Metacognition and UDL Chart**, table 6.4. This chart should be completed with the student. It is a tool that helps the student to buy in to the strategy learning process. ***A blank chart can be found in Appendix 1.11, and blank templates, modifiable versions of materials, and strategy cards can be found at http:// resources.corwin.com/ExecutiveFunctioning.***

TABLE 6.3 Selecting a Strategy for the Student While Integrating UDL Chart

Student: Amanda

Executive Function Deficit: Communication and Cognitive Flexibility/Shifting

Game Plan Goal: Goal 1: I would like to be able to correctly start a writing assignment at the same time my classmates start the same assignment.

MULTIPLE MEANS OF REPRESENTATION				
Things for you to consider:				
1. What information does the student already know?	**2. What are the instructional goals for the student in relation to the executive function addressed?**	**3. What extended activities will be needed?**	**4. What enrichment activities can be implemented?**	**5. What will you need to incorporate when teaching the strategy?**
She is aware that she does not start her written assignments when her classmates start the same written assignment. She knows that she needs a system that will enable her to accurately start her written assignments at the same her peers start their written assignments.	*She needs to accurately start her written assignments accurately and on-time. Amanda cannot determine what the finished product of the written assignment should look like; therefore, she needs to have a graphic organizer in the form of a checklist that provides her a framework for understanding the steps needed to start a written assignment and what the finished product should look like.*	*Use a multisensory approach for teaching how to initiate and complete the steps required when completing a written assignment. Use written directions accompanied by procedural checklist of the steps needed to start and complete an assignment.*	*Have Amanda practice correctly initiating a written assignment by using a procedural checklist across academic settings and at home.*	• *Connect prior knowledge, preteach prerequisite information.* • *Model the expected process for initiating and completing a written assignment.* • *Provide simple verbal directives and visual support.* • *Allow multiple opportunities for practice.*

(Continued)

TABLE 6.3 (Continued)

MULTIPLE MEANS OF ACTION AND EXPRESSION

Things for you to consider:

1. How will you conduct preassessment, formative, and summative assessments for the student's learning?

At the preassessment stage, the student will be given a verbal directive only for starting a written assignment.

During the formative assessment stage, the student will be provided with simple verbal directives and a graphic organizer in the form of a checklist that provides her a framework for understanding the steps needed to start a written assignment and what the finished product should look like.

The teacher will model the process the student will use. Using a prewriting strategy, the student will practice starting a writing assignment at the same time the other students in the class start.

During the summative assessment, the accuracy of the student's performance in completing the task with 80 percent accuracy will determine whether outcomes are met.

2. What platforms will be permitted for the student to demonstrate mastery?

Demonstrate mastery through the completion of a procedural checklist, talking about her progress, and assessing the finished product.

MULTIPLE MEANS OF ENGAGEMENT

Things for you to consider:

1. How will you teach the student in a manner that actively engages the student?

- *Engage student in creating goals that encourage success, using metacognition to self-monitor, and collecting data on effectiveness of strategy to help attain goals.*

- *Chunk information taught, check for understanding by allowing her to share the ideas she has for binder and book organization, provide verbal cues and visual checklist, provide extended time.*

TABLE 6.3 (Continued)

Based on your Considerations of the Principles for this goal, what strategy would you select that aligns with the three Principles and Align with UDL and the Strategy Selected?

Name of Strategy: *Modified Prewriting Strategy*

This strategy is selected because it

1. *Models the expected prewriting process that is to take place* (**Multiple Means of Representation**).

2. *Allows the student to demonstrate mastery and the effectiveness of the strategy through metacognition and self-monitoring* (**Multiple Means of Action and Expression**).

3. *Provides an opportunity to initiate a written assignment at the same time as her classmates, through use of a procedural checklist that is designed specifically for the student with considering the student's input* (**Multiple Means of Engagement**).

Once you and the student have selected a strategy, add the strategy name to the "Things I can do to help with my difficulties in school" column of the Game Plan for an elementary student or the "Action" column of the Game Plan for a secondary student.

Below is Amanda's completed Game Plan, which lists her goals and the strategies she and her teacher have decided she will learn to strengthen her EF skills in the area of communication and cognitive flexibility/shifting. Given her issues, additional strategies such as LLUMP, Say the Message, Timed-Cue and Timed-Cue with Checklist of Tasks, and supportive technology would be taught to Amanda to further strengthen this skill area.

TABLE 6.4 Student Implementation of Strategy With a Focus on Metacognition and UDL Principles

Student: Amanda

Executive Function Deficit: Communication and Cognitive Flexibility/Shifting

Game Plan Goal: Goal 1: I would like to be able to correctly start a writing assignment at the same time my classmates start the same assignment.

METACOGNITION—QUESTIONS THE STUDENT THINKS ABOUT AND RESPONDS TO

Things for you to consider:

1. What am I supposed to do?

Use the Modified Prewriting Strategy.

2. Why is this strategy important for me to use and how will it help me?

This strategy will help me to correctly start my written assignments at the same time my classmates start the same assignment and not miss class time.

3. What are the steps of the strategy?

1. *What does this paper need to look like when I finish?*
   - ✓ *Topic*
   - ✓ *Page length*
   - ✓ *Evidence*
   - ✓ *Punctuation, capitalization, and spelling*

2. *What steps do I need to follow to get to the finished product?*
   - ✓ *Listen to my teacher's directions.*
   - ✓ *On written directions, highlight important directions or words.*
   - ✓ *List the steps I will follow.*

3. *How long do I have to complete the assignment?*

4. *Do I have questions or need help before beginning the assignment?*

4. Is there technology I can use?

- *Kidspiration Software, www.inspiration .com/Kidspiration*

- *Merit Software, https://www .meritsoftware.com/software/process_ writing.php*

- Odyssey Writer, *https://www .time4learning.com/writing-software .shtml*

5. What should I think about when using this strategy?

- *I need to make sure that I follow the steps in sequence and complete each step.*

- If I need extra time to complete my written assignment I will tell the teacher and she will arrange time for me to work.

FIGURE 6.17 Amanda's Completed Game Plan for the Executive Function Skill of Communication and Cognitive Flexibility/Shifting

Student Name: <u>Amanda</u>

What I do best: I am very helpful to my teacher.

What I do best: I try very hard even when I get confused.

What I do best: I am really good at science and love doing science experiments.

THINGS I WOULD LIKE TO DO BETTER		THINGS I CAN DO TO HELP WITH MY DIFFICULTIES IN SCHOOL
Goal 1: I would like to be able to correctly start a writing assignment at the same time my classmates start the same assignment.	→	**Strategy Name:** Modified Prewriting Strategy **Technology I can use:** • *Kidspiration Software, www.inspiration.com/Kidspiration* • *Merit Software, https://www.meritsoftware.com/ software/process writing.php* • *Odyssey Writer, https://www.time4learning.com/writing-software.shtml* **Date Goal Met:** 11/15/18
Goal 2: I would like to understand and correctly interpret the body language and social cues of my friends.	→	**Strategy Name:** LLUMP Strategy **Technology I can use:** • I feel, I say—iPad APP • Social Stories—iPad APP **Date Goal Met:**
Goal 3: I would like to be able to easily switch between activities and conversations.	→	**Strategy Name:** Timed-Cue Strategy **Technology I can use:** Timer **Date Goal Met:**

Step 4

Design and implement data collection tools to measure success in the use of the strategy, teach the selected strategy, and give the student a strategy card.

The following illustrates how step 4 would be applied to the Modified Prewriting Strategy which addresses goal 1.

The data from step 1 show

Amanda does not start her written assignments at the same time as her peers. She states that she does not know how to start the assignment and what it should look like when it is completed. This results in Amanda losing class time, possibly not finishing the written assignment.

We talked with Amanda about her difficulties and started to develop a Game Plan.

Amanda understands that many of her difficulties relate to communication and cognitive flexibility/shifting. She wants to be successful in communicating and being flexible but finds it difficult to follow through. She agreed that she was having trouble with starting her written assignments when her peers start theirs. She also has trouble changing from one activity to another.

The goals Amanda agreed to from step 2 are

Goal 1: I would like to be able to correctly start a writing assignment at the same time my classmates start the same assignment.

Goal 2: I would like to understand and correctly interpret the body language and social cues of my friends.

Goal 3: I would like to be able to easily switch between activities and conversations.

The Strategy you and Amanda selected in step 3 is

Modified Prewriting Strategy. Teach the Modified Prewriting Strategy to Amanda. **Model** the steps of the strategy and incorporate metacognition. Provide motivation for the strategy such as use of a reinforcement and gain a continued commitment by the student. Games such as Role Play, Tell Me the Step That Comes Next, and Sequencing a List of the Steps involved in the strategy can be used to reinforce recall of how to use the strategy. Each game should require the student to explain the strategy and how it helps him or her.

Give the student the strategy card. Have the student practice the strategy using metacognition and referring to the strategy card as needed until he or she can use the strategy with automaticity. The strategy card summarizes the strategy and serves as a reminder of how to use it. It outlines the process and steps that need to be followed to successfully implement the strategy. To make the card, create or purchase a 3" x 5" business-size card. Place the name of the strategy on the front of the card, along with visuals if that is helpful for the student. Place a description of how to use the strategy on the back of the card. It is helpful if this description is stated in the student's own words. Check the description for accuracy. Punch a hole in the top left of the card if you are placing the card on a strategy ring. This strategy ring will provide Amanda with an individualized portable reference system of strategies that supports her EF skills in the area of communicating and cognitive flexibility/shifting.

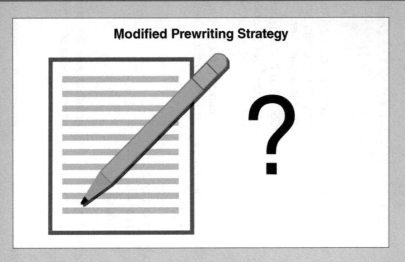

FIGURE 6.18 Modified Prewriting Strategy Card for Early Elementary Students

Modified Prewriting Strategy

Think About

- What do I need to do? Example: Write a sentence about the weather.

- When do I need to finish? Example: Before recess

- What should I do first? Example: Get my paper and pencil.

- Next? Example: Write the sentence.

- Next? Example: Check the sentence to see if I like it.

- Next? Example: Hand in my paper when the teacher collects it.

IMAGE SOURCE: Pixabay.com/clker-free-vector-images

As the student continues to practice the strategy, it is important to determine whether the strategy is appropriate for teaching the student the EF communication and cognitive flexibility/shifting.

Design and collect data and revise as necessary.

Design the data tools, collect data on the success of the strategy, and revise as necessary. A blank reproducible baseline data chart is available in the Appendix. This is the baseline phase of the data collection process. Once the baseline data have been

TABLE 6.5 Baseline Data: Amanda's Usage of the Modified Prewriting Strategy

DAY	BASELINE DATA: AMANDA'S USAGE OF THE MODIFIED PREWRITING STRATEGY ACCURACY OF USAGE—GOAL IS 80%				
	ENGLISH/LANGUAGE ARTS	MATH—WORD PROBLEMS	SCIENCE	SOCIAL STUDIES	COMMENTS
Monday	1 out of 3 possible times 33%	0 out of 5 possible times 0%	1 out of 1 possible times 100%	0 out of 2 possible times 0%	Amanda was cued to use her strategy card in English/language arts. See liked using it and said it helped her. She used it in science without being reminded but she needed to be reminded to use the strategy in her other classes.
Tuesday	0 out of 1 possible times 0%	0 out of 0 possible times n/a	2 out of 3 possible times 66%	1 out of 1 possible times 100%	Amanda is increasing her accurate use of the strategy without being reminded.
Wednesday	1 out of 1 possible times 100%	1 out of 3 possible times 33%	1 out of 1 possible times 100%	1 out of 1 possible times 100%	
Thursday	2 out of 3 possible times 66%	0 out of 0 possible times n/a	1 out of 1 possible times 100%	1 out of 1 possible times 100%	Amanda used her strategy card and did not need to be prompted.
Friday	3 out of 3 possible times 100%	0 out of 0 possible times n/a	0 out of 1 possible times 0%	1 out of 1 possible times 100%	Amanda is familiar with the strategy and likes using it. She no longer needs to be prompted to use the strategy.

collected, analyze the data and go back and make any necessary adjustments. For example, does the baseline data show that this strategy works for the student? Does the student need extra supports such as cues to remind her to use the strategy? Does the student need extended time to complete the steps of the strategy? After the student has been taught the strategy, it is important for you as the teacher to determine whether the strategy is appropriate for the student's needs and if the student is comfortable using the strategy. Not every strategy is appropriate for every student; therefore, it is important to evaluate if the selected strategy is suited to the student and make revisions if needed.

Amanda incorporates metacognition as she uses her strategy card. The Modified Prewriting Strategy is to help Amanda start her work on time with a plan for completion. Amanda and I read the steps on the strategy card for the Modified Prewriting Strategy. She then said the steps to herself as she followed the steps. *Blank templates, modifiable versions of materials, and strategy cards can be found at http://resources.corwin.com/ExecutiveFunctioning.*

Analyze the baseline data and go back and make any necessary adjustments. For example, does the baseline data show that this strategy works for Amanda? Does Amanda need extra supports such as cues to remind her to use the strategy? Does Amanda need extended time to complete the steps of the strategy?

After Amanda has been taught the strategy, it is important for you as the teacher to determine whether the strategy is appropriate for Amanda's needs and if she is comfortable using the strategy. Not every strategy is appropriate for every student; therefore, is it important to evaluate if the selected strategy is suited for Amanda.

Step 5

Continue to collect data for the student's use of the strategy.

Determine the successful use and generalization the strategy. Considerations for Ongoing Data Analysis Chart, table 6.6, provides points you as the teacher need to consider as you continue to analyze the data addressing the student's correct use of the generalization of the selected strategy. Amanda's responses to the questions considered in table 6.6 are posted below. *A blank template of this chart is provided in Appendix 1.12, and blank templates, modifiable versions of materials, and strategy cards can be found at http://resources.corwin.com/ExecutiveFunctioning.*

As explained in step 1, we need to determine whether Amanda has mastered the strategy which includes both using the strategy correctly and generalizing it to a variety of settings. Complete table 6.6, Considerations for Ongoing Data Analysis Chart.

For the Modified Prewriting Strategy, the same data chart was used as used in baseline data collection.

Reviewing the data collected in figure 6.19, it appears that Amanda continues to improve the correct use of the Modified Prewriting Strategy across subjects. Amanda brought her strategy ring and card to school 8 out of 9 days. She continues to have some trouble implementing the strategy during math, but that could be due to a lack of comprehension of what the word problem is asking. Amanda enjoys using this strategy and wishes to continue implementing it in all subjects. She likes that she can start her written assignments at the same time as her friends, and when needed, she does not mind asking the teacher for extra time to complete an assignment.

It is necessary to continually assess the use and generalization of the strategy. An assessment record keeping system is needed to track the student's progress in terms

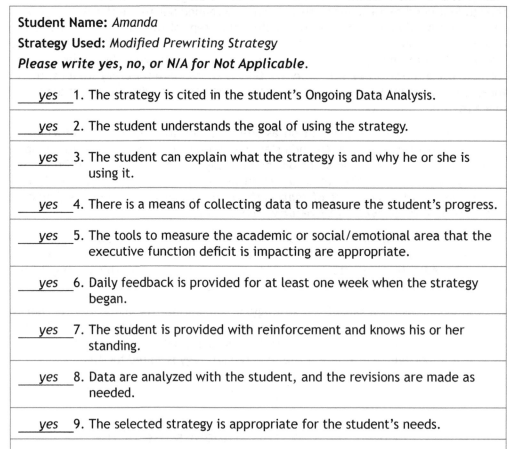

TABLE 6.6 Considerations for Ongoing Data Analysis Chart

Student Name: *Amanda*

Strategy Used: *Modified Prewriting Strategy*

Please write yes, no, or N/A for Not Applicable.

___*yes*___ 1. The strategy is cited in the student's Ongoing Data Analysis.

___*yes*___ 2. The student understands the goal of using the strategy.

___*yes*___ 3. The student can explain what the strategy is and why he or she is using it.

___*yes*___ 4. There is a means of collecting data to measure the student's progress.

___*yes*___ 5. The tools to measure the academic or social/emotional area that the executive function deficit is impacting are appropriate.

___*yes*___ 6. Daily feedback is provided for at least one week when the strategy began.

___*yes*___ 7. The student is provided with reinforcement and knows his or her standing.

___*yes*___ 8. Data are analyzed with the student, and the revisions are made as needed.

___*yes*___ 9. The selected strategy is appropriate for the student's needs.

Comments:

Amanda enjoys using the Modified Prewriting Strategy. She feels that it is easy to use and the strategy helps her remember the steps of the strategy. She likes how she now starts her written assignments at the same time as her classmates. She is good about letting the teacher know when she was unable to finish a written assignment.

She said that practicing the strategy should help with this problem. She has agreed to continue using this strategy.

of the student's learning success and appropriate use of the strategy. Over time, students will be learning many strategies and it is important to assess the maintenance and use of these strategies.

TABLE 6.7 Amanda's Success Implementing the Modified Prewriting Strategy

| WEEK 1 | AMANDA'S SUCCESS IMPLEMENTING THE MODIFIED PREWRITING STRATEGY ACCURACY OF USAGE–GOAL IS 80% | | | | |
	ENGLISH/ LANGUAGE ARTS	MATH–WORD PROBLEMS	SCIENCE	SOCIAL STUDIES	COMMENTS
Monday	2 out of 3 possible times 66%	3 out of 5 possible times 60%	1 out of 1 possible times 100%	0 out of 2 possible times 0%	Amanda needed to be cued to use her strategy card in English/language arts and math. She said that she did not feel well during science and put her head down on her desk. Later in the day, she went home because she had a fever.
Tuesday	Absent from school	Absent from school	Absent from school	Absent from school	
Wednesday	1 out of 1 possible times 100%	1 out of 3 possible times 33%—She stated that she did not understand the word problems so she could not write the answers.	1 out of 1 possible times 100%	1 out of 1 possible times 100%	Amanda had to be reminded to use her strategy card for the first writing assignment in English/language arts. She did not have to be reminded to use her card for the rest of the day.
Thursday	2 out of 2 possible times 100%	1 out of 2 possible times 50%	1 out of 1 possible times 100%	1 out of 1 possible times 100%	Amanda used her strategy card and did not need to be prompted.
Friday	3 out of 3 possible times 100%	0 out of 0 possible times n/a	3 out of 4 possible times 75%	1 out of 1 possible times 100%	Amanda is familiar with the strategy and likes using it. She no longer needs to be prompted to use the strategy.

(Continued)

TABLE 6.7 (Continued)

| WEEK 2 | AMANDA'S SUCCESS IMPLEMENTING THE MODIFIED PREWRITING STRATEGY ACCURACY OF USAGE—GOAL IS 80% | | | | |
	ENGLISH/ LANGUAGE ARTS	MATH—WORD PROBLEMS	SCIENCE	SOCIAL STUDIES	COMMENTS
Monday	1 out of 3 possible times 33%	4 out of 5 possible times 80%	1 out of 1 possible times 100%	2 out of 3 possible times 66%	
Tuesday	1 out of 1 possible times 100%	2 out of 3 possible times 66 %	2 out of 3 possible times 66%	1 out of 1 possible times 100%	Amanda forgot her strategy ring with the strategy card so tried to recall the strategy from memory. The teachers prompted her with the strategy steps during English/ language arts and social studies.
Wednesday	1 out of 1 possible times 100%	3 out of 3 possible times 100%	0 out of 1 possible times n/a	0 out of 0 possible times n/a	Amanda is using the strategy consistently and correctly.
Thursday	4 out of 5 possible times 80%	0 out of 0 possible times n/a	1 out of 1 possible times 100%	1 out of 1 possible times 100%	Amanda is using the strategy consistently and correctly.
Friday	3 out of 3 possible times 100%	0 out of 0 possible times n/a	0 out of 0 possible times n/a	1 out of 1 possible times 100%	Amanda is using the strategy independently.

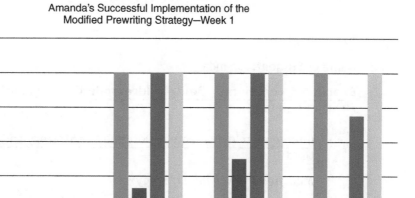

FIGURE 6.19 Amanda's Meeting of the 80% Goal of Successful Implementation of the Modified Prewriting Strategy

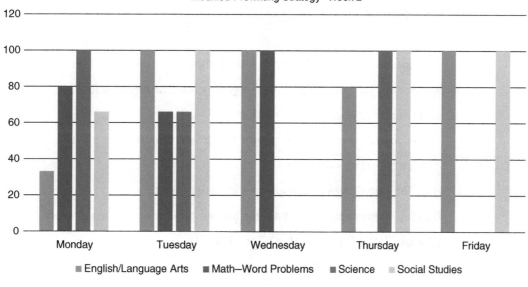

Step 6

Analyze all the data collected and evaluate the student's success in using the strategy; update the Game Plan.

In analyzing Amanda's success in learning and generalizing the Modified Prewriting Strategy, and whether it has helped her, the overarching questions are

- Did she use the strategy in the noted area of executive function difficulty?
- Did she generalize, that is, use the strategy in different scenarios?
- Has the target executive function deficit improved since Amanda started using the strategy?

Sample Template for Final Assessment of the Strategy

Date: 10/21/18

Name of Student: Amanda

Executive Function(s) Being Addressed: Communicating and Cognitive Flexibility/Shifting

☑ Intervention Implemented?(Describe the Strategy and How It Is Being Used).

Modified Prewriting Strategy

This strategy is being used to help Amanda start her written assignments when her classmates start the same written assignment. Using this strategy provides her with a better understanding of what the written product needs to look like when it is finished and a procedure for completing the assignment.

1. **What does this paper need to look like when I finish?**

    ✓ Topic

    ✓ Page length

    ✓ Evidence

    ✓ Punctuation, capitalization, and spelling

2. **What steps do I need to follow to get to the finished product?**

    ✓ Listen to my teacher's directions.

    ✓ On written directions, highlight important directions or words.

    ✓ List the steps I will follow.

3. **How long do I have to complete the assignment?**

4. **Do I have questions or need help before beginning the assignment?**

☑ **Strategy Used From:** 11/1/18 **To:** 11/15/18

☑ **UDL-EF Process Used:**

- Completed Executive Function Planning Chart
- Thought through Selecting a Strategy for the Student While Integrating UDL Chart
- Created with student a Strategy Implementation With a Focus on UDL and Metacognition Chart
- Field-tested the Modified Prewriting Strategy
- Created strategy card for Modified Prewriting Strategy and placed on Amanda's Strategy Ring
- Finalized Modified Prewriting Strategy and Selected this Strategy for Amanda
- Taught the strategy and kept data of usage
- Made revisions as necessary

☑ **Data for Measured Results:** Two weeks of data. See completed Modified Prewriting Strategy **table 6.6**, Amanda's Success Implementing the Modified Prewriting Strategy, and **table 6.7**, Amanda's Meeting of the 80% goal of Successful Implementation of the Modified Prewriting Strategy.

☑ **Anecdotal Report of Results:**

- Amanda liked using the Modified Prewriting Strategy and liked being able to start her written assignments at the same time as her classmates.
- She liked having a visual checklist of the process she needs to complete for starting a written assignment.
- Her difficulty in using this strategy during math is a result of not comprehending what the word problem is asking her to do to solve the problem.

☑ **Review of Results:**

- Improved attitude regarding writing and a willingness to start a writing task without hesitation.
- Was able to be seen as an equal to her classmates when starting a writing task.
- Continues to need support in math in terms of understanding what the word problem is asking so that she can perform the needed operation and complete a written response.

☑ **Summary Report on Game Plan Progress:**

The Modified Prewriting Strategy has helped Amanda to attain "**Goal 1:** "I would like to be able to correctly start a writing assignment at the same time my classmates start the same assignment."*Accomplished 11/15/2018*

(NOTE: Goals 2 and 3 on Amanda's Game Plan will be addressed later once Amanda has mastered and generalized goal 1.)

Summary Report on Implications of Strategy Use on Academic Skills and Social Interactions: Amanda uses the Modified Prewriting Strategy independently across all subjects except math.

We can answer these questions by completing the Final Assessment of the Strategy. A final assessment of the strategy can be used to analyze all the data collected, evaluate Amanda's success and evaluate the effectiveness of the strategy (see table 6.8). *A blank template for the* Final Assessment of the Strategy *can be found in Appendix 1.13, and blank templates, modifiable versions of materials, and strategy cards can be found at http://resources.corwin.com/ExecutiveFunctioning.*

Review the data recording tool and completed Final Assessment Template to determine the following:

- Does Amanda use the strategy in the noted area of executive function difficulty?
  - Yes, Amanda has mastered the strategy and feels the strategy has helped her.

- Does Amanda generalize?
  - Amanda would like to continue using this strategy and has started to use it in other classes and at home.
- Has the noted executive function deficit improved since Amanda started using the strategy?
  - Yes, it appears that Amanda's ability to start a written assignment when her classmates start theirs has improved. She independently uses this strategy.

Conclusion: Based on the data, Amanda is improving in communicating and cognitive flexibility/shifting using the Modified Prewriting Strategy. Amanda will continue to use this strategy, and she will use it independently.

Step 7

Revisit the Game Plan to determine whether the student's goals have been met. Once a goal is met, have the student write a Success Plan.

To determine whether Amanda's first goal has been met, look at the data for the entire period she has been using the strategy. Review the data with her and discuss with her the following key questions:

- Does she feel the use of the strategy is helping?
  - Amanda feels the Modified Prewriting Strategy is helping, and the data collected for two weeks support this.
- Does she feel it would be beneficial to continue to use this strategy?
  - Amanda would like to continue to use this strategy. She has begun to use this strategy at home.
- Does she feel she is ready to move on to another goal for this executive function?
  - Amanda feels ready to work on goal 2 while she continues to work on generalizing goal 1 across settings.

After each goal on the student's Game Plan has been met, help her write a personal Success Plan to communicate what she plans to do to have a successful school year and self-advocate for the assistance she needs to help her on this journey toward success. This should identify the following:

- What I want to do next
- Difficulties I may have
- Strategies I can use to help myself
- What the teacher can do to help

Below is the sample template for Amanda's communicating and cognitive flexibility/ shifting goal 1. *A blank template can be found in Appendix 1.14, and blank templates, modifiable versions of materials, and strategy cards can be found at http://resources.corwin.com/ExecutiveFunctioning.*

What I Want to Do Next

I would like to be able to correctly start a writing assignment at the same time my classmates start the same assignment.

Difficulties I May Have

I have trouble starting written assignments when my peers do. I do not know how to start the writing process.

Strategies I Can Use to Help Myself

To help me start my written assignments, I can use the Modified Prewriting Strategy. For this strategy, I need to have my strategy card so I can remember the steps and start my written assignment right away.

What the Teacher Can Do to Help

When I use the Modified Prewriting Strategy, the teacher might need to help me during math so that I understand what the problem is asking me to do. I might also need some extra time for completing some written assignments.

WHAT HAPPENS THEN?

When all three goals on the Game Plan are met, it is time to identify new challenges on which to focus. Few students experience difficulty in only one executive function. While Amanda will continue to work on strengthening her communicating and cognitive flexibility/shifting, there are other executive function area deficits to be addressed. The next step would be to return to the EF Planning Chart to determine which EF deficits to address.

Summary

The ability to regulate communicating and cognitive flexibility/shifting is a lifelong skill set necessary for one to meet with success on a daily basis. For many students, the ability to efficiently and effectively use this skill set becomes a challenge. What further complicates this situation is the fact that the actions communicating and cognitive flexibility/shifting become interrelated as one sees a task from start to fruition. We acknowledge that a deficit in communicating and cognitive flexibility/shifting looks different for each student. But most students with communicating and cognitive flexibility/shifting deficits have difficulty with or may not appropriately respond to the topic at hand, may demonstrate frustration when writing, or be extremely slow in moving from one activity to another. These difficulties and others have a negative impact on student achievement, behavior, and social/emotional well-being, leading some into the Downward Spiral discussed in chapter 1. Supportive strategies both to improve and compensate for communicating and cognitive flexibility/shifting deficits are available for teachers and students who work together toward student success. Using strategies that help students to moderate communicating and cognitive flexibility/shifting are described in this chapter. Supportive technologies, some of which are listed in the chapter, are available to assist in the improvement of EF skills. Finally, the 7-Step Model is presented in this chapter for an elementary student presenting difficulty in communicating and cognitive flexibility/shifting, as well as other deficits. Through this example in communicating and cognitive flexibility/shifting, you can see how these steps come together working with an individual student. For those using the 7-Step Model Modified, it is helpful to see and select the parts of the model that will fit your particular situation. As teachers, you know your student best and we encourage you to use your knowledge, judgement, and creativity, regardless of whether you are using the 7-Step Model or 7-Step Model Modified. You are the one to best determine what your student's(s') program will look like, keeping in mind that ongoing assessment, determination of what is needed, the consideration of UDL and metacognition in the choice of strategies, the implementation of strategies, and the commitment of the student are all vital components for a successful implementation of communicating and cognitive flexibility/shifting executive function skills training.

Practice

- Practice the 7-Step Model for communicating and cognitive flexibility/shifting using one of the case studies in the Appendix. Note that there is another case study for a secondary student. You may use either Carlos's or Fariha's case study (*see Appendix 1.4*) to practice the 7-Step Model for communicating and cognitive flexibility/shifting.

- Note any challenges and successes you experienced and review the content in chapter 1 for background information relating to this chapter.

- Practice the 7-Step Model for one of your students.

CHAPTER 7

Special Considerations Involving Executive Functions

EARLY CHILDHOOD

Strategies appropriate for use in early childhood and supporting research is included earlier in this book; however, with the current emphasis on early intervention that includes executive function skill training it is important to dedicate a specific section for teaching young children. Was Robert Fulghum (1988), ahead of his time when he wrote the book *All I Really Needed to Know I Learned in Kindergarten* in that he was really addressing executive functioning?

- When he talked about children learning not to hit others, was he referring to the executive function **inhibition**?

- When he talked about teaching children to put their toys and materials away, was he referring to the executive function **organization**?

- When he talked about teaching children to follow rules and procedures, was he referring to the executive function **working memory**?

- When he talked about teaching children to say they were sorry, was he referring to the executive functions **communication and social/emotional**?

We now know that executive function is an important factor in the development of all children including young children. As mentioned in chapter 1, Morgan et al. (2018) reported that executive function difficulties in preschool serve as a predictor of future academic difficulty throughout school and into adulthood. They further recommended that students showing problems in executive functioning in preschool need intervention before they develop academic and behavioral problems that get worse as time goes on without intervention.

Students in preschool demonstrate executive functioning needs when they

- have trouble controlling their behavior,
- have trouble understanding and meeting adult expectations,
- have trouble relating to other children,
- have trouble remembering and following multistep directions,
- have trouble accepting no,
- have trouble sharing,
- have trouble communicating.

Teachers and classmates expect them to have learned to self-regulate these behaviors before moving into higher grades. If they fail to learn to control any of these behaviors, the gap becomes wide very quickly, and the young student starts his or her fall in the Downward Spiral if intervention does not take place. It is important for parents and teachers to work together and keep in mind that some young children are exhibiting executive function deficits and need intervention. Students' executive function issues affect how they think, work, and interact with others. The authors of this book were questioned when, in 2010 and 2011, they included preschoolers into their executive functioning camp. To everyone's surprise, even theirs, the extent to which preschoolers were successful at learning strategies to expand their executive functioning skills was impressive. They not only learned strategies to help them self-regulate especially in inhibition and organization, but they asked for more; planning was an area in which they excelled as a group. Some had difficulties that needed continued attention, but the important thing was they were actively involved in improving these areas.

Research is changing the way we approach executive functioning in preschool every day. Semenov and Zelazo (2018), Morgan et al. (2018), and others go so far as to use executive function skill as a predictor of success in life. For instance, promising research by Semenov and Zelazo (2018) includes looking at "hot EF" and "cool EF," with hot referring to motivational and emotional hot buttons, which children must decide whether to approach or avoid, and cool buttons, referring to EF that are measured by recalling numbers or sorting shapes. Using these skills allows children to pause and reflect on problems. Zelazo (2006) developed the Dimensional Change Card Sort (DCCS) Task to measure cool EF. To complete a task, students needed to use cognitive flexibility, working memory, and inhibitory control. Hot EF tasks most often are tasks that students are motivated emotionally to complete. Additional research in this area will help identify how these findings translate to intervention practices. The important takeaway is that there is important research pointing toward successful early intervention in executive functions.

The Center on the Developing Child (2012) states on their website that "providing the support that children need to build these skills at home in early care and education programs, and in other settings they experience regularly is one of society's most important responsibilities."

With that in mind, there are some special considerations when teaching young children executive function skills.

SPECIAL CONSIDERATIONS WHEN TEACHING PRESCHOOLERS EF SKILLS

- Provide safe, developmentally appropriate settings.
- Select developmentally appropriate tasks.
- Establish routines across a variety of settings.
- Implement situations that require a change from an established routine.
- Model appropriate social behaviors in a variety of settings.
- Provide developmentally appropriate opportunities for problem solving.
- Scaffold activities to connect with what is already known.
- Teach coping skills.
- Provide opportunities for creative play.
- Offer opportunities for practice that leads to mastery and generalization.
- Encourage their efforts to self-regulate.

According to the Center on the Developing Child (2012), "Children are more likely to build effective executive function skills if the important adults in their lives are able to:

- Support their efforts;
- Model the skills;
- Engage in activities in which they practice the skills;
- Provide a consistent, reliable presence that young children can trust;
- Guide them from complete dependence on adults to gradual independence; and
- Protect them from chaos, violence, and chronic adversity, because toxic stress caused by these environments disrupts the brain circuits required for executive functioning and triggers impulsive, 'act-now-think-later' behavior."

The research supports executive function skill intervention for preschoolers, but we as teachers are the ones who will implement the suggestions coming from the findings as we support student growth in such skills as self-regulation and communication. Making all teachers aware of the importance of including attention to executive function skill growth is vital so that all children have the opportunity to receive intervention if needed.

AUTISM SPECTRUM DISORDER (ASD)

Autism spectrum disorder (ASD) is another area that requires special consideration. We recognize that teachers of students with ASD address executive functions in their daily curriculum from early childhood. It is important that others working with students with ASD are cognizant of the fact that executive function difficulties are common especially in students who are verbal and do not have intellectual disabilities (Miller, et al., 2018). One area that especially impacts students with ASD is cognitive flexibility or difficulty shifting from one thought or situation to another. Moyes (2014) provides an example of a student who has a lot of stress regarding shifting. It is difficult for that student to focus on the lesson when he or she is worried about what is happening next. Miller and colleagues (2018) report that it is not clear how the EF difficulties and ASD develop, but stress the importance of accommodations, modifications, and compensatory skills when planning instruction for students with ASD. Following that instruction, they recommend training in self-advocacy early in the child's instructional program (pp. 168–191).

Teachers of students with ASD can provide suggestions to others who have less experience in the area. Below you will find suggestions an Early Childhood Education teacher provided those with less experience in teaching students with ASD.

Teacher Interview with Jessica Gray

Special Educator, Self-Contained Setting

Grade(s) Taught: K-2

Name: Jessica Gray

Jessica Gray

Jessica Gray, a teacher of students with ASD, has this advice to give teachers who have contact with or teach her students:

What do teachers need to know in terms of teaching executive function skills to students with autism?

- Keep in mind that every child is different— what works with one does not work with another child; what did work for a student may not down the line.
- Communication is vital. When working with a student, be sure to offer simple verbal explanations of what content or skill is being learned and why he or she needs to learn it. When possible, the verbal communication is supported with visuals. Jessica emphasizes, "You never know exactly what the child is comprehending so you need to make connections all of the time."
- Consistency is key with implementation.
- All routines are started the first day of school.
- Everyone has roles and responsibility, and if one person is missing, it breaks the chain and throws everything off.
- Students with low-functioning autism are a priority because of the varied and intense needs. When a para is absent additional attention from the teacher must go to this child. The student needs a time reinforcement schedule and token chart implemented so he or she can start to manage his or her own reinforcement. For example, take a star off chart.
- Token charts, timers, and first-then approaches are helpful.

- Things need to be accessible to the student so that he or she sees a clear beginning and a clear ending.
- Routines are established and maintained across activities and settings as possible, and generalization is very difficult to grasp in other settings.
- Clear, succinct goals and objectives that are attainable need to be set for the child, and the child needs to understand the function. This is achieved by verbal (explanation) and visual support (charts, posters, sign language, reinforcement charts), as well as consistency in routine. While it may not be clear how much the child understands, it is important to include the student in verbal and nonverbal conversation.
- My goal for my students is independence.

When asked what works well for her, she reports

- sign language, visuals, and verbal communication;
- Promethean Board, Big Mac, and Classroom iPad.

HOMEWORK AND EF

Our nation is divided not only on whether students should have any homework but also what homework should entail. Some teachers feel it is important for students to have an opportunity to practice what they learned in school through homework. Like-minded teachers also feel it is a bonding experience for parents and their children to read together or review vocabulary works, for example. How much homework should students have? The National Education Association (NEA) and National Parent–Teacher Association (NPTA) recommend the "10-minute rule" increasing by grade according to Robinson and Aronica, (2018). This means thirty minutes each night for students in the third grade but ninety minutes per night for students in ninth grade. While this is the recommendation, it is not what was found in a survey conducted by the University of Phoenix College of Education. They found that students have an average of ten hours of homework per week, and high school is extremely varied because each teacher may assign up to ten hours per week.

Completing assignments in school or at home can be stressful for many students and their families because of problems with executive function skills including organization and planning, initiation, working memory, time management, self-regulation, communication, social/emotional areas, and others (Cooper-Kahn & Foster, 2013; Dawson & Guare, 2010; Kaufman, 2010; Meltzer, 2010). Homework is stressful in many students' homes because of organization and planning issues. Sometimes, the student does not organize the materials he or she needs to complete the assignment. Other times, the student does not know the homework assignment or assignment requirements. It is especially problematic for the family when the student has the materials needed but does not know how to complete the homework. Either the parent helps, or the student is left to try to figure it out. The outcome of this is often upset parents and frustrated students. In the classroom when given the opportunity to work on an assignment, students with executive function skill problems often do not make the progress needed in the time allotted. They are left to work on it at home or try to catch up in the next class period.

Homework is especially problematic for students with executive function issues. Anecdotally, it appears that parents become so stressed that they may resort to doing the homework for their child. Some parents find that their children do not want to expose their difficulties in learning to the parent. It is just not the parent who is anxious about their student's homework, but students are also upset when they do not know what the assignment is, do not have their materials, or know what they should be doing or how to do it. Even in the best-case scenario when the student has recorded the assignment, brought it home, and tried to complete it, there can be frustration if the work is too difficult for the student. The very nature of the student's executive function difficulty may make it difficult for the student to manage all the prerequisites for successful homework completion. While there are some supportive technologies to help in situations where students forgot to bring the assignments home, many of our students with and without executive function issues do not have access to the Internet due to poverty or lack of connectivity in their area. Strategies help students meet the requirements of the school where homework is required.

SOME SUPPORTIVE STRATEGIES TO ASSIST STUDENTS, TEACHERS, AND PARENTS

NOTEBOOK ORGANIZATION AND EF

Students displaying problems with executive function skills in organization often have notebooks that are described as sloppy with pages not secured, as well as missing and misfiled assignments. It is advantageous to organize a notebook with the student to help with executive functioning difficulties. Discuss what the student likes in a notebook and incorporate those features if possible. Encourage keeping the organization simple by doing the following: (1) use one notebook with a zipper, (2) use dividers for each subject, and (3) make a homework section with three parts. As described in earlier chapters, the first part of the homework section consists of homework to be completed, materials or supplies needed, and due date. The second part consists of homework partially complete, and the third part consists of homework completed that is ready to be handed in.

Students can self-monitor with checklists and to-do lists. They may need reinforcement to begin using them, but once they experience success, they usually agree to their use. It is important that the lists are not too long.

INSTRUCTIONAL HINTS FOR ENHANCING ASSIGNMENT SUCCESS

- ☐ Post all assignments every day on the board and on your website.
- ☐ Always post assignments in the same place in the classroom.

☐ Include assignments on your teacher website; however, keep in mind that some students do not have access to the Internet.

☐ Explain all assignments and give students notice of challenging items.

☐ Think Universal Design for Learning (UDL). When possible, give choices as to how the assignment may be completed: for example, write, word process, or dictate.

☐ Address how homework will be evaluated so that students know the weight of homework assignments in grading.

☐ Consider make-up options for homework not turned in as part of your homework policy and make certain students know and understand the policy.

☐ Remind students of the materials they will need to complete these assignments.

☐ Remind students to record their assignments and provide time for the students to do so.
   ○ Note that some students may need to dictate or record the assignment in to an electronic device or have someone else write it.
   ○ Allow students to take photos of posted assignments with their device or with an instant camera.

☐ Plan to give students time at the beginning of class to record assignments so they are not rushed to do so at the end.

☐ For some assignments, begin the assignment in class to make certain students understand what they need to do.

☐ Give students time at the end of class to ask questions about the assignment and gather materials.

☐ Consider assigning homework buddies.

☐ Check assignment sheets and initial at the beginning of the academic year; let students know they are prepared for homework success.

ASSIGNMENTS AND EXECUTIVE FUNCTIONING CHECKLIST

Homework is stressful in many students' homes because of difficulty with a variety of executive functioning issues. The chart below touches on some of the problems and the accompanying executive function. This serves as an informal record of the students' difficulties and progress. Instructors and students can complete it together and determine difficulties. It can be used daily or weekly, for example, to keep record of the student's progress. Note that difficulties in any of the executive function skills may result in unsuccessful completion of assignments. ***Blank templates, modifiable versions of materials, and strategy cards can be found at http://resources.corwin.com/ExecutiveFunctioning.***

FIGURE 7.1 Assignments and Executive Functioning Checklist

Prioritizing, Organizing, Sequencing, Managing Time, and Planning

_____Records the assignment in writing, on an app, or in a photo

_____Has the materials needed

_____Sets priorities

_____Backward Maps long-term projects

_____Plans the homework session

_____Follows the homework plan

  • Includes study time

  • Includes time to work on long-term projects

_____Puts items in the homework section of the notebook when finished

_____Puts notebook near the door

_____Monitors time with a timer to stay on track

_____Checks off each item when it is complete

_____Other

Attending, Initiating, and Focusing

_____Starts on time

_____Asks questions if he or she does not understand the assignment or process

_____Chunks assignments

_____Takes a timed break when needed

_____Other

Working Memory

_____Remembers to bring home notebook and materials each day

_____Uses homework learning strategies

_____Other

Communication and Cognitive Flexibility/Shifting

_____Checked with teacher to confirm

_____Asks questions for clarification

_____Meets with parents briefly before and following homework session

_____Determines whether there are any messages to the teacher regarding the work

_____Stops one assignment when time has expired and moves on to the next

_____Other

Social/Emotional and Inhibiting

_____Does not become upset during homework and study time

_____Ignores impulses to play a game or watch TV

_____Monitors time with a timer to stay on track

_____Checks off each item when it is complete

FAMILY PLANNING MEETINGS STRATEGY

Families are complex, and some may have to plan by phone, e-mail, and or FaceTime, or Skype. The important point is that if families can give fifteen minutes once a week to discuss the family schedule, it helps all members to know what is coming up in the following seven days. All families have their own schedules and ways of addressing the complicated lives that intertwine within their home. For that reason, a time that communication among family members occurs should be determined by the ones who know the family best, the parents.

However, here are some helpful hints that may guide their thinking:

- ☑ Cooper-Kahn and Foster (2013) suggest the family meet with the student on Thursday to determine what still needs to be completed for the current week and to plan for that completion and the week ahead. This way the student can speak with the teacher about a plan to complete any work that may involve the weekend to catch up.

- ☑ It is important to keep in mind that the schedule is no larger than any of its parts which, when derailed, can cause chaos for several or all family members. The discussion is not a time to debate on the merits of the tasks at hand or the meeting will drag on and the younger family members will feel left out. Also, any person or persons in the family with ADHD may tune out, and the meeting will not help.

- ☑ It may be that families will have a group meeting and follow up with individuals who have questionable activities. This could happen with any child, not only the child with homework issues. It is helpful to post the calendar where everyone can view it. In the case of family members living in other homes, the calendar content can be shared through the Family Meeting Record. It can be emailed or texted, for example, to all concerned.

ASSIGNMENT RESPONSIBILITY

Parents and their children who have difficulty with homework may find that **spending five minutes together** per night planning assignment and study completion time helps get the process started. **Spending five minutes reviewing homework** completion and discussing any needs the student may have in completing the requirements helps students with accountability. The goal is for the student to self-start and work independently. Parents should **not** do their children's homework under any circumstances. When an impasse occurs, a note to the teacher to explain the situation should be written by the parent and taken to the teacher by the student. In addition, the parent should send the same information in an e-mail to the teacher. The reason for this is that the teacher may not see their e-mail before class, and it is good advocacy training for the child to deliver the note. The e-mail is essential in case the student loses or forgets to deliver the note.

FIGURE 7.2 My Weekly Calendar Reminder Strategy Card

My Weekly Calendar Reminder

1. Take a photo of the calendar from your family meeting.

2. Place the picture on your strategy ring as a reminder of your responsibilities for the week.

3. Meet with your parents to monitor your progress.

Blank templates, modifiable versions of materials, and strategy cards can be found at http://resources.corwin.com/ ExecutiveFunctioning

IMAGE SOURCE: iStock.com/realstockvector

Some parents dread projects or study time because they become frustrated with their child's work behavior. Students who have problems with executive function skills need the support of their parents as they navigate the "assignment dilemma together."

- Students and parents should complete a plan. Give the student a form to complete with his or her parents. See figure 7.3 for a sample plan. ***Blank templates, modifiable versions of materials, and strategy cards can be found at http://resources.corwin .com/ExecutiveFunctioning.*** The form should have a place for the student to fill in when and where assignments and study will be completed. A time limit should be set for assignments, and if the student has worked on an assignment for the scheduled time and has not finished, the parent should write a note to the teacher describing the difficulty the student had completing the assignment.

FIGURE 7.3 Sample Study and Assignment Plan Template

Sample Study and Assignment Plan Template

When will I study?

Where will I study?

How long will I spend on my work?

What will I do if I have difficulty with my work?

What if I have tried to complete all my assignments but did not get finished in the time scheduled?

By signing this form, we are agreeing to this plan.

Signatures

Parent_____ **Date**_____

Student_____ **Date**_____

HOME AND DONE STRATEGY (FOR MIDDLE AND HIGH SCHOOL)

Once you and your parents complete a homework plan, it is important to follow the plan as written. If there are changes needed, the plan should be revised with the needed changes. There are several steps you need to follow in the Home and Done Strategy, and they include:

1. **Bring the assignments and materials home.**
   Think outside the box when recording assignments. If the assignments are posted on the internet, print the assignments on Sunday evening and take the list to school. Make notes if there are any changes. For example, your teacher may change the quiz scheduled for Thursday to Friday.

   If your teacher posts homework, if permitted, take a photo of the assignment on your device.

   If you use an agenda, write the assignments in your agenda.

   In addition, many students find apps like iHomework helpful. The point is that you have to find what works for you and use it consistently.

   Now that you know what the assignments are, make certain you have all of the materials you will need with you before leaving school. Go through the list of assignments and check that you do indeed have all of the books and papers you will need before leaving school.

2. **Before you begin the assignments, make a plan.** Ask yourself the following questions: What do I need to complete? How long should each assignment take (including work on long-term projects, study for upcoming quizzes, tests, etc.)? What will I do first, second, etc.? Students often find it helpful to use the assignment sheet to look at the assignments as a whole, estimate the time each assignment will take, place a number beside each item to note the order in which you will complete the assignments.

3. **Start your homework**. Highlight or check off each assignment as you complete it. If you have difficulty with an assignment and need help, do not check it off. Circle it to remind you that you need to share with your parents and teacher the difficulty you are experiencing. For long-term projects, use your long-term project checklist to keep track of where you are in terms of completing it. For study, make certain you take five or ten minutes daily to review your notes, study guide, vocabulary, etc. This will help you prepare for an upcoming quiz or test.

4. **When you are finished, share your assignment sheet with your parents**. Summarize what you did and explain why you were unable to complete any assignments not finished. Discuss next steps with your parents if you were unable to complete one or more of your assignments.

5. **Pack your book bag to include all assignments** in the appropriate folder (in progress or complete) so that you can easily find them and turn them in.

6. **Done!**

Home and Done Strategy	Bring assignments and materials home Make a plan Start your homework Share your assignment sheet Pack your book bag Done

Some Other Strategies Covered in the Book That Relate to Homework Situations and Long-Term Assignments

For some more specific strategies and technologies that can help with completing assignments, projects and homework please refer to the chapters listed below. *A copy of* **Some Other Strategies Covered in the Book That Relate to Homework Situations and Long-Term Assignments,** *and blank templates, modifiable versions of materials, and strategy cards can be found at http://resources.corwin.com/ExecutiveFunctioning.*

All Chapters

Self-Monitoring Checklists

Chapter 2—Working Memory

Visual Schedules Strategy

This strategy is helpful for students to see what they will be doing during the homework period.

Teach-It Strategy

This strategy is helpful for students to test their understanding of the material they are studying.

Study Cube Recall

This strategy is helpful for students to determine their mastery of the material they are studying.

Prewriting Strategy Graphic Organizer

This strategy is helpful for students to organize their thoughts prior to writing.

Chapter 3—Prioritizing, Organizing, Sequencing, Managing Time, Planning, and Supportive Strategies

Binder Organization Strategy

This strategy is helpful for students to organize their binder specifying homework dividers.

Backpack Organization Strategy

This strategy is helpful for students to organize their backpack and find the materials they have brought home from school.

Steps for Completing a Long-Term Project Strategy

This strategy is helpful for students to follow as they approach, work on, and complete a long-term project.

Time Needed Strategy

This strategy is helpful for students to determine how long it will take to complete an assignment.

Big Rocks Strategy

This strategy is helpful for students to set priorities among their homework parts.

(Continued)

FIGURE 7.5 (*Continued*)

Backward Mapping Strategy

This strategy is helpful for students to schedule the completion of an assignment.

Specific Location Strategy

This strategy is helpful for students to keep track of materials they need to complete homework assignments.

Chapter 4—Attending, Initiating, Focusing, and Supportive Strategies

Prewriting Strategy for Getting Started Self-Check Card Strategy

This strategy is helpful for students to move a bead on a card to indicate how they are doing in terms of completing an assignment.

Break Pass Cards

This strategy is helpful for students to take breaks as needed.

Self-Monitoring for Attending, Initiating, and Focusing

This strategy is helpful for students to maintain attention and focus during the homework session.

COPS Strategy Checklist

This strategy is helpful for students to find errors in writing and correct them. Scaffolding is provided based on age and grade expectations.

Chapter 5—Social/Emotional and Inhibiting and Supportive Strategies

Take a Breather Strategy

This strategy is helpful for students to use when feeling stressed about their homework.

Self-Monitoring Chunking Strategy

This strategy is helpful for students to use when planning homework by dividing assignments into parts.

I Am Able Strategy

This strategy is helpful for students who are afraid to try.

Chapter 6—Communicating and Cognitive Flexibility/Shifting and Supportive Strategies

COPS Strategy Play

This strategy is helpful for students to find errors in writing and correct them.

FIGURE 7.5 (Continued)

Simply Note It Strategy

This strategy is helpful for student note taking. The notes can then be used to study for tests.

Modified Pre-writing Strategy

This strategy is helpful for students to plan their writing assignment before writing.

Checklists of Tasks With Time Limits Strategy

This strategy is helpful for students to maintain a schedule for homework completion.

SOME SUPPORTIVE TECHNOLOGIES TO ASSIST STUDENTS, TEACHERS, AND PARENTS

TABLE 7.1 Supportive Technologies Chart Example

TECHNOLOGY TOOL CATEGORY (WEBSITE, SOFTWARE, APP)	NAME OF TECHNOLOGY	EXECUTIVE FUNCTION AREA ADDRESSED	AGE GROUP
Website	Your school website	All Areas	Most ages
Website	www.KhanAcademy.com	Communication	K to Grade 6
iPhone App	Homework, my Homework, and the HW App	Prioritizing	All ages
iPad App	Study Blue, Quizlet	Organization	Grade 4 to Grade 12

A copy of Some Supportive Technology to Assist Students, Teachers, and Parents, *and blank templates, modifiable versions of materials, and strategy cards can be found at http://resources.corwin.com/ExecutiveFunctioning.*

OTHER CONSIDERATIONS

Recently, flipped classrooms have come on the scene and while there is not a lot of research regarding the effectiveness of this approach, there is a loyal following that finds it helpful to all involved (Pierce, n.d.). In flipped classrooms, time in the classroom is spent in hands on activities our students with EF difficulties may find motivating, but the collaboration component can be difficult for students with EF issues in social areas. Content is often covered in homework when the student may be required to read about or watch a video explaining the content. Proponents of flipped learning state that it helps all students and is changing classrooms especially for students with disabilities. Technology is key, and in some cases, students may watch a video at home several times before attending the class. If this approach is expanded, the impact on homework philosophy is bound to be affected. The impact on students with executive function deficits is yet to be determined.

Students with executive functioning deficits also have need for learning that helps them not only in the classroom but as they transition to life after high school. Personalized Learning is designed to meet the individual interests and needs of students. With each student, a learning plan is developed that designates their learning needs and manner in which they learn. Students in middle school and high school benefit from knowing that they will be using what they are studying in their life beyond school. Learning fits their life plan. Personalized Learning is found helpful for general and special educators to make inclusion more personalized for students with disabilities. The idea that students have a choice in what they will study and how they will study it is key to the popularity of this approach. Instead of telling students what they will study and what tools they will use to access information, teachers listen to what the student would like to learn *that meets his or her life goals* and how he or she would like to move forward. Students and teachers may find the arrangement more motivating than traditional learning. For students with significant executive function difficulties, this type of learning may help to rekindle the motivation to learn and to escape the Downward Spiral (retrieved from https://www.understood.org/en/school-learning/partnering-with-childs-school/instructional-strategies/personalized-learning-what-you-need-to-know).

Summary

Looking at these special considerations prepares you for some of the more challenging issues students with EF deficits face every day at every stage of development. It is no wonder that many students start with such high hopes but end up in the Downward Spiral. The challenges are great for teachers, students, and parents alike; students will not magically get over all these issues. It takes explicit instruction in strategies and use of metacognition to self-regulate, but the important point is that executive function skills can be improved. Furthermore, this instruction should be informed by Universal Design for Learning (UDL) and supportive technologies. It is vital that all teachers working with students with EF difficulties stay in touch with the latest research that is being made available. New knowledge can give us a means to provide students a great boost in learning socially and academically resulting in improved self-confidence.

References

Altemeier, L. E., & Abbott, R. D. (2008). Executive functions for reading and writing in typical literacy development and dyslexia. *Journal of Clinical and Experimental Neuropsychology, 30*(5), 588–606.

American Speech, Language and Hearing Association. (2014) *Statistics of communication disorders.* Retrieved from https://identifythesigns.org/statistics-of-communication-disorders/

American Speech, Language and Hearing Association. (n.d.). *Written language disorders: Causes.* Retrieved from https://www.asha.org/PRPSpecificTopic.aspx?folderid=8589942549&section=Causes

American Speech, Language and Hearing Association. (n.d.). *Written language disorders: Overview.* Retrieved from https://www.asha.org/Practice-Portal/Clinical-Topics/Written-Language-Disorders/

American Speech, Language and Hearing Association. (n.d.). *Signs and symptoms of written language disorders.* Retrieved from https://www.asha.org/Practice-Portal/Clinical-Topics/Written-Language-Disorders/Signs-and-Symptoms-of-Written-Language-Disorders/

Barkley, R. A., Murphy, K. R., & Fischer, M. (2008). *ADHD in adults: What the science says.* New York, NY: Guilford Press.

Boyle, J. (2014). Notetaking and secondary students with disabilities: Challenges and solutions. *Learning Disabilities Research and Practice. 27*(2), 90–101.

Brown, J. (2013). *Potato Head activity.* Retrieved from https://trello.com/c/yboWRH5d/18-mr-potato-head

Brown, T. E. (2005). *Attention deficit disorder: The unfocused mind in children and adults.* New Haven, CT: Yale University Press.

Business Dictionary. (2018). Non-verbal communication. Retrieved from http://www.businessdictionary.com/definition/non-verbal-communication.html

Case, L., Mamlin, N., Harris, K., & Graham, S. (1995). Self-regulated strategy development: A theoretical and practical perspective. In T. E. Scruggs & M. A. Mastropieri (Eds.), *Advances in learning and behavioral disabilities* (vol. 9, pp. 21–46). Greenwich, CT: JAI Press.

Center for Applied Special Technology (CAST). (2013). *Universal Design for Learning, Version 2.0.* Wakefield, MA: Author.

Center for Applied Special Technology (CAST). (2011). *Universal Design for Learning Guidelines, Version 2.0.* Wakefield, MA: Author.

Center on the Developing Child. (2017). *Executive function & self-regulation.* Retrieved from https://harvardcenter.staging.wpengine.com/science/key-concepts/executive-function/

Center on the Developing Child. (2012). *InBrief: Executive function.* Retrieved from https://developingchild.harvard.edu/resources/inbrief-executive-function/

Child Mind Institute. (2015). *Executive functioning.* Retrieved from https://www.understood.org/en/about/sea

Common Sense Media: https://www.commonsensemedia.org/

Cooper-Kahn, J., & Dietzel, L. (2008). *Late, lost and unprepared: A parent's guide to helping children with executive functioning.* Bethesda, MD. Woodbine House.

Cooper-Kahn, J., & Foster, M. (2013). *Boosting executive skills in the classroom: A practical guide for educators.* San Francisco, CA: Jossey-Bass.

Covey, S., & Harris, D. (1999). *The 7 Habits of highly effective teens.* Salt Lake City, UT: Franklin Covey.

Crozier, S., & Sileo, N. M. (2005). Encouraging positive behavior with social stories: An intervention for children with autism spectrum disorders. *Teaching Exceptional Children, 37*(6), 26–31.

Dawson, P., & Guare, R. (2009). *Smart but scattered.* New York, NY: Guilford Press.

Dawson, P., & Guare, R. (2010). *Executive skills in children and adolescents* (2nd ed.). New York, NY: Guilford Press.

Diamond, A., & Lee, K. (2011, August 19). *Science, 333,* 6045, pp. 959–964.

Durlak, J. A., Weissberg, R. P., Dymnicki, A. B., Taylor, R. D., & Schellinger, K. B. (2011). The impact of enhancing students' social and emotional learning: A meta-analysis of school-based universal interventions. *Child Development, 82*, 405–432.

Ellis, E. (1991). *SLANT*. Retrieved from https://kucrl.ku.edu/slant

Every Student Succeeds Act: www.ed.gov/ESSA

Ezell, D., Klein, C., Decker, T., Golden, J., Lanza, L., Meints, L., Roth, A., Murphy, T., & Spaulding, C. (2002). Courtesy of the University of Central Florida/Cocoa Campus Student Council for Exceptional Children #1050.

Feifer, S. G. (2016). *Neuropsychology fundamentals for educators*. Sparta, WI: Schoolhouse Educational Services.

Fulghum, R. (1988). *All I really need to know I learned in kindergarten*. New York, NY: Ivy Books, Random House.

Garner, J. K. (2009). Conceptualizing the relations between executive functions and self-regulated learning. *Journal of Psychology, 143*(4), 405–426.

Gioia, G. A., Isquith, P. K., Guy, S., & Kenworthy, L. (2002). *Behavior Rating Inventory of Executive Function* (BRIEF). Austin, TX: WPS.

Gray, C. A. (2000). *The new social story book*. Arlington, TX: Future Horizons.

Gray, C. A. (2002). *My social stories book*. London, England: Jessica Kingsley.

Harris, K. (2013). *Self-regulated strategy development*. Retrieved from http://iris.peabody.vanderbilt.edu/interview/self-regulated- strategy-development-srsd-a-framework-for-teaching-instructional-strategies/script-karen-harris/

Harris, K. R., & Graham, S. (1996). *Making the writing process work: Strategies for composition and self-regulation*. Cambridge, MA: Brookline.

Hulme, C., & Snowling, M. (2014). The interface between spoken and written language: Developmental disorders. *Philosophical Transactions: Biological Sciences, 369*(1634), 1–8. Retrieved from http://www.jstor.org/stable/24499216

IDEA Partnership and the Common Core. (n.d.). *Common Core State Standards and assessments collection: Tools: Tools to assess knowledge and level of agreement*. Retrieved from http://www.ideapartnership.org/index.php?option=com_content&view=article&id=1522

Individuals with Disabilities Education Improvement Act [IDEA] of 2004, Public Law No. 108–446, 118 stat. (2004).

James, W. (1990). *Principles of psychology*. New York, NY: Holt.

Johnson, S. (1999). *Who moved my cheese?* New York, NY: Putnam's Sons.

Johnson, S. (2002). *Who moved my cheese for teens?* New York, NY: Putnam's Sons.

Johnson, S. (2003). *Who moved my cheese for kids?* New York, NY: Putnam's Sons.

Kaufman, C. (2010). *Executive function in the classroom: Practical strategies for improving performance and enhancing skills for all students*. Baltimore, MD: Paul H. Brookes.

Kouyoumdjian, H. (2002). *Learning through visuals: Visual imagery in the classroom*. Retrieved from https://www.psychologytoday.com/us/blog/get-psyched/201207/learning-through-visuals

King, D. (1986). *Keyboarding skills*. New York, NY: Educators Publishing Service.

Landmark College. (n.d.). *Working memory, attention, & executive function*. Retrieved from http://ussablealgera.landmark.edu/instructor-training/working-memory-attention-executive-function

Mahone, E. M. (2008, August). ADHD and executive functions: Lessons learned from research. *Exceptional Parent Magazine, 38*(8), 48–51.

McCloskey, G., Perkins, L., & Van Diviner, B. (2001). *Assessment and intervention for executive function difficulties*. New York, NY: Taylor & Francis.

Medina, J. (2018). *Attack of the teenage brain! Understanding the weird and wonderful adolescent learner*. Alexandria, VA: ASCD.

Meltzer, L. (Ed.). (2007). *Executive function in education: From theory to practice*. New York, NY: Guilford Press.

Meltzer, L. (2010). Function processes: The why, what, and how. In K. R. Harris & S. Graham (Eds.), *Promoting executive function in the classroom* (pp. 3–27). New York, NY: Guilford Press.

Meltzer, L. (Ed.). (2018). *Executive function in education: From theory to practice* (2nd ed.). New York, NY: Guilford Press.

Meltzer, L., Katzir, T., Miller, L., & Reddy, R. (2004). Academic self-perceptions, effort, and strategy use in students with learning disabilities: Changes over time. *Learning Disabilities Research & Practice, 19*(2), 99–108.

Meltzer, M., Reddy, R., Pollica, L. S., Roditi, B., & Sayer, J. &. (2004). Positive and negative self-perceptions: Is there a cyclical relationship between teachers' and students' perceptions of effort, strategy us, and academic performance. *Learning Disabilities Research and Practice, 19*(1), 33–44.

Meyer, A., Rose, D. H., & Gordon, D. (2014). *Universal design for learning: Theory and practice.* Wakefield, MA: Center for Applied Special Technology.

Miller, M., Schetter, P., & Ozonoff, S. (2018). Executive function in autism disorder: From research to practice. In L. Meltzer. (Ed.), *Executive function in education: From theory to practice* (2nd ed., pp. 168–191). , New York, NY: Guilford Press.

Morgan, P., Farkas, G., Wang, Y., Hillemeier, M., Oh, Y., & Maczuga, M. (2018). *Does a lack of executive function explain why some kids fall way behind in school?* Retrieved from https://hechingerreport.org/does-a-lack-of-executive-function-explain-why-some-kids-fall-way-behind-in-school/

Morin, A. (n.d.). *6 ways kids use flexible thinking to learn.* Retrieved from https://www.understood.org/en/learning-attention-issues/child-learning-disabilities/executive-functioning-issues/6-ways-kids-use-flexible-thinking-to-learn

Moyes, R. (2014). *Executive function "dysfunction": Strategies for educators and parents.* London: Jessica Kingsley Publishers.

National Commission on Education. (1983). *A nation at risk.* Retrieved from www2.ed.gov/pubs/NatAtRisk/risk.html

Newhall, P. W. (2012). Language-based learning disabilities. In P. W. Newhall (Ed.), *Language-based teaching series.* Prides Crossing, MA: Landmark School Outreach Program. Retrieved from http://www.ldonline.org/article/56113/

No Child Left Behind Act, 20 U.S.C. (2002).

Pandey, A., Hale, D., Das, S., Goddings, A., Blakemore, S., & Viner, R. M. (2018). Effectiveness of universal self-regulation–based interventions in children and adolescents: A systematic review and meta-analysis [Original Investigation]. *JAMA Pediatrics, 172*(6), 566–575. doi:10.1001/jamapediatrics.2018.0232

Reading Rockets. (2008). COPS Editing Checklist. In I. Mevs, *Think write book.* Bloomington, IN: AuthorHouse. Retrieved from http://www.readingrockets.org/content/pdfs/COPSchecklist.pdf

Reid, R., & Lienemann, T. O. (2006). *Strategy instruction for students with learning disabilities.* New York, NY: Guilford Press.

Rief, S. (2015). *The ADD/ADHD book of lists: A practical guide for helping children and teens with attention deficit disorders.* San Francisco, CA: Jossey-Bass.

Reynolds, C. R., Horton, A., & Decker, S. L. (2008). Assessing executive functions: A life-span perspective. *Applications of Neuropsychology in the Schools, 45*(9), 875–892.

Robinson, K., & Aronica, L. (2018). *How much homework is enough? Depends who you ask.* Retrieved from https://edweek.org/ew/articles/2018/04/19/how-much-homework-is-enough-depends-who.html

Rosen, P. (n.d.). *Flexible thinking: What you need to know.* Understood. Retrieved from https://www.understood.org/en/learning-attention-issues/child-learning-disabilities/executive-functioning-issues/flexible-thinking-what-you-need-to-know

Rosen, S. M., Boyle, J. R., Cariss, K., & Forchelli, G. A. (2014). Changing how we think, changing how we learn: Scaffolding executive function processes for students with learning disabilities, *Learning Disabilities: A Multidisciplinary Journal, 20*(4), 165–176.

Sasser, T. R., Bierman, K. L., Heinrichs, B., & Nix, R. L. (2017, December). Preschool intervention can promote sustained growth in the executive-function skills of children exhibiting early deficits. *Psychological Science, 28*(12), 1719–1730. doi: 10.1177/0956797617711640

Scruggs, T., & Mastropieri, M. (2000). The effectiveness of mnemonic instruction for students with learning problems: An update and research synthesis. *Journal of Behavioral Education, 10*(2/3), 163–173.

Semenov, A., & Zelazo, P. (2018). *The development of hot and cool executive function.* In L. Meltzer, *Executive function in education: From theory to practice* (2nd ed., pp. 329–391). New York, NY: Guilford Press.

Songlee, D., Miller, S., Tincani, M., Sileo, N., & Perkins, P. G. (2008). Effects of test-taking strategy instruction on high-functioning adolescents with autism spectrum disorder. *Focus on Autism and Other Developmental Disabilities, 23*(4), 217–228.

Strosnider, R., & Sharpe, V. (2015). *Using technology for executive function training.* Presentation manual, Preconvention workshop, Council for Exceptional Children Convention, San Diego, CA, April 8, 2015.

Strosnider, R., & Sharpe, V. (2016). *Ensuring success: Executive function skill training for ALL students.* Presentation manual, Preconvention workshop, Council for Exceptional Children Convention, St. Louis, MO, April 13, 2016.

Strosnider, R., & Sharpe, V. (2017). *Ensuring success for ALL students: Executive function skill t raining through a universal design for learning approach.* Presentation manual, St. Louis, MO, Public School Teachers, March 7, 2017.

Strosnider, R., Sharpe, V., & Weaver, J. (2017). Visual Association Strategy.

Strosnider, R., & Sharpe, V. (2018). *Executive function training.* Presentation manual for teacher assistants, Hilo, HI, January 31, 2018.

Strosnider, R., & Sharpe, V. (2018). *Executive Function Training.* Presentation manual for teachers, Hilo, HI, February 1, 2018.

Strosnider, R., & Sharpe, V. (2018). *Executive function training.* Presentation manual for administrators, Hilo, HI, November 14, 2018.

Tam, N. (2014). *Executive functions.* Denton, TX: Author.

Tannock, R. (2007). The educational implications of attention deficit hyperactivity disorder. *Research Monograph* #3. Toronto, Ontario: University of Toronto.

Tucker, G. (2015). *Neuropsychological-evaluations: What you need to know.* Retrieved from https://www .understood.org/en/learning-attention-issues/treatments-approaches/educational-strategies/ neuropsychological-evaluations-what-you-need-to-know

Understood. (n.d.). *The difference between universal design for learning (UDL) and traditional education.* Retrieved on 1/20/2018 from https://www.understood.org/en/learning-attention-issues/treatments-approaches/educational-strategies/the-difference-between-universal-design-for-learning-udl-and-traditional-education?cm_ven=ExactTarget&cm_cat=012918_ToolsTipsEmail&cm_pla=All+Subscribers&cm_ite=https%3a%2f%2fwww.understood.org%2fen%2flearning-attention-issues%2ftreatments-approaches%2feducational-strategies%2fthe-difference-between-universal-design-for-learning-udl-and-traditional-education&cm_lm=vssharpe@frostburg.edu&cm_ainfo=&utm_campaign=outreach&utm_source=weeklytools&utm_medium=email&utm_content=012918_ToolsTipsEmail&&&&

Understood. (n.d.). *Signs of executive functioning issues at different ages.* Retrieved on from https://www .understood.org/en/learning-attention-issues/signs-symptoms/could-your-child-have/ executive-function-disorder-symptoms

Understood. (n.d.). *Understanding your child's trouble with spoken language.* Retrieved from https://www .understood.org/en/learning-attention-issues/child-learning-disabilities/issues-involving-spoken-language/understanding-your-childs-trouble-with-spoken-language

Understood. (n.d.). *The difference between ADHD and executive functioning issues.* Retrieved from https:// www.understood.org/en/learning-attention-issues/child-learning-disabilities/executive-functioning-issues/difference-between-executive-functioning-issues-and-adhd

Understood. (n.d.). *Hamburger paragraph* (Prewriting graphic organizer). Retrieved from https://www .understood.org/~/media/f27fa769f3c74e3298981008d4f771c2.pdf

Welsh, M. C., Pennington, B. F., Ozonoff, S., Rouse, B., & McCabe, E. R. B. (1990). Neuropsychology of early-treated phenylketonuria: Specific executive function deficits. *Child Development, 61,* 1697–1713.

Women's and Children's Health Network: Child and Youth Health. (2018). *Language delay—young children.* Retrieved from http://www.cyh.com/HealthTopics/HealthTopicDetails.aspx?p=114&np=306&id=1877#1

Zelazo, P. D. (2015). The Dimensional Change Card Sort (DCCS): A method of assessing executive function in children. *Nature Protocols, 1*(1), 297–301.

Index

THE EXECUTIVE FUNCTION GUIDEBOOK

homework assignments and, 287 (table)

keyboarding skill development and, 1

learning strategies and, 2, 11, 22, 22 (table)

movement for use of, 11–12

online calendars and, 113

organizing/planning/prioritizing/sequencing/
time management skills and, 118, 119–121
(table)

reading fluency/comprehension aids and, 64

social/emotional and inhibition behaviors and,
202, 202–204 (table)

supportive technologies and, 2, 11, 22, 22
(table), 83

Universal Design for Learning and, 3, 11–12,
15 (table)

visual-sequential memory aids and, 60

working memory and, 73, 74–75 (table)

TheHwApp, 120, 121

Think It, Become It Strategy, 193, 193 (figure)

Time-Cue Strategy, 243, 244 (figures)

Time management skill, 6 (figure), 7

assessment of, 24, 25 (table)

deficits, impact of, 100–102

definition of, 98

difficulties with, 8 (table), 100

Downward Spiral and, 101

student achievement, impact on, 100–102

supportive technologies for, 118, 119–121
(table)

Time Needed for Time Management Strategy
and, 110–111, 112 (figures)

See also Amanda's organizational skills
case study; Executive functioning
(EF); Organizing skill; Planning skill;
Prioritizing skill; Sequencing skill

Time Needed for Time Management Strategy,
110–111, 112 (figures), 152, 285

Time Timer app, 161

Timer app, 74

Timer+ app, 121

Todoist: Organize your life app, 120

Toso, B., 18–19, 20, 21

Understood.org, 73, 119, 161, 203, 247

Universal Design for Learning (UDL)
framework, 3, 4, 11

action/expression, multiple means of, 12, 12
(figure), 14–15 (table), 17 (figure), 27, 28
(table)

affective networks and, 12, 12 (figure)

barriers to learning, reduction in, 13

development of, 12

engagement, multiple means of, 12, 12 (figure),
14–15 (table), 17 (figure), 27, 28 (table)

enlightened instructional practices and, 11, 12,
13–16, 13 (table), 14–15 (table)

executive function strategies, explicit teaching
of, 13–16, 13–15 (tables)

instruction delivery, individual learning and, 13,
13 (table)

learner participation, encouragement of, 13

learner variability, emphasis on, 13

metacognition and, 15, 16–17, 17 (figure)

networks in learning and, 12

neuroscientific findings and, 12

one-size-fits-all model and, 12, 13 (table)

premises of, 12

principles of, 12, 12 (figure), 27

recognition networks and, 12, 12 (figure)

representation, multiple means of, 12, 12
(figure), 14–15 (table), 17 (figure), 27, 28
(table)

7-Step Model, UDL considerations and, 12, 12
(figure), 27, 28–29 (table), 51

skill-building strategies, metacognition and,
15–16

skill fluency/mastery, flexible demonstration of, 13

strategic networks and, 12, 12 (figure)

student needs/strengths and, 12, 13

technology, use of, 3, 11–12, 15 (table), 22, 22
(table)

tools for, 14 (table), 22, 22 (table)

See also Case studies; Learning strategies;
Metacognition; 7-Step Model for
Executive Function Skills Training;
Teaching/instructional strategies

Van Diviner, B., 6

Venn Diagrams, 58

Ventura, J., 192

Verbal communication, 226, 227, 228, 230–236

Viner, R. M., 188

Visual learning aids, 66–70

Visual Planning Schedule Strategy, 117, 118
(figure)

Visual Schedules Strategy, 59, 59 (figure), 284

Voice Dream software, 64

Voice Thread app, 248

Wang, Y., 9, 273, 274

Weissberg, R. P., 190

What is the Next Integer? app, 74, 120

What's On My Mind Strategy, 32, 192, 193
(figure)

Whiteboard app, 22, 119, 248

Who Moved My Cheese?, 242–243

Women's and Children's Health Network, 226

Word walls, 66

Working memory, 6 (figure), 7, 47

ABC Memory Strategy and, 51–52, 52–53
(figures)

assessment of, 24, 25 (table)

attending/initiating/focusing and, 150–160

auditory memory and, 47, 49 (figure), 60

auditory-sequential memory and, 60

behavioral effects, memory deficits and, 50

Chunking Strategy and, 60

cognitive desktops, limited capacity of, 50

Concentration Games Strategy and, 60

concrete external storage systems and, 56, 58
(image)

decay of information and, 49 (figure)

deficits, impact of, 50

definitions of, 47
Desktop Photo Strategy and, 58, 58 (image)
difficulties with, 8 (table), 48, 50
functions of, 47, 48, 49 (figure)
GOP Memory Strategy/elementary students
    and, 53–54, 55 (figure)
GOP Memory Strategy/secondary students
    and, 54–55, 56 (figure)
Home Keys Keyboarding Strategy and, 71,
    72–73 (figures)
Human Number Line Strategy and, 60
information synthesis function and, 47, 73
lifelong impact of deficits in, 50
long-term memory, linkage with, 47, 49 (figure)
Matching Cards Memory Strategy and, 60
mathematics visual aids and, 67–69, 67–68
    (figures), 70 (figures)
metacognition, role of, 58, 64
mnemonics and, 51, 54
modeling writing processes and, 58
multisensory approach to learning and, 50,
    71–73
multistep problems, solving of, 47
Number Line Strategy and, 67–68, 67 (figure)
Online Research Strategy and, 73
Post-it Note Modified Strategy and, 64–65,
    65–66 (figures)
prewriting graphic organizers and, 56–58, 57
    (figure)
problems with, manifestations of, 48
reading fluency/comprehension strategies and,
    64–66
repetition, utility of, 50

retrieval of stored information and, 228
rules/procedures, forgetting of, 50
See-It-in-Your-Mind Association Strategy and,
    53, 54 (figure)
sensory activities, learning from, 50
7-Step Model and, 50–51
Skip Counting Strategy and, 67, 68–69, 68
    (figure), 70 (figures)
social/emotional well-being and, 50
student achievement, impact on, 50
study aid strategies and, 60–63
supportive strategies with cards for, 50–56
supportive technologies and, 73, 73–74 (figure)
Teach-It Strategy and, 60–62, 61 (figures)
visual-kinesthetic strategies and, 60
visual learning aids and, 66–70
Visual Schedules Strategy and, 59, 59 (figure)
visual-sequential memory and, 60
visual-spatial memory and, 47, 49 (figure)
See also Amanda's working memory case study;
    Executive functioning (EF)
Writing process:
    metacognition, role of, 58
    modeling writing process and, 58
    prewriting graphic organizers and, 56–58, 57
        (figure)
    software programs for, 58
    See also Communication/cognitive flexibility
        skills; Written communication
Written communication, 226, 227, 228,
    237–242

Zelazo, P., 274

A SAGE Publishing Company

Helping educators make the greatest impact

CORWIN HAS ONE MISSION: to enhance education through intentional professional learning.

We build long-term relationships with our authors, educators, clients, and associations who partner with us to develop and continuously improve the best evidence-based practices that establish and support lifelong learning.

Solutions YOU WANT | Experts YOU TRUST | Results YOU NEED

EVENTS

>>> **INSTITUTES**

Corwin Institutes provide large regional events where educators collaborate with peers and learn from industry experts. Prepare to be recharged and motivated!

corwin.com/institutes

ON-SITE PD

>>> **ON-SITE PROFESSIONAL LEARNING**

Corwin on-site PD is delivered through high-energy keynotes, practical workshops, and custom coaching services designed to support knowledge development and implementation.

corwin.com/pd

>>> **PROFESSIONAL DEVELOPMENT RESOURCE CENTER**

The PD Resource Center provides school and district PD facilitators with the tools and resources needed to deliver effective PD.

corwin.com/pdrc

ONLINE

>>> **ADVANCE**

Designed for K–12 teachers, Advance offers a range of online learning options that can qualify for graduate-level credit and apply toward license renewal.

corwin.com/advance

Contact a PD Advisor at (800) 831-6640 or
visit www.corwin.com for more information